GA DOCUMENT EXTRA is a new series of publications. Each issue is dedicated to an architect and documents the latest works through photographs, drawings and interviews.
Each issue contains three chapters.
The first chapter illustrates the architect's past, present and future through and in-depth interview at his/her atelier.
The second chapter focuses on recently built projects illustrated with abundant color and black-and-white photographs and interviews.
The third chapter introduces projects currently in progress in order to examine the architect's philosophy for the future.

いま，世界の第一線で活躍する建築家群像に，写真，図面，インタヴューで迫り，その過去・現在・未来を三部構成でつづる新しい発想の建築書——GAドキュメント・エクストラ。
第1章では，彼らの創造の場であるアトリエを訪問。設計の現場をくまなくルポルタージュ。建築を志すに至った背景，どのようにして建築を学んできたか，そして今，建築の現在に向けて何を思うかを聞く。
第2章では最近実現した建築作品を紹介。そのデザインの核心を問い，それぞれの作品についてルポルタージュ。
第3章では，現在進行中のプロジェクトを中心に，明日に向けての建築思考をインタヴュー。

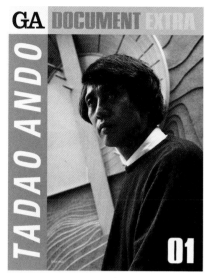

01 TADAO ANDO
安藤忠雄

WORKS
Suntory Museum／Inamori Auditorium／Maxray Headquarters Building／Museum of Gojo Culture／Nariwa Municipal Museum／Harima Kogen Higashi Primary School

PROJECTS
Oyamazaki Museum／Rokko Housing III／FABRICA／Awajishima Project／Naoshima Contemporary Art Museum II／Annex for Museum of Literature, Himeji／Meditation Space, UNESCO／Tate Gallery of Modern Art／Seaside & Hilltop Housing

168 total pages, 64 in color, 定価2,990円

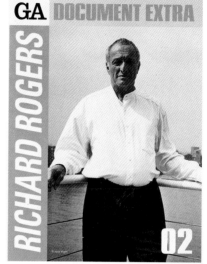

02 RICHARD ROGERS
リチャード・ロジャース

WORKS
Channel 4 Headquarters／European Court of Human Rights

PROJECTS
Terminal 5 Heathrow／Zoofenster Building／Shanghai Lu Jia Zui／Turbine Tower／Bordeaux Cité Judiciare／Daimler Benz Offices and Housing／VR Techno Center／Lloyd's Register of Shipping／Thames Valley University／Saitama Arena／South Bank Redevelopment／Parc BIT／Yokohama Port Terminal

176 total pages, 56 in color, 定価2,990円

03 ZAHA M. HADID
ザハ・ハディド

WORKS
IBA Housing／Moon Soon Restaurant & Bar／Vitra Fire Station

PROJECTS
Cologne Rheinauhafen Redevelopment／Düsseldorf Art and Media Center／Cardiff Bay Opera House／Spittelau Viaducts／New York City 42nd Street Hotel Project

160 total pages, 64 in color, 定価2,990円

04 CHRISTIAN DE PORTZAMPARC
クリスチャン・ド・ポルザンパルク

WORKS
Cité de la Musique／Rue Nationale, Paris／Apartment in Bercy／Crédit Lyonnais Tower

PROJECTS
Nara International Convention Hall／Law Courts in Grasse／Cultural Center for Bandai Corporation／Extension of the Palais des Congrès／New Cultural Complex, Renne／School of Architecture, Marne la Vallée／Porte Maillot

160 total pages, 64 in color, 定価2,990円

PLANNED ISSUES

JEAN NOUVEL ジャン・ヌヴェル
RICHARD MEIER リチャード・マイヤー
RICARDO LEGORRETA リカルド・レゴレッタ
ERIC OWEN MOSS エリック・オーエン・モス
MORPHOSIS モーフォシス
ENRIC MIRALLES エンリック・ミラージェス
FRANK O. GEHRY フランク・O・ゲーリー
STEVEN HOLL スティーブン・ホール
and others

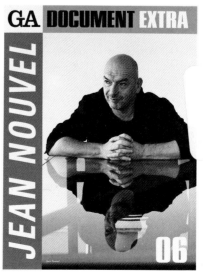

GA HOUSES

GA HOUSES documents outstanding new residential architecture from all over the world. Included in each issue also are retrospective looks at residential works of the past which are now considered epoch-making. This magazine is essential not only for architects and architectural students but for those who wish to master the art of living.

世界各国の住宅を現地取材により次々に紹介してゆくシリーズ。最近の作品はもちろん、近代住宅の古典の再検討、現代建築家の方法論、集合住宅のリポートなど、住宅に関わる問題点を広い範囲にわたってとりあげてゆく。

Vols. 1–16, 18–24, 28, 31, 34 are out of print.
1–16, 18–24, 28, 31, 34号は絶版。　　Size: 300×228mm

17
作品：ゲーリー／マイヤー／ヴェンチューリ／タイガーマン／アルキテクトニカ／クレック＆オルセン／ヤコブセン／他
Gehry; Meier; Venturi; Tigerman; Arquitectonica; Jacobsen; Krueck & Olsen; Quigley; and others
160 pages, 64 in color.　¥3,400

25
近代住宅：グロピウス自邸
特集：R・レゴレッタ／S・ホール
作品：篠原／安藤／早川／斎藤
Gropius; Legorreta; Holl; Shinohara; Ando; Hayakawa; Saito
232 pages, 68 in color.　¥3,800

26
近代住宅：R・M・シンドラーの住宅
作品：プリンス／アルキテクトニカ／グワスミー／村上／早川／斎藤／他
Schindler; Prince; Arquitectonica; Cunningham; Gwathmey Siegel; Murakami; Saito; and others
176 pages, 56 in color.　¥2,903

27
近代住宅：ライトの山邑邸
作品：ウィルソン／クールハース／ホール／クリエ／ムーア／原／山本／他
Wright; Wilson; Koolhaas; Holl; Krier; Moore; Kappe; Kada; Hara; Yamamoto; and others
176 pages, 56 in color.　¥2,903

29
特集：ケンドリック・バングス・ケロッグ
作品：ガフ／ゲーリー／ブルックス／ホジェッツ＋ファング／飯田／石田／他
Kellogg; Goff; Gehry; Hodgetts+Fung; Iida; Ishida; Saitowitz; Scully; Brooks; and others
160 pages, 48 in color.　¥2,903

30
作品：マイヤー／スコーギン・エラム・ブレイ／ボッタ／シュヴァイツァー／ペリ／サントス／村上／妹島／西本／他
Meier; Scogin Elam and Bray; Botta; Schweitzer; Murakami; Sejima; Nishimoto; and others
160 pages, 56 in color.　¥2,903

32
特集：ジョン・ロートナー
作品：ソットサス／プリンス／ナイルズ／プレドック／PAPA
Lautner; Sottsas; Prince; Niles; Predock; PAPA
160 pages, 48 in color.　¥2,903

33
作品：レゴレッタ／マック／キャピー／エリクソン／グワスミー＆シーゲル／ヒューバート＆ゼルニオ／葉／村上／他
Legorreta; Mack; Kappe; Yoh; Murakami; Gwathmey Siegel; Hubert Zelnio; Koning Eizenberg
160 pages, 56 in color.　¥2,903

35
作品：オーブレリー／モーフォシス／ウォルドマン／ノタ／デニソン＆ルキーニ／エリクソン／安藤／斎藤
Oubrerie; Morphosis; Waldman; Nota; Denison Luchini; Erickson; Ando; Saito
160 pages, 56 in color.　¥2,903

36
作品：クールハース／ボッタ／ロトンディ／プリンス／イスラエル／アルキテクトニカ／BAM／安藤／他
OMA; Botta; Rotondi; Prince; Israel; Arquitectonica; Sunyer/Badia; BAM; Ando; and others
160 pages, 64 in color.　¥2,903

37
特集号：プロジェクト1993
Special Issue: Project 1993
144 pages, 24 in color.　¥2,505

38
連載：巨匠の住宅―ル・コルビュジエ1
作品：ホール／シゴル＆コールマン／モス／石田／ナイルズ／早川／他
Essays on Residential Masterpieces–Le Corbusier 1; Holl; Moss; Niles; Standing; Hayakawa; and others
168 pages, 56 in color.　¥2,903

39
連載：巨匠の住宅―ル・コルビュジエ2
作品：マック／ノタ／レゴレッタ／シュヴァイツァー／安藤／ボッタ／他
Essays on Residential Masterpieces–Le Corbusier 2; Ando; Botta; Mack; Schweitzer; Legorreta; and others
160 pages, 64 in color.　¥2,903

40
連載：巨匠の住宅―フランク・ロイド・ライト1
作品：フライ／プレドック／ソットサス／クイグリー／ブルーダー／他
Essays on Residential Masterpieces–F.L.Wright 1; Frey; Predock; Quigley; Sottsass; Bruder; and others
160 pages, 56 in color.　¥2,903

41
特集号：プロジェクト1994
Special Issue: Project 1994
168 pages, 20 in color.　¥2,903

42
連載：巨匠の住宅―フランク・ロイド・ライト2
作品：村上／早川／妹島／飯田／レゴレッタ／ミラージェス／プレドック／他
Essays on Residential Masterpieces–F. L. Wright 2; Murakami; Legorreta; Miralles; Predock; and others
160 pages, 48 in color.　¥2,903

43
連載：巨匠の住宅―フランク・ロイド・ライト3
作品：OMA／クイグリー／グワスミー＆シーゲル／石田／北山／ヌヴェル／他
Essays on Residential Masterpieces–F. L. Wright 3; OMA; Gwathmey; Nouvel; Ishida; Kitayama; and others
160 pages, 48 in color.　¥2,903

44
連載：巨匠の住宅―ルイス・I・カーン
作品：ブルーダー／プリンス／岸和郎／北川原温／ロートナー／他
Essays on Residential Masterpieces–Louis I. Kahn; Lautner; Bruder; Waldman; Koenig; Prince; and others
160 pages, 56 in color.　¥2,903

45
特集号：プロジェクト1995
Special Issue: Project 1995
184 pages, 24 in color.　¥2,903

46
連載：巨匠の住宅―ジョン・ロートナー
作品：カラチ／ノルテン／イスラエル／近藤／北川原／ミラージェス／他
Residential Masterpieces– John Lautner; Kalach; Norten; Israel; Niles; Rotondi; Miralles; and others
160 pages, 64 in color.　¥2,903

47
特集号：日本の現代住宅　第4集
論文：原広司　エッセイ：石山修武
座談会：山本理顕、岸和郎、妹島和世
Special Issue: Japan Part IV
176 pages, 48 in color.　¥2,903

48
特集号：プロジェクト1996
Special Issue: Project 1996
176 pages, 32 in color.　¥2,903

49

表記価格には消費税は含まれておりません。

GA

Global Architecture

An Encyclopedia of Modern Architecture

企画・撮影: 二川幸夫
Edited and Photographed by Yukio Futagawa

現代建築の名作をじっくり見ていただくために企画された大型サイズのシリーズ。現代建築の巨匠たちの古典的名作から，今日最も新しい傾向を示す作品に至るまで1軒ないし2軒の建築を総48頁で構成し，現代建築の持つ空間の広がり，ディテール，テクスチュアなどを確実に，明確に，見事に表現。加えて，原稿執筆にあたっては世界の建築界の最高峰の協力を得た文字どおりグローバルな規模の企画であり，回を重ねるごとに現代の名建築の百科事典となろう。

Having now published more than 70 volumes, GLOBAL ARCHITECTURE has become a classic among architectural publication. GA is meant for those who would like to "experience" masterpieces of modern architecture. Apart from those seminal works of architecture which imply new directions, those columns also introduce some of the classic work by such masters of modern architecture. Each volume thoroughly documents one or two works illustrated by the stunning photography of Yukio Futagawa in a large format (364×257mm), accompanied by a critique written by a prominent architectural critic or historian. As the columns accumulate in your library, they will gradually become an encyclopedia of modern architecture.

~67

Size: 364×257mm
48 total pages, 8 in color and 24 in gravure

Vols. 33, 43, 45, 61, 62, 64, 65, 67: ￥2,400 each

残部僅少
Supply low

GA68
Gerrit Thomas Rietveld
The Schröder House
Text by Ida van Zijl
設計：ヘリット・T・リートフェルト
シュローダー邸
文：イダ・ファン・ゼイル

GA69
Arata Isozaki
Tsukuba Center Building
Text by Alessandro Mendini
設計：磯崎新
つくばセンタービル
文：A・メンディーニ

GA70
Walter Gropius
Bauhaus & Fagus Factory
Text by Dennis Sharp
設計：ヴァルター・グロピウス
バウハウス校舎，ファグス工場
文：デニス・シャープ

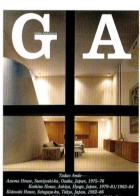

GA71
Tadao Ando
Azuma House & others
Text by Vittorio M. Lampugnani
設計：安藤忠雄
東邸（住吉の長屋），小篠邸，城戸崎邸
文：ヴィットリオ・M・ランプニャーニ

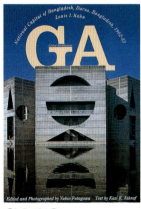

GA72
Louis I. Kahn
National Capital of Bangladesh
Text by Kazi Khaleed Ashraf
設計：ルイス・カーン
バングラデシュ国政センター
文：カジ・カレード・アシュラノ

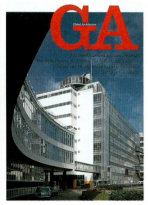

GA73
J. A. Brinkman &
L. C. van der Vlugt
Van Nelle Factory
Text by Jeroen Geurst
設計：J・A・ブリンクマン／
L・C・ファン・デル・フルーフト
ファン・ネレ工場
文：イェルン・ヒョルスト

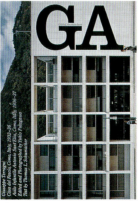

GA74
Giuseppe Terragni
Casa del Fascio, Asilo Infantile, Antonio Sant'Elia
Text by Thomas L. Schumacher
設計：ジュゼッペ・テラーニ
カサ・デル・ファッショ，
A・サンテリア幼稚園
文：トーマス・L・シュマッハー

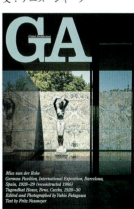

GA75
Mies van der Rohe
German Pavilion & Tugendhat House
Text by Fritz Neumeyer
設計：ミース・ファン・デル・ローエ
バルセロナ・パヴィリオン，
トゥーゲントハート邸
文：フリッツ・ノイマイヤー

68~

Size: 364×257mm
48 total pages, 8 in color and 24 in duo-tone

Vols. 68～：￥2,806 each

To be continued.
以下続刊

Planned issues:

Ricardo Legorreta
*House in Southern California
& Greenberg House*

Frank O. Gehry
*Gehry Residence
& Winton Guest House*

GA JAPAN
ENVIRONMENTAL DESIGN BIMONTHLY
Global Architecture

19

1996年3-4月号 発売中

特集／一戸建て住宅に未来はあるのか
論文「建て売りパークを行く」
　　　石山修武
インタヴュー「商品化住宅はここまで考えられている」
　　　田原晋（松下電工住宅システム研究所所長）
座談会「お客様は神様か？」
　　　石山修武
　　　山根千鶴子（積水ハウス技術本部副本部長）
　　　二川幸夫
論文「工業化住宅の未来」
　　　松村秀一
記事「アメリカからの報告」
　　　ウエイン・藤井

[クライアント登場]
[1] 安藤忠雄設計／城戸崎邸
　　　城戸崎博孝・裕子夫妻
[2] 山本理顕設計／岡山の住宅＋山本クリニック
　　　山本智之・恵子夫妻
時評／内田祥哉　伊東豊雄　坂茂　山田脩二

作品
斎藤裕　坂茂
北山恒　村上徹
小川晋一　岸和郎
山本理顕　中東壽一
スタジオ建築計画
インターデザインアソシエイツ

隔月刊：1, 3, 5, 7, 9, 11月 年6回発行
年間購読料：14,400円（送料弊社負担）
サイズ：300×228mm　総176頁（カラー72頁）
定価：2,400円

「GA JAPAN」「GA DOCUMENT」「GA HOUSES」「GA DOCUMENT EXTRA」を確実にご購入いただくためには、最寄りの書店に「定期購読」の申込みをして下さい。刊行時に書店にお届けいたします。なお、品切れの場合は書店にご注文下さい。

購入の難しい地域の方は、年間購読制度をご利用下さい。（送料弊社負担）
GA DOCUMENT 11,960円　　GA JAPAN 14,400円　　GA HOUSES 11,960円
年間購読専用電話番号　Tel: 03-3403-7497　Fax: 03-3404-1462

書店での各シリーズのご購入は
建築書籍のコーナーで
お求め下さい

LIGHT & SPACE 光の空間
MODERN ARCHITECTURE

企画・撮影＝二川幸夫
序文＝パオロ・ポルトゲージ
文＝三宅理一

Edited and Photographed by Yukio Futagawa
Introduction by Paolo Portoghesi Text by Riichi Miyake

空間を構成する根源的な要素である光。
あふれる自然の光をとらえ，
絞り込み，屈折させ，形を与えて内部に導き入れる。
近代建築の黎明期から現代にいたる，光と影を主役
として織りなされてきた建築空間の集大成。

Light is a fundamental element of architecture.
Through the finest examples
from the beginning of Modernism to the present,
this compendium examines
the way natural light is captured, altered,
and shaped in architectural space.

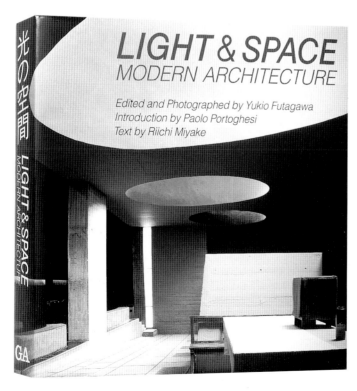

Vol. 1
Size: 300×297mm／216 pages, 30 in color／¥5,806

光と近代建築—パオロ・ポルトゲージ　Light and Modern Architecture *by Paolo Portoghesi*
鉄とガラスの神話　The Myth of Iron and Glass
空の簒奪　Usurpation of the Sky
樹木のアレゴリー　Allegory of Trees
世紀末の光と影　Light and Shadow in the Fin-de-Siècle
胎内への窓　Window to the Womb
透明な質感　The Texture of Transparency
形而上学的な光　Metaphysical Light

Vol. 2
Size: 300×297mm／216 pages, 24 in color／¥5,806

輝く額　The Shining Brow
建築の快楽　The Pleasure of Architecture
東方への旅　Travel to the Orient
ガラス箱の神話　The Myth of the Glazed Box
透視できる建築　See-Through Architecture
影のない光　Light without Shadow
始原の光　Primitive Light
ねばっこい空間　Sticky Space
メカニカルな空　The Mechanical Sky
被膜の建築　Architecture of Membrane

COMBINED ISSUE 合本 (HARD COVER 上製)
Size: 300×297mm／426 pages, 54 in color／¥14,369

GA
HOUSES

Global Architecture

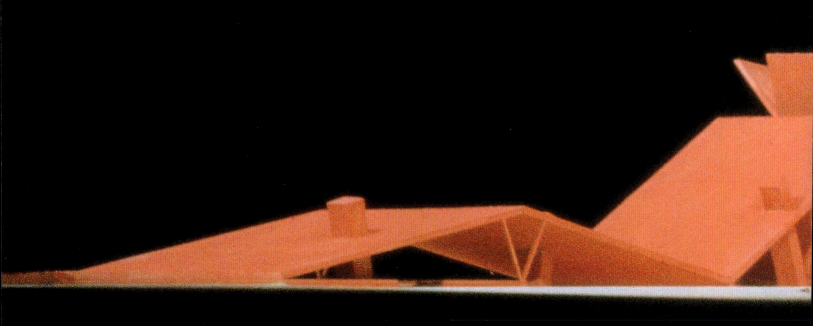

A.D.A. EDITA Tokyo

PROJECT 1996 48

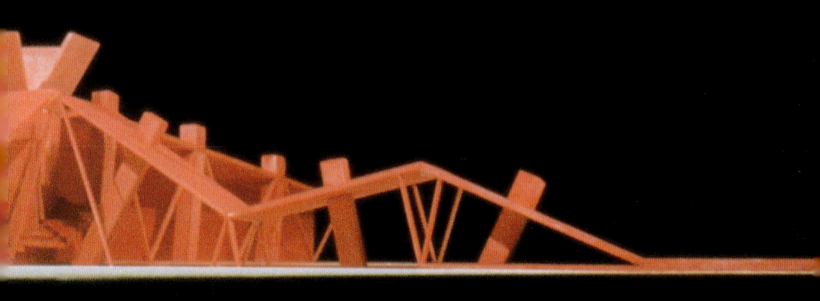

PROJECT 1996

GA HOUSES

目次 / Contents

安藤忠雄	10	TADAO ANDO
平野区の町屋		Town House in Hirano
ARO	12	ARCHITECTURE RESEARCH OFFICE
ニューヨーク・ロフト		Loft Apartment
アーキテクチャー・プロジェクト	14	ARCHITECTURE PROJECT
APIXV.01		APIXV.01 Residence
アンジェリル／グラハム	16	ANGELIL/GRAHAM
砂漠の家		Desert House
ブライアン・アルフレッド・マーフィー	20	BRIAN ALFRED MURPHY
ケイ邸		Kaye Residence
ジョセフ・N・ビオンド	22	JOSEPH N. BIONDO
アディロンダックの夏の家		Summer Cabin
ウィリアム・P・ブルーダー	24	WILLIAM P. BRUDER
ビュリアン邸		Burian Residence
二至の家 I		Solstice I
パット・マシューズ邸		Pat Matthews Residence
ウォーレス・E・カニングハム	30	WALLACE E. CUNNINGHAM
ソルトマン邸		Saltman Residence
シゴル＆コールマン	32	CIGOLLE & COLEMAN
スカイ・ランチ・ハウス		Sky Ranch House
コーシア・デイ	36	COSCIA・DAY
トパンガ渓谷の家		Topanga House
グワスミー／シーゲル	40	GWATHMEY SIEGEL
メイヤー邸		Meyer Residence
丘の家		Hilltop Residence
サン・オノフレの家		San Onofre Residence
アレキサンダー・ゴーリン	52	ALEXANDER GORLIN
グラス・スパインの家		House of the Glass Spine
ジン＋デザイン・ワークショップ	56	GIN+Design Workshop
Eeハウス		Ee House
ハンラハン・メイヤース	58	HANRAHAN MEYERS
デュプリケート・ハウス		Duplicate House
石山修武	62	OSAMU ISHIYAMA
世田谷村		Setagaya Village
飯田善彦	66	YOSHIHIKO IIDA
J山荘ゲストハウス		J Villa Guest House
石田敏明	68	TOSHIAKI ISHIDA
T²		T²
ジム・ジェニングス	70	JIM JENNINGS
アーティストのための宿泊施設		Visiting Artist Suites
グドゥムンドゥール・ヨンソン	72	GUDMUNDUR JONSSON
アイスランドの夏の家		The Wall
ハマロイ島の夏の家		The Elevating Intersection
アン・M・ペンデルトン＝ジュリアン	74	ANN M. PENDLETON-JULLIAN
テネリフェ島の生物気候住宅		Bioclimatic House for Tenerife
岸和郎	78	WARO KISHI
東灘の家		House in Higashinada
北川原温	80	ATSUSHI KITAGAWARA
C邸		C House
リカルド・レゴレッタ	81	RICARDO LEGORRETA
カーサ・オファー		Casa Offer
マーク・マック	84	MARK MACK
リトナー邸		Ritenour House
タオスの家		House in Taos
リチャード・マイヤー	86	RICHARD MEIER
ラチョフスキー邸 II		Rachofsky House II

メカノ	90	MECANOO
オランダ大使公邸		Dutch Ambassador's Residence
村上徹	92	TORU MURAKAMI
今治の家		House in Imabari
タレク・ナガ	94	TAREK NAGA
スキャンダース邸		The Scandars Residence
西本圭敦	98	TAEG NISHIMOTO
キム=ライダー邸		Kim-Ryder House
エドワード・R・ナイルズ	102	EDWARD R. NILES
マッケイ邸		McKAY RESIDENCE
プレスコウ+ラエル	104	PLESKOW+RAEL
アヴネット邸		Avnet House
スコット・パーカー	106	SCOTT PARKER
ポワリエ邸		Poirier Residence
シェーファー・アーキテクツ	108	SHAFER ARCHITECTS
渓谷の家		Residence in Salt Lake County
ソットサス・アソシアーティ	110	SOTTSASS ASSOCIATI
スティールのプレファブ・エレメントによる住宅コミュニティ		Project for Residential Community in Pre-Fabricated Steel Elements
ジャスミン・ヒル		Jasmine Hill
ファン・アンプ邸		Casa Van Impe
首藤廣剛	117	HIRO SHUDO
松永邸		Matsunaga House
三浦邸		Miura House
シスコヴィッツ+コワルスキー	120	SZYSZKOWITZ + KOWALSKI
リッツィ邸		House Rizzi
ジョセフ・ヴァレリオ	122	JOSEPH VALERIO
シンシナティ・ドリーム・ハウス		Cincinnati Dream House
カルロス・ザパタ	124	CARLOS ZAPATA
クライン邸		Klein Residence
ピーター・ゼルナー	128	PETER ZELLNER
埠頭の家		Jetty House
モーターサイクリストの家		MotoHouse
ハウジング		**HOUSING**
フレデリック・ボレル	134	FREDERIC BOREL
集合住宅と学校		Housing Program and School
E.o.E.	138	P. EBNER / G. ECKERSTORFER
学生寮		Students' Housing
コープ・ヒンメルブラウ	140	COOP HIMMELBLAU
ウィーンの高層集合住宅		Highrise Building with Climate Facade
ガソメター B-2		Gasometer B2
ウィーンの集合住宅		Apartment Building Remise Vorgartenstrasse
マーク・マック	149	MARK MACK
ウィーンの集合住宅		Vienna Housing
エンリック・ミラージェス	152	ENRIC MIRALLES
サルデーニャの海辺のリゾート		Seaside Resort in Sardinia
エリック・オーエン・モス	158	ERIC OWEN MOSS
ウィーンの集合住宅		Vienna Housing
ガソメター D-1		Gasometer D-1
パウホフ	166	PAUHOF
リンツの再開発計画		New Urban Complex
マイケル・ソーキン	168	MICHAEL SORKIN
ウィーンの集合住宅		Vienna Housing
デイヴィッド・ロックウッド	170	DAVID ROCKWOOD
高層集合住宅プロトタイプ		Residential Tower Prototype

《世界の住宅》48
編集・発行人：二川幸夫

1996年3月15日発行
エーディーエー・エディタ・トーキョー
東京都渋谷区千駄ヶ谷3-12-14
電話(03)3403-1581(代)
ファクス(03)3497-0649

ロゴタイプ・デザイン：細谷巖
印刷：日本写真印刷株式会社
製本：(株)丸山製本所

取次店
トーハン・日販・大阪屋
栗田出版販売・誠光堂
西村書店・中央社・太洋社

禁無断転載

ISBN4-87140-348-3 C1352

GA HOUSES 48
Publisher/Editor: Yukio Futagawa

Published in March 1996
© A.D.A. EDITA Tokyo Co., Ltd.
3-12-14 Sendagaya,
Shibuya-ku, Tokyo, 151 Japan
Tel. 03-3403-1581
Fax. 03-3497-0649

Logotype Design: *Gan Hosoya*

Printed in Japan by
Nissha Printing Co., Ltd.

All rights reserved.

Copyright of Photographs:
© *GA photographers*

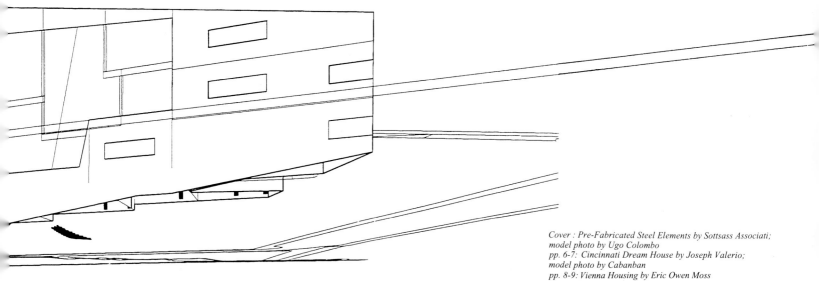

Cover : Pre-Fabricated Steel Elements by Sottsass Associati;
model photo by Ugo Colombo
pp. 6-7: Cincinnati Dream House by Joseph Valerio;
model photo by Cabanban
pp. 8-9: Vienna Housing by Eric Owen Moss

TADAO ANDO

TOWN HOUSE IN HIRANO
Hirano-ku, Osaka, Japan
Design: 1995
Construction: 1996

Site plan

計画：平野区の町屋／大阪市平野区
用途：専用住宅／夫婦＋母親
建築主：能見康一
建築設計：安藤忠雄建築研究所　担当／安藤忠雄, 水谷孝明, 小杉宰子
構造設計：アスコラル構造研究所
施工：ハンドハウス建築工房
敷地面積：120.48m²／第1種居住専用地域
建築面積：72.11m²／建蔽率59.85％（許容60％）
延床面積：92.13m²／容積率65.05％（許容160％）
建築規模：地上2階, 最高高さ5.7m
主体構造：鉄筋コンクリート造
主要仕上：ベニヤ型枠コンクリート打放し

Roof plan

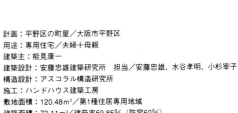
First floor plan

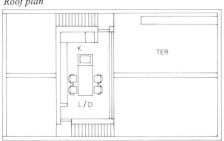
Second floor plan

Section

The house is located in downtown Osaka where many traditional row houses and small family businesses still abound. Designed for a young couple and a mother, it stands as if it were completely cut off from the outside world by four walls. The plan consists of equal volume of indoor spaces and open courts. The occupants' mutual privacy is retained by placing the common living room on upper level and two bedrooms on the ground level each opening to its own courtyard. Thus the building holds two households, each holding its own by having a courtyard as a nucleus but sharing the rest of more public spaces with the other.

The house is entered through the only opening in the perimeter wall. A small court leads you to the stairs to the upper level where the living area with a open terrace welcomes you. From here the private quarters are reached by way of respective stairs and courtyards. The living area is open and lively, filled with even light filtered by a wide overhang. In contrast, the bedroom quarters below are calm and serene with only dimmed light entering through the courts. A big tree in the back court is the only link, in this concrete enclosure, to the outside world which provide a token dialogue with nature.

From a purely functional standpoint, the house demands some getting used to. The two-court solution provides, however, good ventilation and quality of light throughout, and furthermore the courtyards reflect the duality of family structure this house embraces.
Tadao Ando

この住宅は，今も町工場や長屋が多く残る，大阪の下町に位置している。若い夫婦とその母親のための2世帯住宅は，周辺から切り取られるように立ち上がった四周の壁の内側に，内部空間と同等のヴォリュームの外部空間を持ち，2階に居間，1階に2つの寝室を配し，各世帯の寝室がそれぞれ専用の庭に面することで，お互いのプライバシーを確保している。ここでは，個室以外を共有しながら，庭を核にしていわば2つの家を内包しているといえる。

外部に向かって唯一開かれた入口から，前庭，外階段を通ってこの家族の生活の中心となる2階の居間へと至る。前面に広いテラスを持ったこの場でお互いに顔を合わせてから，それぞれの個室へ向かうことになる。再び階段を降りて，庭を通り，公的な場からより私的な場，寝室へと移行していく。庇が大きく突き出した2階の居間が，均質な光が入り込み明るく開放的な場になっているのとは対照的に，1階の寝室は，光の量が限られ落ち着いた場になっている。後庭では，大木が根を下ろし，コンクリートの壁に囲まれた中で，唯一取り込まれた緑との対話がなされる。

機能一辺倒でないところに，生活するには難しい部分もあるが，通風，採光の機能面でも庭が中心的な役割を果たし，専用の庭を持つ各部屋が，立体的に配されている。
（安藤忠雄）

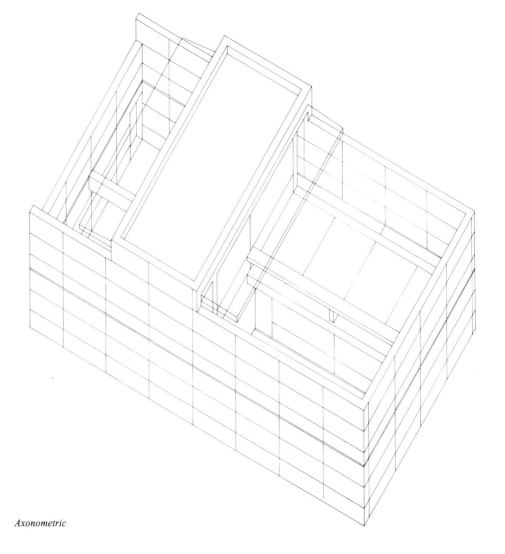
Axonometric

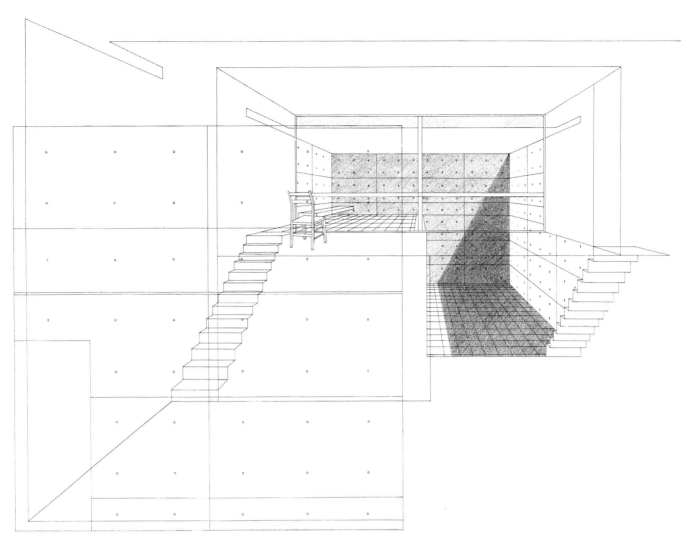
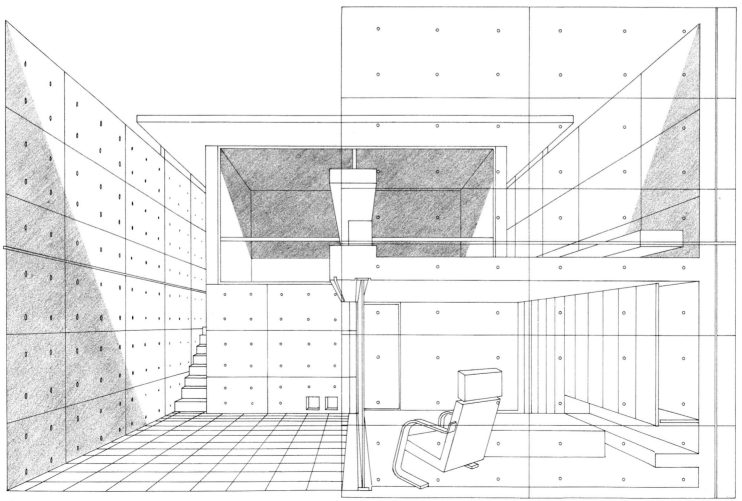

Perspectives

ARCHITECTURE RESEARCH OFFICE

LOFT APARTMENT
Flatiron District, New York, U.S.A.
Design: 1995–96
Under construction

This project occupies two floors of a former factory in the Flatiron district of Manhattan. The main living areas are located on the third floor, while the floor below contains a guest suite and gallery for the owner's art collection. A double-height space and a mezzanine connect the two levels. The design evolves from several conditions: an economy of means necessitated by a limited budget, the display of a beautiful collection of art and furniture, and the owner's desire to live in the open space of a loft, while simultaneously enjoying the enclosed rooms of a townhouse.

The design establishes a spatial framework for programmatic relationships that vary according to day-to-day living. On the third floor, the west half of the loft is subdivided into a series of rooms with discrete programs: sleeping, bathing, studying, exercising and playing. Between these rooms and the main open living space, sliding screens and solid panels establish a variable edge. Screens of silk act like a theatrical scrim —when lit from the living area they are opaque, displaying the owner's photography collection which hangs on them. When an activity occurs within a room, the fabric screens become translucent as they are illuminated from both sides. For rooms where greater privacy is needed, solid doors control view, sound and movement. The experience of the loft changes through the interaction of particular rooms with the main living space caused by different configurations of panels and screens. Similarly, the dining area, the library on the mezzanine and the second floor guest room are experienced both separate from or a part of the loft's continuous space. The partitions defining these areas do not extend to the ceiling, allowing daylight to penetrate into the loft.

The overall spatial and program relationships established by the screens are reinforced by the use of other materials elsewhere in the loft. Wall and floor planes of unusual materials contrast with the roughness of original wood factory floor. These elements have a large scale and minimal detail, leaving the middle ground to be occupied by the client's art and furniture. The dining area has a leather tile floor and a translucent beeswax wall. Floating between the second and third floor, the library is partially defined by a cork floor and a wall of books. Panels of sandblasted water-white glass divide the guest suite from the second floor gallery. The material qualities of these program areas distinguish them from the continuous space of the loft.

マンハッタン, フラティロン地区にある, 元は工場だった建物の2つの階を占めている。主要な住空間は3階にあり, その下の階にはゲスト・スペースとオーナーの美術コレクションが置かれている。2層吹き抜けた空間とメザニンがこの2つの階を結んでいる。いくつかの条件からこのデザインが生まれた。限られた予算のため経済的な方法をとること。芸術作品や家具の美しいコレクションを飾ること。オーナーが, ロフト特有のオープン・スペースに住みたいと同時に, タウンハウスの囲まれた部屋も楽しみたいと考えていることなどである。

毎日の生活に対応して変化する, 計算されたスペース・フレームをつくりあげる。3階では, ロフトの西半分が別個のプログラム——眠る, 風呂を浴びる, 勉強する, 体操する, 遊ぶ——をもつ一連の部屋へ細分されている。これらの部屋と開放的な主リヴィング・スペースの間は, 引き込み式のスクリーンとソリッドなパネルで多彩な端部を構成する。絹のスクリーンは劇場の沙幕のように働き, リヴィング・エリアから照明すると, スクリーンは不透明となり, そこに下げられているオーナーの写真コレクションを浮き立たせる。その部屋が使われているときは, 両側から照明されるので布製のスクリーンは半透明となる。さらにプライヴァシーを必要とする部屋は, ソリッドなドアで, 見通し, 音, 動きを制御する。ロフト内での体験は, パネルやスクリーンの異なった布置が引き起こす, メイン・リヴィング・スペースと個室との相互作用を通して変化する。同じように, ダイニング・エリア, メザニンの書斎, 2階のゲスト・ルームもまた, ロフトの連続する空間の一部としても, 個別の空間としても経験することができる。これらのエリアを分けているパーティションは, 天井までの高さがないので, 日差しはロフトのなかに浸透して行く。

スクリーンがつくりだす空間とプログラムの全体的関係は, ロフト内に使われている材料によって補強される。珍しい材料を用いた壁や床は, 元の工場の荒々しい木の床と対照をなしている。これらのエレメントは大きな尺度とミニマルなディテールを備え, 中央のスペースを美術作品や家具のために残している。ダイニング・エリアはレザー・タイルの床にワックスを塗った半透明の壁。2階と3階の間に浮かぶ書斎は, コルクの床と書棚壁で部分的に境界がつけられている。サンドブラスト仕上げ, ウォーター・ホワイトのガラス・パネルがゲスト・スイートと2階ギャラリーの間を分けている。使われている材料の質が, これらのエリアをロフトの連続空間と区別する。

Architects: Architecture Research Office—Stephen Cassel, principal-in-charge; Stephen Rogers, project architect; Tom Jenkinson, Adam Yarinsky, Tim Archambault, John Quale, Joon Paik, Josh Pulver, Monica Rivera, Wanda Willmore, project team
Consultants: IP Group Consulting Engineers, MEP

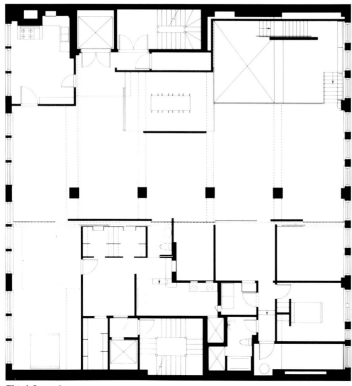

Third floor plan

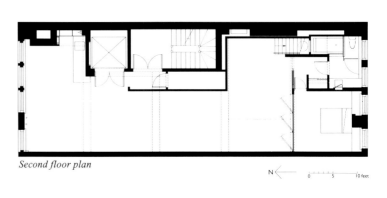

Second floor plan

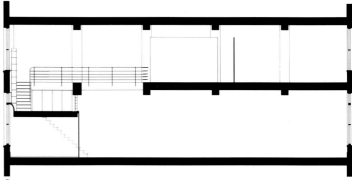

Section

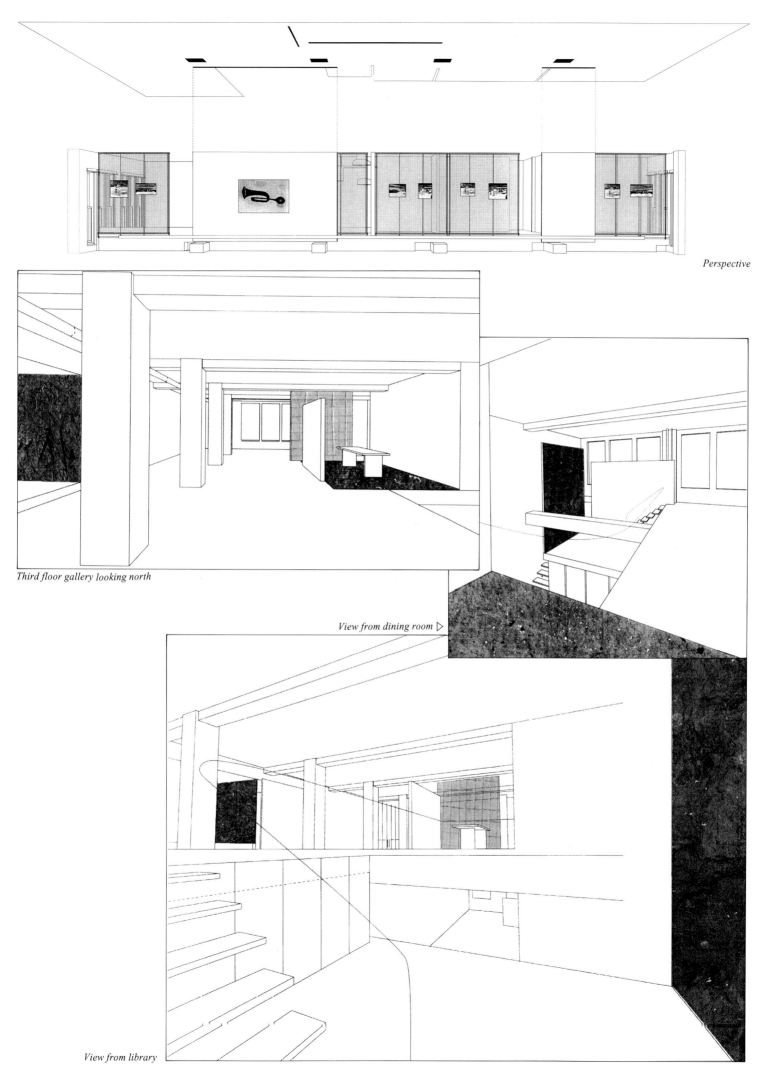

Perspective

Third floor gallery looking north

View from dining room ▷

View from library

ARCHITECTURE PROJECT

APIXV.01 RESIDENCE
Cortlandt Manor, NY, U.S.A.
Design: 1995
Completion: 1996

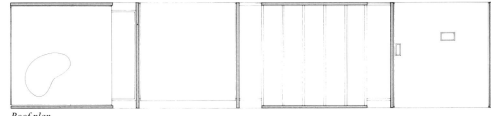
Roof plan

Floor plan

A weekend house in upstate New York, located on a densely wooded site. The program calls for a bedroom, bath, kitchen, living area and swimming pool with an existing barn to be converted to a guest house.

The site has an access road to the south, a stream to the north and an old stone wall to the east. The site does not have a dominant element (lake, view, etc.) to respond to; rather, it is made up of several events and experiences that define place: a vegetable and flower garden, the sound and movement of water in the stream, movement and entry along the stone wall, a rock outcropping, and two existing barn structure.

The proposed house is made up of four sets of parallel concrete structural walls that respond to each other and alternate their orientation with each change of programmatic event (1. bathing 2. resting 3. gathering 4. dining). Glass and wood are laid in-between the concrete walls to complete enclosure and provide opportunities for natural light within.

Light and color variations experienced on the interior are also perceived from the exterior. The bedroom and living areas have a warm glow from teak wood floors and wood fixtures, whereas the bath/spa has a cool glow from the aqua marine glass mosaic floor. The kitchen is in a blue granite stone, with stainless steel fixtures balanced by a teak table and work island. The combination of the above creates a color, tone and light sequence that the user perceives upon approach and experiences within. A sequence that changes throughout the day and season.

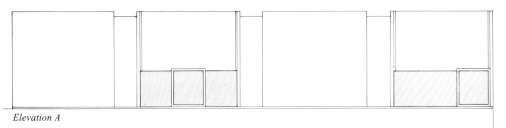
Elevation A

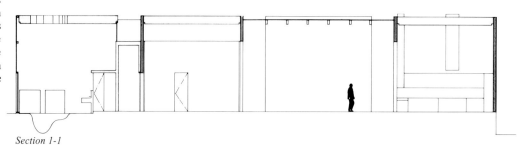
Section 1-1

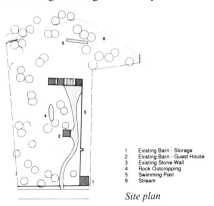

1. Existing Barn - Storage
2. Existing Barn - Guest House
3. Existing Stone Wall
4. Rock Outcropping
5. Swimming Pool
6. Stream

Site plan

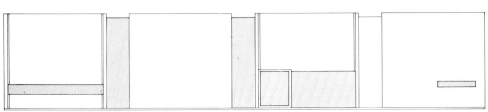
Elevation B

Architects: Architecture Project—Mark Janson, Hal Goldstein, principals
Consultant: Friedman & Oppenheimer, LLP, structural
General contractor: Michael Hord & Company

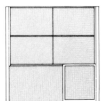
Elevation C

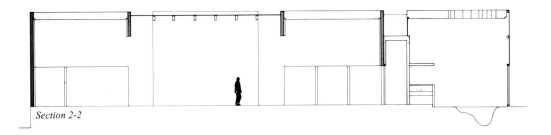
Section 2-2

ニューヨーク北部，深い木立のなかに位置する週末住宅。寝室，浴室，キッチン，リヴィング・エリア，水泳プール，そして既存の納屋をゲスト・ハウスに改造することが求められている。

南にアクセス路，北に小川，東に古い石造りの塀がある。この敷地には湖や景観など，応答すべき支配的な存在はない。むしろ，場所を定めて行く幾つかのイヴェントや経験によって建物を構成するのがよい。野菜畑や花壇，小川のせせらぎの音や水の流れ，動きと石塀に沿ったエントリー，頭をのぞかせている岩，そして元からある納屋。

建物は平行して置かれた4つのコンクリート壁で構成されている。これらの壁は互いに呼応し，それぞれに異なるプログラム（1.水浴び　2.休息　3.集い　4.食事）によって方位を交互に変えている。コンクリート壁の隙間にはガラスと木がはめられ被膜を完結すると同時に光を内部に呼び込む。

内部で経験できる光と色彩の変化は外からも感知できる。寝室とリヴィングはチーク材の床と建具によって暖かく輝き，浴室／スパはアクアマリンのガラス・モザイク・タイルの床が冷たい輝きを放っている。キッチンは青い御影石貼りで，ステンレス・スティールの建具がチーク材のテーブルとワーク・アイランドとのバランスをとっている。こうした組み合わせが色彩，色調，光の連なりをつくりだす。それはアプローチに立つとともに感知され，内部に入って実際に体験することになる。こうしたシークェンスは，一日を通して，季節を通して変転する。

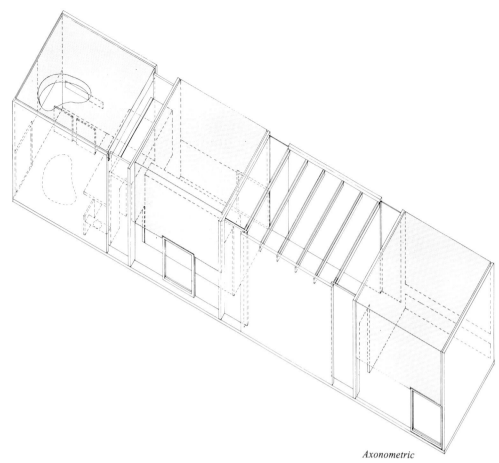

Axonometric

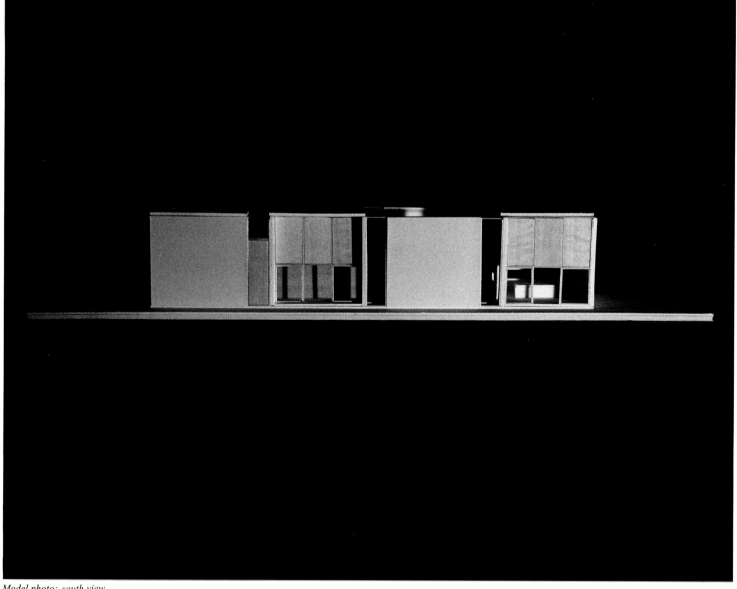

Model photo: south view

ANGELIL/GRAHAM

DESERT HOUSE
La Quinta, California, U.S.A.
Design: 1995
Construction: 1996

Architects: Angélil/Graham—Sarah Graham, Marc Angélil, principals-in-charge; Scott Hudgins, Cynthia Salah, Juan Villalta, Sidhartha Sabikhi, Shevjit Sidhu, project team
Consultant: William Koh, structural

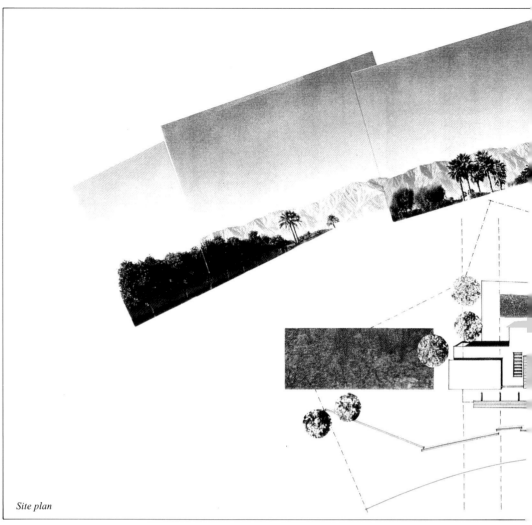

Site plan

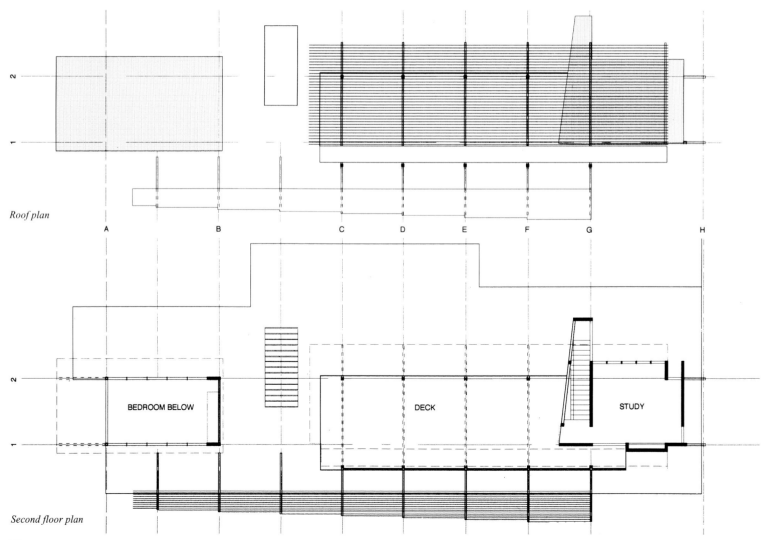

Roof plan

Second floor plan

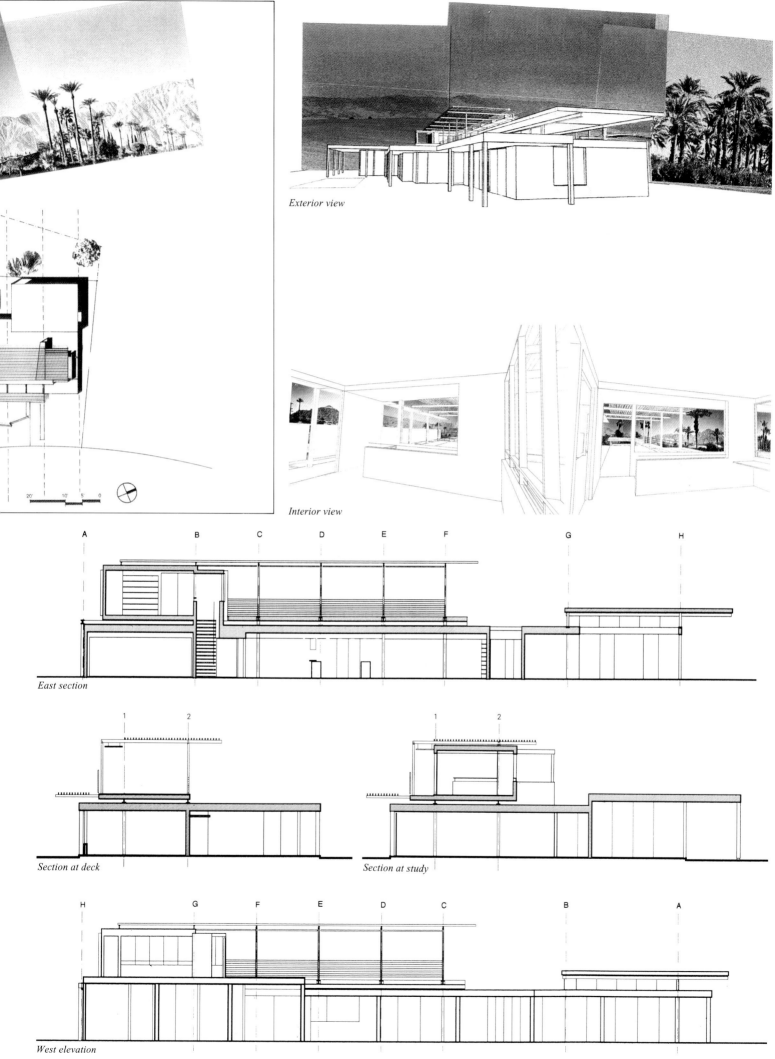

The project is a renovation and addition of an existing house in the Southern California desert.

Dry rugged mountains and vast expanses of sandy scrub lands reflect the omnipresent heat of the American Southwest desert. A primeval beauty prevails, emphasized by the sculptural forms of native cactus and the non-Euclidean geometry of the rock formations. The wildlife of the desert, an existence based on survival, can be heard at night by those who look beyond the newly defined confines of the community.

The climate is extreme: immensely hot in the summer yet cold during winter nights. The warm daytime weather is the source of urban settlement.

The light can be blinding white, when winds carry the desert sands into the air, or sharply clear, bringing the mountains into immediate confrontation. The light reflects the constant panorama of changing colors of those arid mountains: purples and yellows and blues which never remain fixed or solid.

From above, the urban settlement can be viewed as a patchwork of random green shapes which are pieced together to form an oasis community. Water from the aquifer below the desert surface has been brought up to irrigate farms and resort lands. The intensity of such green in the desert light always carries some degree of the surreal, parallel to the relationship between the stark survival code of the desert wilderness and the artificial landscape devoted to recreation.

An existing single family house within the desert community is to be expanded in such a way as to reflect the demands of the climate. The house as stands is within a modernist vernacular, a compilation of horizontal volumes which respect the problems of light and shade but conform to local 2 × 4 light wood construction and dubious craft. This is construction based on the values of expediency, unrelated to the timelessness of the immediate landscape.

The house will be updated, accommodating new services and functions: kitchen, library, and master bedroom complex will be renovated on the ground floor. Finishes will be reworked throughout, emphasizing the changing quality of light reflected from without.

Above, a study and terrace are added onto the existing house. Both utilize the 360 degree views of the dry mountains and function as a series of articulated layers to promote shade and shadow to the house and its inhabitants. Floating above the roof with minimal penetrations, the upper level encourages air movement within its spaces and between its layers.

A steel frame holds the second floor layers apart from the lower construction while seismically reinforcing the existing house. The principle of layering carries onto the construction and the details, with roof planes, shade louvers, retractable fabric awnings, and ventilator apertures articulated in response to the desert environment.

Model photo: east view

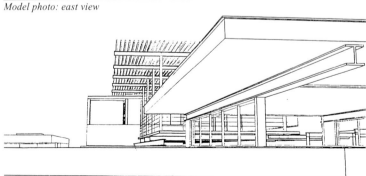

South view

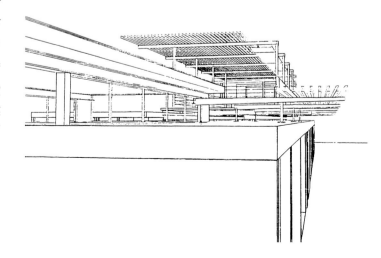

南カリフォルニアの砂漠にある既存住宅の改造と増築である。乾燥した岩山と低木の続く砂地の広大な土地は、アメリカ南西部の砂漠に遍在する熱を反射する。サボテンと非ユークリッド幾何学をかたちづくる岩の広がりによって強調された原始的な美しさが席巻している。夜には、適者生存に支配されている砂漠の野生生物の声が、新たに形成されたコミュニティの境界に佇む者の耳に聞こえる。

極限の気候である。夏は非常に暑いが、冬の夜は厳しい寒さである。都市化した定住のためには、日中の温暖な気候が根源的条件である。

風が砂漠の砂を空中に吹き上げると、光は目のくらむような白さとなり、あるときはまた、山並みを間近に運んでくるほどくっきりと澄み渡る。光はこれらの乾ききった山々の移り変わる色彩のパノラマを写し出す。紫、黄、青とその色彩は決して留まることなく変転し続ける。

上空からは、集落はオアシスの町を形成するように繋ぎ合わさり、不規則な緑色の形からなるパッチワークのように見えるだろう。砂漠の地表下の帯水層から水が汲み上げられて、農地やリゾートを潤す。砂漠の光のなかのこうした緑の集中は、砂漠という荒野の厳しいサヴァイヴァル・コードと、レクリエーションに捧げられた人工の風景との間の関係と平行する、いくぶん、シュールな趣をもたらす。

砂漠のコミュニティ内にある既存の戸建て住宅は、気候の求めるものに対応するように拡張することになる。既存家屋はモダニスト・ヴァナキュラーの範疇に入るもので、光と影の問題を尊重した水平のヴォリュームで編集されているが、ローカルな2×4の軽量木構造とおぼつかない職人技術でつくられている。これは間近の風景のもつ無限性とは無関係な便宜的な価値に基づいた建物である。

この住宅に新しいサーヴィスや機能を供給し、最新なものにする。1階のキッチン、ライブラリー、主寝室は改造されることになる。仕上げは、外部から反射する光の変化する質を強調するように、全体にやり直す。

既存家屋の上に、書斎とテラスを増築する。どちらからも360度に渡り、乾燥した山々が見え、建物と住み手に日陰や影を多く与えるための一連の分節されたレイヤーとして機能するように活用する。上の階は、最小限の光の浸透を許す屋根の上に浮かべられ、そのレイヤーの間を空気が流れていくように構成する。

スティール・フレームが、既存住宅の耐震力を強化する一方で、低層階の構造は別として、2階のレイヤーを支持している。レイヤリングの原則は、屋根、日除けのルーヴァー、伸縮自在の布製天幕、砂漠環境に対応するように分節された換気孔など、構造やディテールに取り入れられている。

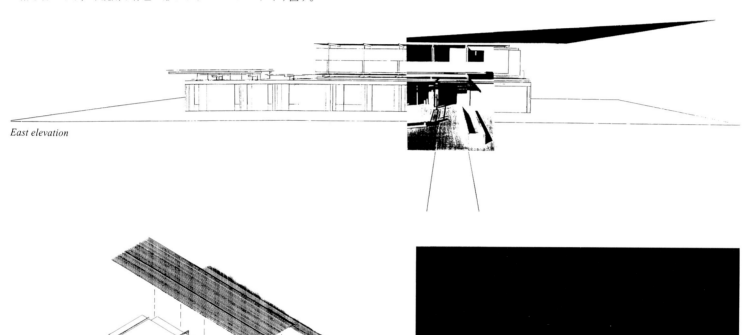

East elevation

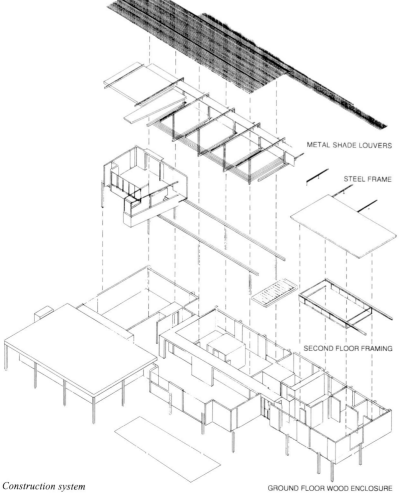

Construction system

South view

BRIAN ALFRED MURPHY

KAYE RESIDENCE
Santa Monica, California, U.S.A.
Design: 1995
Completion: 1996

They bought a Tudor but they really wanted a 4-door,...

An existing retro-Mansion who's new owners first request was to "Make it disappear." Their preference was to have a clean gallery/exhibit space along with studio/work environment;... minimal interaction with the surrounding neighborhood. A safe, comfortable/stimulating domicile in which their young family might grow...

Program
—3500-square-foot exhibit area in the existing 6000-square-foot structure.
—Very private and exciting entry.
—Secure play area for children and dogs.
—Provisions for entertaining.
—3-car covered parking and vehicular access from both ends of the property. Controlled lighting in the art exhibit area.
—Sequestered access to lap pool at second story with deck.
—Consideration for flexible guest/staff quarters.
—Security.
—"Clean, minimal, Clean, Minimal, Clean Minimal," (PRINTER RUN TO END OF PAGE).

Sketches

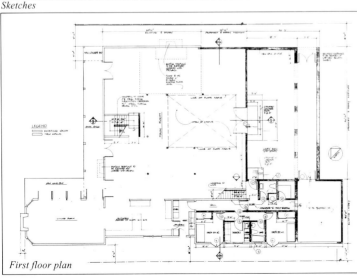
First floor plan

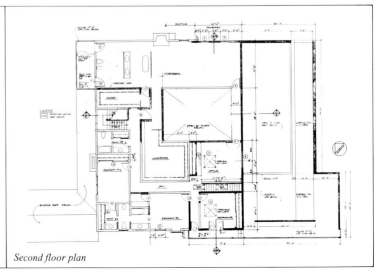
Second floor plan

彼らはチューダー様式の住宅を購入したのだが，実際に欲しかったのはフォードアの，……

このレトロなマンションの新しい持ち主の最初の要望は「それを消してしまう」ことだった。スタジオやワークスペースの付いた，クリーンな展示スペース，……近隣との関係は最小限にとどめる——というのが希望である。子供たちが育って行くことになる，安全で居心地良く，それでいて刺激的な住居。
プログラム：
——もとの6,000sq. ft. の建物に，3,500sq. ft. の展示エリアを設ける。
——外からはわかりにくい，興味をかきたてるエントリー。
——子供たちと犬たちのための安全な遊び場。
——娯楽設備。
——3台収容できる屋根付きの駐車場。敷地両端から車でアクセスできること。
——美術品の展示エリアには制御可能な照明装置をつける。
——2階にあるラップ・プールへのデッキを経由して行く孤立したアクセス。
——ゲスト／スタッフのためのフレキシブルなエリアを考えること。
——保安。
——「クリーン，ミニマル，クリーン，ミニマル，クリーン，ミニマル」（プリント・アウトはページの終わりまでこのまま続く）。

Architects: BAM Construction/Design, Inc.—Brian Alfred Murphy, principal-in-charge; Julie Hart, Suza Ferenx, Eva Held, project team
Consultant: Joseph Perazzelli, structural

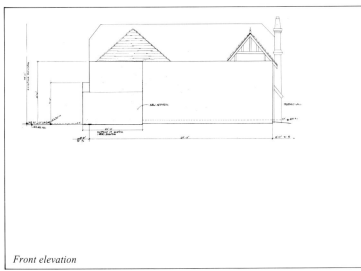

Front elevation

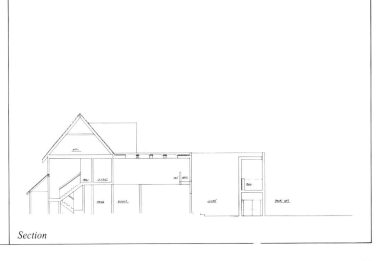

Section

JOSEPH N. BIONDO

SUMMER CABIN
Adirondack Park Region,
New York, U.S.A.
Design: 1995
Construction: 1997

サマーキャビン：敷地はニューヨーク州アディロンダック地方。敷地の特徴に従い，コンテクストに応答したデザインである。材料，工法，空間構成，建築形態は，この地方の実用的な建物のタイポロジーの影響を受け，それを翻案している。

建物と敷地：木々が生い茂る場所に，敷地の長手に直角に向き合うように建物を配置する。屋根の開口を南に向け，光は非常に幅の狭くなっている南側のファサードを抜けて差し込む。オーヴァーハングが強い夏の直射日光を遮り，ベネシャン・ブラインドの付いた窓から湖水からの微風が入り，キャビン全体を流れる。

アプローチ：敷地の方に降りて行くと，キャビンが見え始める。ウェザード・スティールの擁壁と屋根が早くから見え，アディロンダック地方によくある岩の露頭のように，山から切り出したように現れる。

レイヤー・システム：建物の側に来ると，層状の構成で組み立てられているのが分かる。屋根は宙に舞い上がり，メーソンリーのヴォリュームは，その内部に別のレイヤーを包むに充分な大きさ，広がり，規則性を備え，全体を編成するエレメントとなる。

自然光を捕らえ，南側の景色を取り入れたいということから，メーソンリーの壁は薄くされた。これによって荷重を受ける力は減り，補強のために西と

Summer cabin
Situated in the Adirondack Region of New York State, this cabin was conceived as a contextually responsive, site-specific structure. Materials, construction methods, spatial organization and building form reflect and interpret a local functional typology.

Building and site
Building placement is perpendicular to the length of the site, within a densely wooded area. Oriented with the roof opening to the south, natural light is admitted through a highly subtractive south facade. The overhang will omit the direct entry of the intense summer sun, while jalousie windows will allow the lake breezes to flow through and ventilate the cabin.

Approach
Descending towards the site the building begins to reveal itself. A series of weathered steel retaining walls and roof become visible early on and appears to be carved out of the mountain, much like the natural rock outcroppings of the Adirondack Region.

Systems layering
Once adjacent to the building, the layering becomes evident. The roof appears to hover, while the masonry volume becomes an organizing element with sufficient size, closure and regularity to serve as a figure that can embrace the other layers being organized from within.

The desire to capture natural light and to provide views to the south results in a masonry wall with subtractive characteristics. This reduces the shear and load bearing capabilities of the masonry wall, thus a timber truss is introduced at the south and west walls to complete the structure.

The fenestration layer, additive in nature, fastens directly to either side of the masonry wall always revealing the wall thickness. The introduction of jalousie windows creates visual richness in the south and west facades while optimizing air flow throughout the cabin.

Interior casework consists of delicate layers of volumes and planes which together define edges of zones within the cabin. The open design of the casework permits visual continuity of the masonry wall and truss. Hardware, conduit and fixtures are exposed to view and comprise the final layer of the whole.

Materials
Concrete block, wood and weathered steel were chosen for their site sensitive characteristics and natural tones.

Architects: Joseph N. Biondo Architects—Joseph N. Biondo, principal-in-charge; Michael J. Revit, Michael G. Yusem, David L. Everett
Consultant: Michael F. Salley, PE., structural

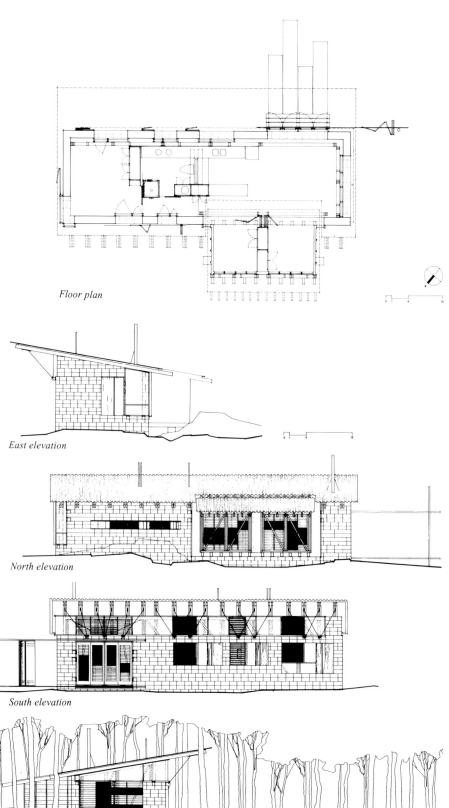

Floor plan

East elevation

North elevation

South elevation

West elevation

Model photo: south view

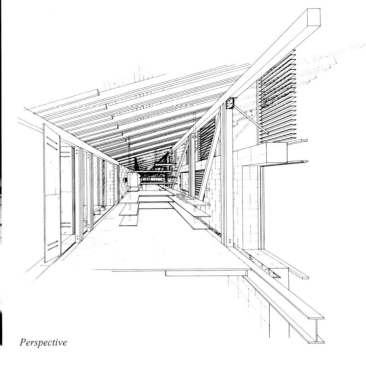
Perspective

南側の壁に丸太のトラスが組み込まれた。
　窓割りのレイヤーは，付加的な性格をもち，メーソンリー壁の両側に直接固定され，壁の厚さを常に見えるものにしている。ベネシャン・ウィンドーによって南と西のファサードは豊かなものとなり，キャビン全体に空気が流れる。
　内部はヴォリュームと面の繊細な層で構成され，それが各ゾーンを分けている。開かれた構成なので，室内は連続したものとして感じられる。ハードウェア，配管，設備は外に露出され，最後のレイヤーを構成する。
材料：敷地の繊細な性格と自然の色調を考えて，コンクリートブロック，木，ウェザード・スティールを選択した。

South edge

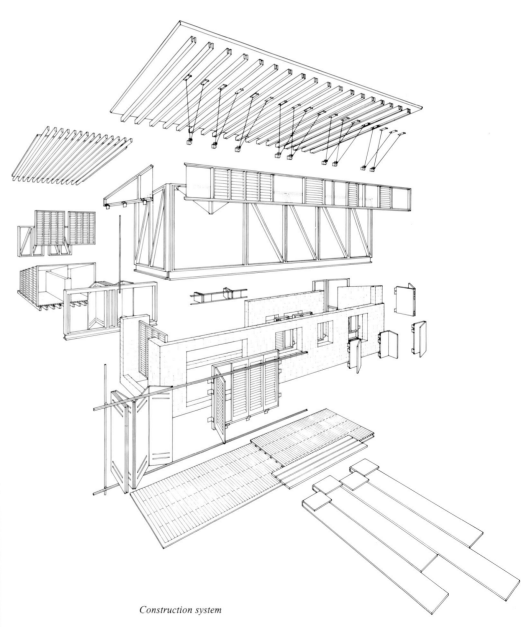
Construction system

WILLIAM P. BRUDER

BURIAN RESIDENCE
Desert Hills, Arizona, U.S.A.
Design: 1995
Construction: 1996

The challenge of this project is to create a desert retreat for a retired librarian and her pets for a modest budget of 70,000 dollars. Located on a ten acre, creosote covered flat desert site, the program of the home includes a vestibule entry for animal safety, a small guest suite, and a shared living, dining, sleep space for the owner with a total area of 985 net square feet. A linear dog/cat garden reaches out to the east and a curved masonry wall defines the west guest garden. A half-round storage room and a pipe and shade mesh carport to the north will shelter a vw "bug" and a pick-up truck from the sun.

In brief, the design solution is a celebration of a simple plan and building section, the use of very basic and low-maintenance materials, and very minimal and inexpensive construction detailes. It is scheme of "one-stroke" systems which come to their finality in the architecture immediately upon placement by a few crafts/tradesmen.

A softly curved, randomly perforated north facing exposed (inside and out) insulated "integra" concrete unit masonry wall serves as an entry foil and winter wind shield for the house. A simple shed roof sloped to a fully glazed, sun sheltered south overhang defines the shape and scale of the homes interior spaces. With a standard corrugated galvanized metal roof and overhang system, standard recycled wood truss "I" joist members, 10 inches insulation batting and a ceiling of sandblasted oriented strand board combined with the masonry walls and polished concrete floors the construction should be accomplished in less than two months. Standard cabinets, storage systems and a large used cast-iron free standing bath tub will be simply customized to serve detailed program functions. All materials will be natural in finish and represent long term low maintenance service to the owner. In winter the sun, minimal gas heaters, and a fire feature provide heat, in the summer, natural ventilation, ceiling fans and evaporative cooling provide space comfort.

The architecture of this desert basic shelter looks back on a design heritage of Wright's Usonians of the 1930s, Mies "pavilion" studies of the 1940s, and the California case study homes of the 1950s to create an exciting, elegant and affordable housing model for the 21st century. The experience of the sensual pleasures of real architecture should be accessible as an option to people of any economic position. An alternative to poorly designed and crafted mobile and tract homes is something that our communities and our citizens desperately need.

停年退職した司書と彼女のペットのために，7万ドルの予算でつつましい住宅を人気のない荒れ地に建てることが課題である。クレオソートで覆われた10エーカーの平坦な不毛の土地である。動物からの安全のために前室となった入口，小さなゲスト・スイート，そして持ち主のためのリヴィング，ダイニング，寝室空間からなる985sq.ft.の住宅。犬と猫のためのリニアーな庭が東に延び，湾曲するメーソンリーの塀が西側のゲスト・ガーデンを囲んでいる。北側の半円形の倉庫とパイプと日除け用のメッシュでできたキャノピー付きのカーポートが，フォルクスワーゲンのかぶと虫とピックアップトラックを日差しから守るだろう。

簡単に言えば，単純な平面と断面構成をもち，非常に基本的で，メンテナンスもあまり必要としない材料，ミニマルで安価なディテールを使うことがこのデザインの解法である。数人の職人や熟練工によって敷地に据えられるやいなや直ちに完成するような，「ひと仕事」ですむシステムによるスキームなのである。

ゆるやかに湾曲し，不規則に穴を穿たれ，北面する，むき出しになった（内も外も）断熱コンクリート・ユニットのメーソンリー壁が入口を引き立て，冬の風から家を守る。ガラス張りの，日差しから守られた南側のオーヴァーハングに向かって傾斜する単純な片流れ屋根が，内部空間の形とスケールを決めている。規格の波形亜鉛メッキメタル製の屋根とオーヴァーハング・システム，規格のリサイクル品である木製トラスのI型ジョイスト，10インチ厚断熱押縁と繊維の流れを揃えたサンドブラスト仕上げの板を使った天井をメーソンリーの壁と磨き仕上げのコンクリート床と組み合わせた建物は，2ヶ月以下の工期で完成できる。規格のキャビネット，収納システムと再生鋳鉄製の大きな浴槽はプログラムの要求する細かな機能に簡単に対応する。材料はすべて自然仕上げとし，メンテナンスも長期間，最小限ですむようなものとする。冬は太陽熱，最小限のガスヒーター，火が熱源となり，夏は，自然換気，天井の扇風機，熱蒸発により部屋を快適にする。

砂漠地のためのこのベーシックなシェルターは，30年代のライトのユーソニアン・ハウス，40年代のミースの"パビリオン"に対する一連のスタディ，50年代のカリフォルニアにおけるケース・スタディ・ハウスを回顧し，21世紀のための，斬新かつ優雅で実現可能な住宅モデルをつくろうというものである。現実の建築のもつ感覚的な楽しさは，どのような経済力の人にも実現可能であるべきだ。劣悪なデザインと仕上げのモビールハウスや建て売り住宅に代わるものが，早急に求められている。

Architects: william p. bruder–architect, ltd.—Will Bruder, Jack DeBartolo 3, Ben Nesbeitt, design team
Consultants: Brickey, Rudow and Berry, structural

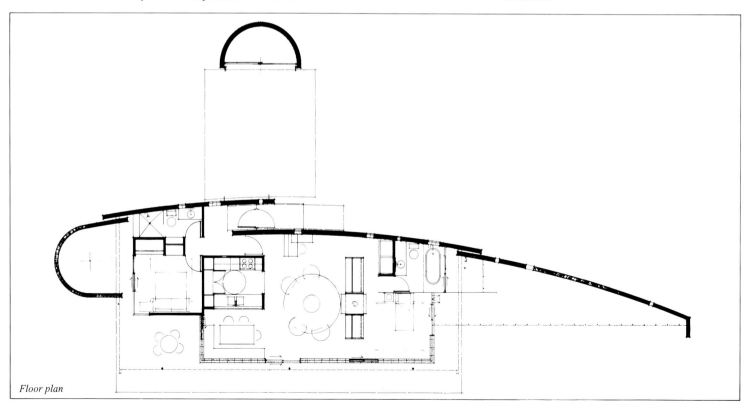

Floor plan

Model photos

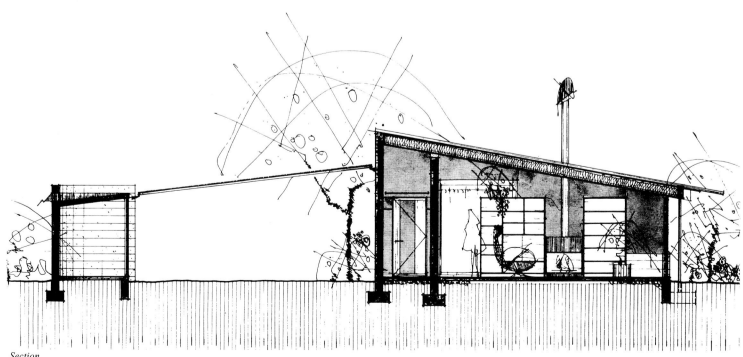

Section

WILLIAM P. BRUDER

SOLSTICE I
Canmore, Alberta, Canada
Design: 1994–95
Construction: 1996

Architects: william p. bruder–architect, ltd.—Will Bruder, Jack DeBartololo 3, Dan Harding, design team
Consultants: Brickey, Rudow and Berry, structural

A retirement retreat for a professional couple to be located on a densely wooded lot overlooking the Bow River with vistas in all directions of rugged snow covered, granite peaks. The residence will be their winter and summer base and thus the name *Solstice*. The owner's are very into personal fitness and outdoor sports, i.e. cross country skiing, mountain and road biking, kayaking, and aerobics. Program functions include sports equipment storage, maintenance, and preparation areas, a workout room and spa like bathing and changing areas. Other unique program features include a serious library, a film viewing room, an on-line computer center and a writer's den. The clients are extremely private and the house has been conceived to enjoy distant as well as micro views while having a mysterious sense of enclosure and security from the street and adjacent lots.

Working with a very restrictive set of community design guidelines the project has grown as a multileveled metaphorical "rock" like mass which diagonally straddles the natural rock outcrop of the site's escarpment position. With a southeastern elevation that is, in large part an insulated translucent glass scrim, north and northwestern elevations that deal with the site's dramatic forest and mountain peak vistas and a series of rooftop skylight penetrations, the architecture is designed to make the internal environment a pavilion of daylight. By carefully framing and editing the views from interior spaces as well as manipulating the fall of light across the reflective plaster wall and concrete floor surfaces, the project's interior architecture will dynamically be enhanced by passage of day and each season's unique sunlight. Combined with the reflective neutral whites and grays of the primary surfaces will be the warm glow of wood veneers and resawn board elements and several powerful colored planes. The scheme's primary staircase along the translucent scrim wall of the entry facade will have more the presence of a "hilltown street" as its surface textures and movement patterns are varied and articulated than a traditional staircase.

From the exterior a natural rock entry wall and porch, a vertical random pattern of weathered

Lower floor plan

gray cedar board and batten siding, an acid etched galvanized metal roof and several deep colored plaster walls will make the house most "stealth" like in the shadows of the surrounding trees. In the spirit of the great lodges of the Canadian Rockies at nearby Banff and Lake Louise, this house is designed to be both rustic and modest, and at the same time sophisticated and elegant. Foremost, however, it is wanting to be a warm, cozy, and comfortable retreat for all seasons.

専門職をもつ夫妻が引退後，閑居する場で，ボウ川を望み，雪を頂いた険しい花崗岩の峰々を四方に見晴らせる，木々の生い茂る敷地である。夫妻が冬と夏に利用する家であるので，Solstice 二至（夏至冬至）と名付けた。二人は，スキーのクロスカントリー，バイク，カヤック乗り，エアロビクスなど，フィットネスや戸外スポーツに熱心である。プログラムにはスポーツ用具の収納，補修，準備のための部屋，トレーニング室，スパのような沐浴場，更衣室が含まれている。その他に特徴のある施設として，ライブラリー，映写室，オンラインのコンピュータ・センター，著作用のデンがある。クライアントは非常にプライヴァシーを重んじており，建物は，謎めいた感じに囲い込まれ，道路や隣接地から守られている一方，近景も遠景も楽しめるように考えた。

この地域には非常に制限されたデザイン上のガイドラインがあり，建物は，'岩'のメタファーのような多層のマッスを構成し，断崖に位置する敷地の岩の露頭に斜めにまたがっている。南東の立面は大半が絶縁した半透明のガラスの沙幕，北と北西の立面は森や山々の景色に向き，屋根には一連のスカイライトが取られ，内部には昼の光の溢れるパヴィリオンがつくられるようにデザインされている。眺めを細心に枠取り編集すると同時に，よく反射するプラスター壁とコンクリート床の表面を横断して差し込んでくる光を操作することによって，内部空間は，毎日の，そして季節ごとに固有の日差しの推移によって強調される。主要な面に光をよく反射するニュートラルな白やグレイの組み合わせは，木の合板やのこぎり引きの板，いくつかの強い色彩を塗った面の暖かい輝きとなるだろう。入口ファサードの半透明の沙幕のような壁に沿った主階段は，従来の階段よりも表面のテクスチュアや動きのパターンが多様に分節され，'丘の町の通り'以上の存在感をもつだろう。

外からは，自然石の入口壁とポーチ，風雨にさらされて変色したように見せかけたグレイのシーダー・ボードの不規則な縦羽目，小割板の下見，酸で食刻した亜鉛メッキメタルの屋根，いくつかの濃い色のプラスター壁が，この住宅を周囲の木立の影のなかに密やかに置くことになるだろう。バンフやレイク・ルイーズに近いカナディアン・ロッキーの大きなロッジのもつスピリットのなか，この家は野生味があり，質実であると同時に洗練され優雅なものとなるように設計されている。しかし，最も大切にしたのは，四季を通じて暖かく，居心地よく快適な隠棲の場をつくることである。

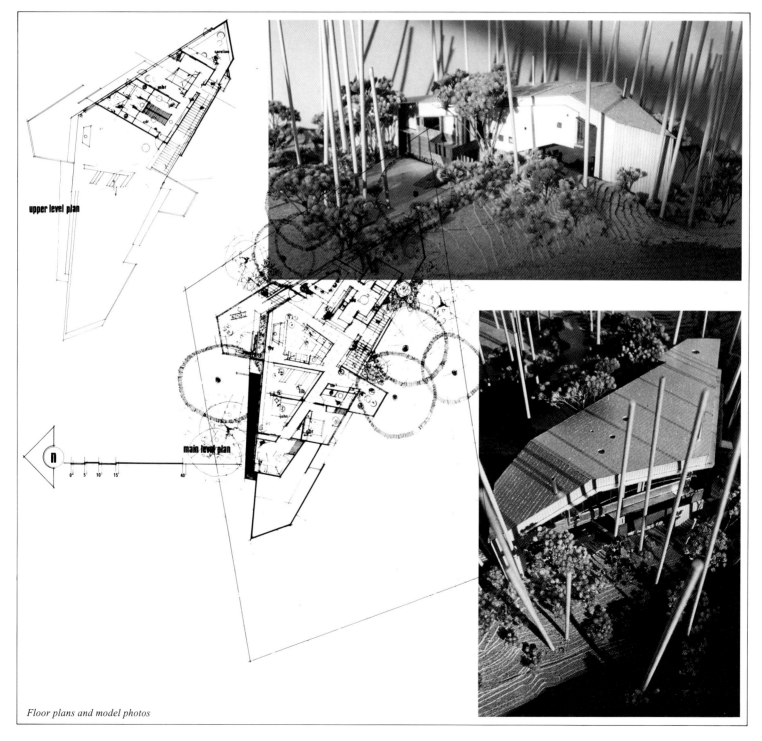

Floor plans and model photos

WILLIAM P. BRUDER

PAT MATTHEWS RESIDENCE
Glacier View Meadows, Red Feather, Colorado, U.S.A.
Design: 1995
Construction: 1996

Architects: william p. bruder–architect, ltd.—Will Bruder, Jack DeBartolo 3, Ben Nesbeitt, design team
Consultants: Brickey, Rudow and Berry, structural

This retirement retreat for one of my original clients (1972) is located on a 10+ acre site in the mountains of north central Colorado. The site is unique in that no man made object is visible between it and the distant peaks of the Rocky Mountain National Park more than fifty miles away. A modest program of 1800 square feet plus an auto storage structure will provide for a guest suite, general living, a subterranean level computer/crafts studio, and a sleeping/bathing loft level suite for the owner. As contextually appropriate and owner required the primary construction materials will be traditional log and corrugated galvanized metal roofing common to the region.

Designed to work with the topography, focus on the views and capture the southern sun, the scheme is composed of two asymmetrically triangular plan forms. The logs of the primary walls throughout the geometry form interesting tensions and adjacencies. The crisp geometry will be softened by the rusticated wild random cantilevers of the log tips and butts at all corners in the manner of Reima Pietila's "SARESTO" of 1972, a studio and gallery in "Nordic" lapland. Interior walls of fabric, veneered plywood, and translucent glass, a floor of exposed smooth sanded aspen oriented strand board and ceiling of sandblasted strand board will work in tension and contrast to the textures of the logs and the landscape. With the flat roofed mass of the log garage playing against the steeply pitched metal roof of the house, the architecture in form is very much a landscape sculpture played against the site's unique natural geological features.

A third triangular form adjacent to the residence's south window wall is an exposed aggregate cantilevered cast concrete "rock like" platform with a rustic log, pole, and woven reed bench and railing system. Beneath this element

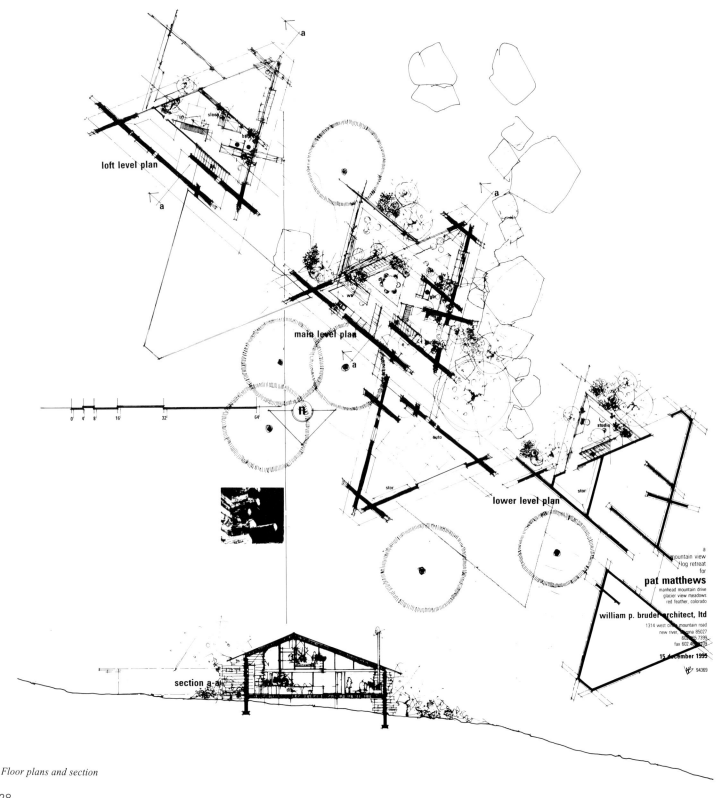

Floor plans and section

is the owner's computer and craft studio with strip glazing set at grade to give it a cave like perspective of the flora and fauna (birds and animals) of the site.

This architectural concept uses the traditional materials of the place, bonds with natural features of its site setting and strives to create a poetic and timeless marriage of geometry and light for the owner to continue her journey through life.

1972年に住宅を設計したことのあるクライアントの依頼による引退後の住宅で，コロラド北部の中央部に聳える山中にある10エーカー余の敷地である。敷地から50マイル先のロッキー山系国立公園の峰々まで，人の建てたものは皆無という珍しい場所である。1800sq.ft.の住宅＋ガレージという簡素な建物で，ゲスト・スイート，リヴィング全般，コンピュータ／工芸の仕事場のある階，主寝室／浴室のあるロフト階がある。周辺のコンテクストに相応しいこととオーナーの要望もあって，主要な建築材料はこの地方に一般的な昔ながらの丸太と波形亜鉛メッキメタル葺きの屋根となるだろう。

地形に合わせ，眺望に焦点を定め，南からの日差しを捕らえるようにデザインした建物は，非対称な2つの三角形プランで構成されている。この幾何形態全体を貫く丸太の壁が，興趣ある緊張感をつくりだす。このきっぱりした幾何学形態は，レイマ・ピエティラが1972年に，北方のラップランドに建つスタジオとギャラリー「サレスト」で行った同じ方法を使って各コーナーに施した，丸太の先端と元口による不規則で野趣のある片持ちによって和らげられる。布，化粧張り合板，半透明ガラスの内壁，滑らかに砂で磨いたアスペン材の繊維ボードの床とサンドブラスト仕上げの繊維ボードの天井が丸太のテクスチュアや風景と対比を描くだろう。丸太造のガレージの平坦な屋根が，住宅の急傾斜の金属屋根と対立を演じ，この家はその形態において敷地固有の地質に対するまさに景観彫刻としての役割を演じる。

建物南面のウィンドー・ウォールに隣接する3つ目の三角形は，一団になったキャスト・コンクリートの「岩のような」プラットフォームが片持ちで露出したもので，丸太，柱，アシを編んだベンチ，手摺が付いている。この下はオーナーのコンピュータと工芸用の仕事場で，地盤面の高さにガラス張りの帯状の開口が取られ，仕事場に，この敷地の植物相や動物相（鳥や動物）の洞穴のような見通しを与える。

この場所にある伝統的な材料を，敷地の備えている自然の特徴で結んで，幾何学形態と光が，詩的で，無限に融合するような，オーナーが生涯にわたる旅を続けるための場所をつくりたいと考えた。

View from site

Model photos

WALLACE E. CUNNINGHAM

SALTMAN RESIDENCE
La Jolla, California, U.S.A.
Design: 1995
Construction: 1996

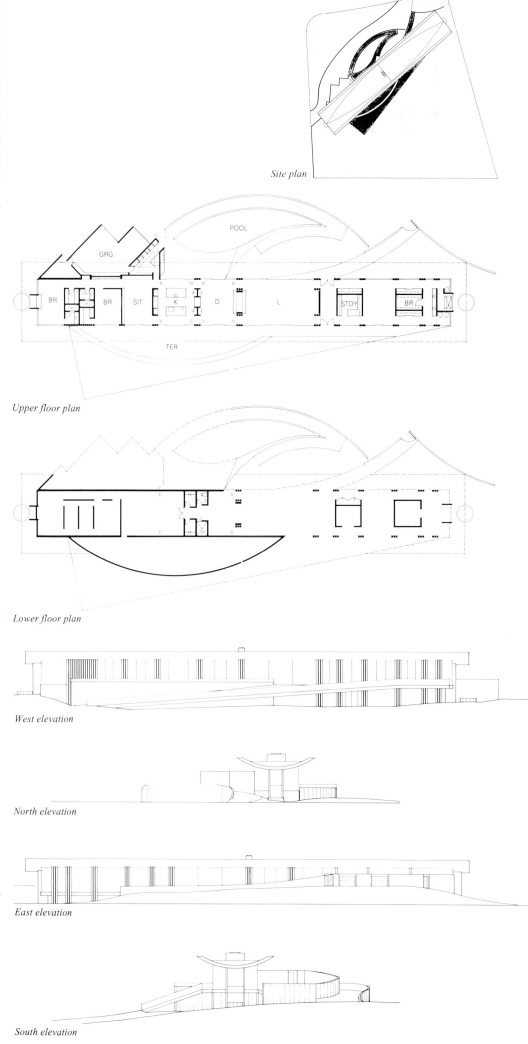

Site plan

Upper floor plan

Lower floor plan

West elevation

North elevation

East elevation

South elevation

This design replaces a 30-year-old house on a one acre ocean view site near the University of California San Diego and Louis Kahn's Salk Institute. It was commissioned by Dr. Paul Saltman, a prominent biologist at UCSD, and his wife Barbara, an artist, and one of the founders of the La Jolla contemporary crafts gallery, Gallery Eight.

The site is gently rolling land set back from the ocean front cliff, with a handsome, existing mature landscape of black pines, melaleucas and several varieties of bamboo, designed by Joseph Yamada, ASLA, of the prestigious San Diego landscape firm Wimmer Yamana. During the years the Saltmans inhabited the original ranch-style house, the ocean view became impaired by surrounding residential development. The new one level design is oriented for distant views and has the house floating like a platform above the ground. The landscape rolls down underneath and through it toward the ocean. This lifting of the living level restores a full view of the ocean.

With references to antiquity, the three-bedroom residence hovers in the landscape like a contemporary temple or shrine, subtly reflecting the owners admiration for Oriental and native American art. The sense of ceremonial platform is further enhanced by the knowledge that this land was home to the Kumeyaay tribe of native Americans many centuries ago and nearby was the site of their ancient burial ground.

The approach to the house is up a driveway of random quarried stone to the living level. The open breezeway beneath houses mechanical and service areas. A ramp leads below grade around the perimeter of an abstract fish or leaf-shaped pool with a vanishing edge waterfall. Dark gray unpolished stone is the flooring material both inside and out contrasted with wood paneled walls. The entrance is on the main living level where all rooms take advantage of a completely open plan and clear views east and west through expanses of glass. Space separation occurs through the use of walls for the owners' extensive collection of books, contemporary glass and pottery, allowing easy circulation in each room. Special consideration was given to the owners' fine collection of mid-century furnishings and contemporary-crafted furniture. The west, ocean-view side of the house opens on to a large elliptical entertainment terrace with built-in poured concrete bench which acts as railing.

The residence comprises 4500 square feet of living space plus 660 square feet of garage. Several clusters of three columns of aged wood, emulating the trunks of ancient trees, support the 210-foot-long steel frame roof the length of the house. Overhangs on two sides are an expansive 10 feet. Rainwater that collects on the roof's elastomeric surface is engineered to drain as miniature waterfalls into pools located at each end of the house. Due to its lifting, rolled edges,

the roof seems to disappear into infinite space. This design is truly both of the earth but in the air...
Phyllis Van Doren

カリフォルニア大学サン・ディエゴ校とルイス・カーンの設計したソーク研究所に近い，海の見える場所に建つ，30年ほど経つ住宅の建て替えである。依頼者はUCSDの著名な生物学者，ポール・ソルトマン博士とバーバラ夫人。夫人はラ・ヨラの現代工芸ギャラリー，「ギャラリー・エイト」の創設者の一人で芸術家である。

敷地は海に面した崖から後退した，なだらかに起伏する土地で，サン・ディエゴの高名な造園会社，ウィマー・ヤマダのジョセフ・ヤマダが設計した，クロマツや何種類かのタケの構成する成熟した庭園が広がっている。何年もの間，ソルトマン夫妻は元々のランチ・スタイルの住宅に住んできたが，周辺の住宅開発によって海がよく見えなくなってきていた。この新しい1層の建物は，遠くの眺めに焦点を合わせて，地面上方のプラットフォームのように浮かんでいる。その下を風景が，海に向かってゆるやかに起伏して降りて行く。リヴィング階を持ち上げたことによって海が再び前面に見晴らせる。

古代への参照をこめて，3寝室の住宅は，オーナーの東洋や固有のアメリカン・アートに対する賛美の念を微妙に反映させて，現代の神殿か寺院のように，風景のなかに浮かんでいる。儀式的な台座の感覚は，この土地が何世紀も前に，アメリカ先住民であるクメヤイ族の本拠地であり，彼らの古代の墳墓に近いという知識によっても強められている。

住宅へのアプローチは，リヴィング階へと登っていく，不規則に切り出された石のドライヴウェイである。真下にあるブリーズウェイには機械室，サーヴィス・エリアが置かれている。地盤面の下方からランプが，先端で滝のように流れ落ちる，抽象化された魚あるいは木の葉のかたちをしたプールの周辺へと続いている。濃い灰色の磨いていない石が内外の床に敷かれ，木製のパネル壁と対比を描く。エントランスは主階にあり，この階はすべての部屋が完全にオープン・プランで広いガラス面を通して東西に眺望が開けている。オーナーの蔵書や，現代ガラス工芸，陶器のコレクションを収めた壁が間仕切りの役割を果たし，各部屋には簡単に行き来できる。今世紀半ばの家具や職人の手になる現代家具のコレクションの置き場には特に配慮されている。西側，海が見える側には長円形のテラスがあり，コンクリート打ちのベンチが造り付けになっていて，これが手摺の役割も果たしている。

建物は4,500sq.ft.のリヴィング・スペースと660sq.ft.のガレージで構成されている。古代の樹木の幹に見習って，古い木を3本束ねたコラムの束がいくつか，210フィートの長さのスティール・フレームの屋根を建物全長に渡って支えている。両側面のオーヴァーハングは10フィートの広がりをもっている。屋根のゴム製の表皮が，雨を集め，家の両端に置かれているプールへ小さな滝となって落ちるように排水路がつくられている。軽快な，巻き上げられた端部によって，屋根は無限空間のなかへ消えていくように見える。この住宅はまさに地上にありまた空中にある。　（フィリス・ファン・ドーレン）

Architect: Wallace E. Cunningham, Inc.
Client: Dr. Paul and Barbara Saltman
Drawings and model: Peggy Walter

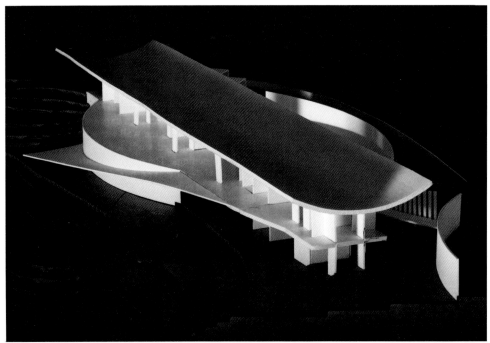
Model photo: west view

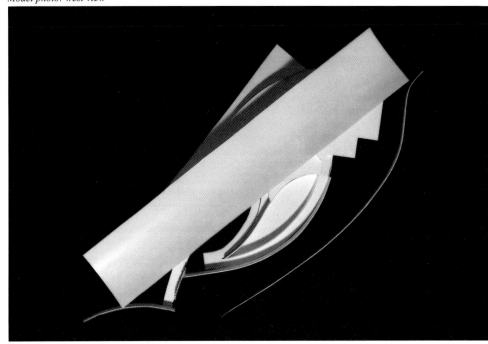
Site view

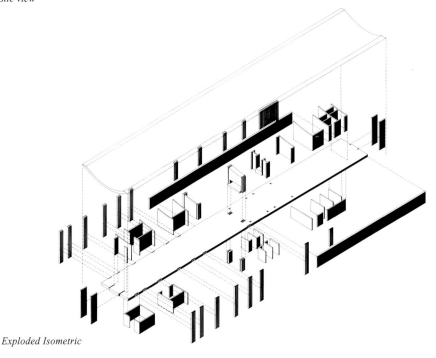
Exploded Isometric

31

CIGOLLE & COLEMAN

SKY RANCH HOUSE
Carmel Valley, California, U.S.A.
Design: 1995
Construction: 1996–97

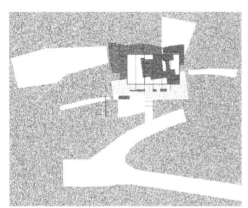

Site plan

The SITE is a twelve acre hillside in a rural ranch area several miles from the Pacific Ocean in Central California. South, up the hill, is a grove of live oaks, beyond which is the road. To the east, are lichen-covered trees and shrubs. North, there are views down the hills and across the valley to hills and ranch land extending to the horizon. To the west, is a view of the ocean beyond the ranch land.

The program is that of an open plan live/work house for a couple, a graphic designer and a photographer. The house is comprised of three different forms: the FRAME, the BAR, and the FIGURE.

The FRAME, a steel structure open to the light and view on all sides, contains the primary residential functions of the house and frames the relationship between the view and the other parts of the house. It is a neutral container, with elements forming their own spaces within. Low walls define spaces without enclosing them. Trusses span beyond the walls to provide overhangs that welcome winter sun from the south, but protect from the summer sun. The walls of this volume are wrapped with sheet metal. The slope of the roof follows the slope of the ground. Steel frame decks with wood joists and decking cantilever off of the frame, providing perches above the view.

The BAR is a wall/datum element that sets up the relationship between figure and frame and anchors the composition to the site. It is a wood frame construction with exposed joists on the interior. Plaster is the wall surface both inside and out and exposed studs are revealed at the window openings. The bar represents a slice through the landscape. The bar contains study/studio spaces at either end as well as storage, entry, and circulation.

Emblematic of silos and the machines of farm production, the FIGURE, wrapped in corrugated metal, is an object set against the more neutral elements of bar and frame. It is molded to fit its circumstances, having been pushed and pulled in response to its context. It presents a solid face to the front, excepting of a single window that focuses a view towards the oak trees from the large studio within.

The family of forms developed for Sky Ranch House is abstract and ambiguous, derived from prefabricated farm buildings, sheds, and silos. Each form is expressed individually, suggesting readings that differentiate scale, material, and method of construction, but each reciprocates and is modified by the next. The collection of forms fits loosely together, providing less determined spaces in between. A pair of stairs and a series of pleated storage walls occupy the areas of overlap and mitigate the spaces between volumes. The composition is a collective, conceived around a number of different experiences, views, and activities both inside and outside the walls.

カリフォルニア中央部，太平洋から内陸へ数マイル入った農場のなかにある丘の斜面に広がる12エーカーの敷地。南側，丘の上にライヴ・オークの木立があり，その向こうは道路。東側は地衣類に被われた木々と潅木。北を見ると，丘を下って谷を越え，地平線まで丘や農場が広がっている。西には農場の果てに海が見える。

グラフィック・デザイナーと写真家夫妻のための，オープン・プランをもつ住宅兼仕事場。＜フレーム＞＜バー＞＜フィギュア＞という，3つの異なった形が建物を構成する。

＜フレーム＞は鉄骨で，四方が光や眺めに開き，家の主要機能を収め，景色とこの家の他の部分との関係を枠取る。その内部を区画するエレメントを内蔵した，中性的なコンテナだ。間仕切りは低い壁なので，空間は閉ざされたものにならない。トラスは外壁を越えて延び，オーヴァーハングとなって，冬の日差しを呼び込み，夏の日差しを遮る。外壁はシート・メタル被覆。屋根の傾斜は地盤面の傾斜にあわせた。スティール・フレームに木製の小梁と床で構成されたデッキが，片持ちで突き出し，高い位置から景色を見晴らす場所となる。

＜バー＞は，フィギュアとフレームの間を関係づけ，この構成体を敷地に繋ぎ留める役割を果たす，壁／基準面だ。木造で，内部からは小梁が見える。内外部とも壁はプラスター仕上げで，間柱が窓の開口から覗いている。バーは風景を貫く切片を表現したものだ。バーには書斎／スタジオ空間が両端部に置かれ，そのほか，収納，エントリー，動線が配されている。サイロや農耕機械を象徴し，波形メタルで包まれた＜フィギュア＞は，無性格なバーやフレームに対立するオブジェである。敷地のコンテクストに対応して押し出し，引き寄せながら，周辺環境にぴったりはめこむように形づくった。広いスタジオからオークの木立に焦点を合わせている窓一つの効果に期待をこめて，正面にはソリッドな顔を見せている。

スカイ・ランチ・ハウスのために展開した形態は，プレファブの農家，小屋やサイロに由来する抽象的で曖昧なものである。それぞれの形態は，異なったスケール，材料，工法が分かるように，個別に表現されているが，互いに交換しあい，隣にくるものによって修正されている。それぞれの形はゆるやかな束となり，その間に曖昧なスペースを残している。対の階段と倉庫のプリーツをつけた壁の連なりが，このオーヴァーラップする空間を占め，ヴォリュームの間に挟まれたスペースを和らげている。つまり，全体の構成は，壁の内側でも外側でも，いくつもの異なった空間体験，眺め，活動が起こるように考えた，集合体といえよう。

Architects: Cigolle & Coleman—Mark Cigolle, Kim Coleman, principals-in-charge

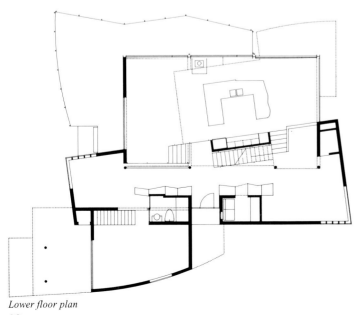

Lower floor plan

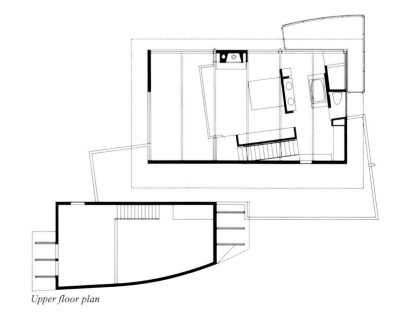

Upper floor plan

Section perspective

View from northwest

West elevation

Section perspective through frame, bar and entry canopy

View of figure from southwest

Exploded front view

View into living space from northeast

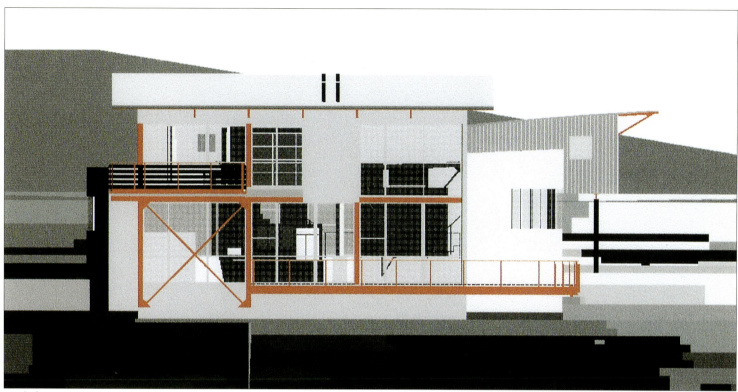
North elevation

Entry view

View of living space

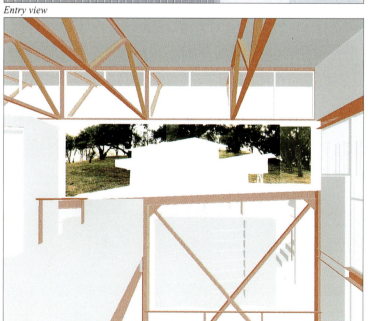
Composite: through the looking glass

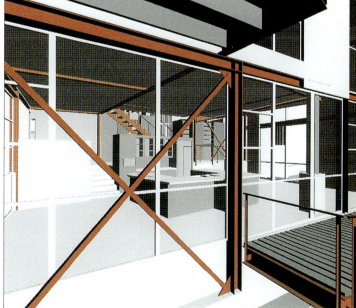
View into living space from north

COSCIA · DAY

TOPANGA HOUSE
Malibu, California, U.S.A.
Design: 1995
Construction: 1996–

The residence is a 6000 square foot private home for a family of four located on a sloped two acre parcel within Topanga Canyon. The project is a hybrid composed of both site formative solids referred to as geodes and subverted iconographic elements of wall, frame and plane. A process of abstract figuration was used to create the house's vocabulary of form. The overall massing of the project was produced through a planar sectional integration of three dimensional forms related through body geometry.

The site was manipulated to create an interrelational dialogue between built form and unbuilt landform. A sheltered outdoor dining terrace and a semi-enclosed car gallery result from a mounding of the topography into an extruded relational form. The adjacent reflecting pool's terraced earthwork reveals the houses' large geode component through an excavation of the site. The geode form grounds the project to the landscape through its placement and materiality.

The circulation space is an interstitial axis formed by the interplay of the major and minor, open and closed components. Unoccupiable space produced by the hovering roof plane folding under itself is used to capture and redirect light into the central interior fissure.

The private spaces of the bedrooms and study area are cavities carved out of the large geode form. The public space of the walled volume is organized into salon, kitchen, dining and living areas by freestanding cabinet geodes underneath the multipurpose family room and deck. The frame deck is a sectional object equipped with automated louvers that respond to the sun's movement depending on the hour of the day and the time of year. A full height moveable glass wall allows for a reconfiguration of interior and exterior space within the frame volume depending on the season or event.

Architects: Coscia·Day—Anthony Coscia, Jonathan Day, principals-in-charge; Lili Ishihara, James Wolf, project team
Clients: Jeff and Lela Shenton
Consultant: David Lau & Assoc. Inc., structural; CoDa West, interior designer
General contractor: Dauntless Construction

トパンガ・キャニオンにある2エーカーの斜面が敷地である。4人家族のための6,000sq.ft.の住宅。晶洞石を思わせる形をつくりあげているソリッドと，壁・フレーム・面からなるイコン的なものの転覆との両方から成るハイブリッドな構成である。形態の抽象化のプロセスからこの住宅の形態ヴォキャブラリーが生まれている。全体のマッシングは，躯体のもつ幾何学全体を通して関わっている三次元形態の平坦で断面的な統合を通して生みだされた。

敷地は建てられるかたちと，何も建っていない大地のかたちとの間の相互に関係をもった対話をつくりだすように操作する。被われた戸外のダイニング・テラスと半分囲まれたカー・ギャラリーが，突き出している関連形態へと地形を盛り土する結果として生まれる。そこに隣接するリフレクティング・プールの造成された雛壇は，敷地の根切りを通して，この住宅の大きな晶洞石形コンポーネントを外に見せている。ジェオデ・フォームはこのプロジェクトをその配置の仕方と材料によって風景のなかに着地させる。

動線は，主と縦，開と閉，それぞれのコンポーネントの相互作用によって形成された隙間のつくる軸線といえよう。宙に浮かぶような屋根面の下に包まれた何も占めることのできないスペースは光を捉え，内部中央の裂け目へと送り込むだろう。

寝室や書斎などの私的な部屋のあるエリアは，大きなジェオデ・フォームに切り取られた窪みである。壁で囲まれたパブリック・スペースは，多目的なファミリー・ルームとデッキの下，独立したキャビネット式ジェオデ・フォームによって，サロン，台所，食堂，リヴィングへと編成されている。枠取られたデッキは，一日の，そして一年の太陽軌道の動きに合わせて自動的に調節されるルーヴァーのついた組み合わせ式のオブジェである。天井まである可動のガラス壁によって，季節やイヴェントに応じて枠取られたヴォリュームのなかのスペースを内外とも変えることができる。

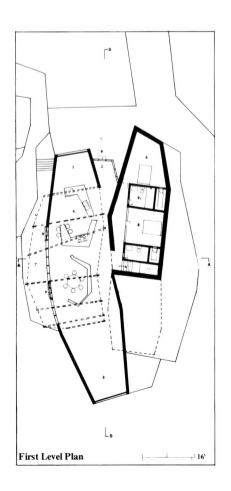

First Level Plan

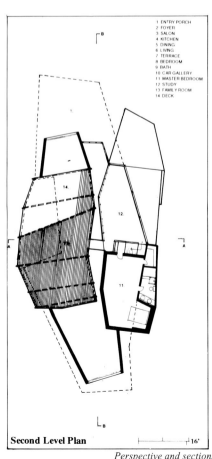

Second Level Plan

Perspective and sections ▷

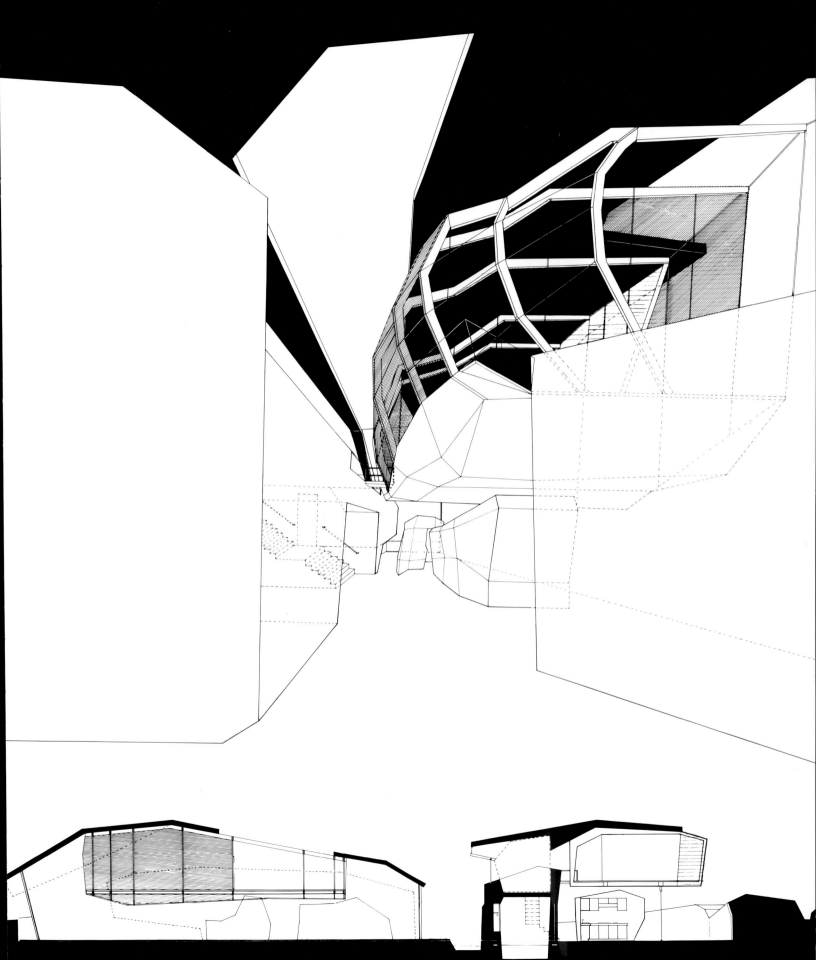

East view   Model photo: Marvin Rand

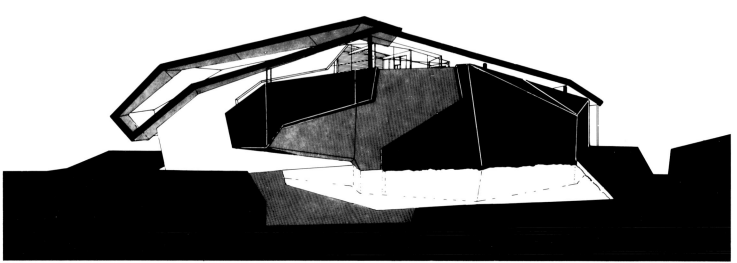

Section

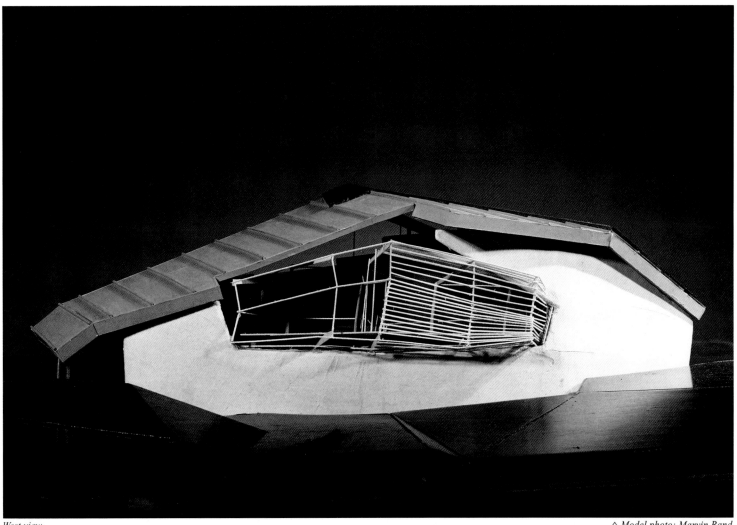

West view

△ Model photo: Marvin Rand

South view

Site view

GWATHMEY SIEGEL

MEYER RESIDENCE
California, U.S.A.
Design: 1994–95
Completion: 1997–98

Architects: Gwathmey Siegel & Associates Architects—Charles Gwathmey, principal; Dirk Kramer, associate; Lilla Smith, project architect; Mark Hill, Joseph Hsu, Chris Liu, Juan Miro, Meta Brunzema, Daniel Sullivan, Tom Lekometros, Karen Brenner, project staff
Project manager: The McGregor Company
Engineers: Robert Newlon & Associates, civil; Siavash Bahador, structural; The Sullivan Partnership, Inc., mechanical; Athans Enterprise, Inc., electrical
Consultants: Hillmann Dibernardo & Associates, Inc., lighting; Burton & Company, landscape; Charles M. Salter, acoustical
Contractor/construction manager: ARYA

Although located on a small plot of land (less than 1.25 acres), with a limited buildable area (7200 sq.ft), the Meyer Residence was designed to create the perception of an expansive site, as well as to maximize the actual size of the building to accommodate an extensive program.

In order to comply with the 24-foot-height zoning restriction, two guest bedrooms, a music/dance room, study, gymnasium, mechanical room, four-car garage and caretaker's suite were located below the existing grade in a "basement" level, behind a landscaped berm overlooking the Pacific Ocean. This below-grade level becomes a plinth for the remainder of the house, which is developed in a layered series of indoor and outdoor spaces from the street to the ocean.

A landscaped autocourt creates a transitional zone between the street and the north wing of the house, which contains a screening room on the ground floor and bedrooms above. A gallery leads past the kitchen and a small sculpture court to the main living space, which captures both a vista of the ocean and Point Dume, as well as a more intimate view of the private courtyard and pool. A gull-wing roof extends beyond the master bedroom above, forming the ceiling of the double height living room. The final site layer is the bermed courtyard next to lower level bedrooms.

建築可能な面積の限られた(7,200sq.ft.)小さな敷地(1.25エーカー以下)であるにもかかわらず，広い敷地と感じさせるように，かつまた広範なプログラムに対応する現実の大きさを最大限にするように設計されている。

24フィートという高度制限に従うために，ゲスト用寝室2つ，音楽／ダンス室，書斎，体操室，機械室，4台収容のガレージ，管理人室は，太平洋を見晴らす修景された崖径の背後，既存の地盤面より低い「地階レベル」に置いている。この地盤面より低いレヴェルは，道路から海に向かって続いていく外部と内部スペースのレイヤーから成る，この建物の残る部分の基壇となる。

修景されたオートコートが道路と1階に映写室，2階に寝室のある建物の北翼の間に転換領域をつくりだす。ギャラリーがキッチンから，小さな彫刻の中庭，そしてメインのリヴィングへと通じている。リヴィングからは，海とデューム岬が見晴らせると同時にプライヴェートな中庭やプールも見える。カモメの翼のような屋根が主寝室の上を越えて延び，2層吹き抜けのリヴィング・ルームの天井を形成する。最後に来る層は下のレヴェルの寝室に隣接する汀段になった中庭である。

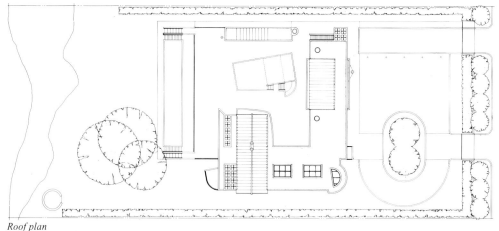
Roof plan

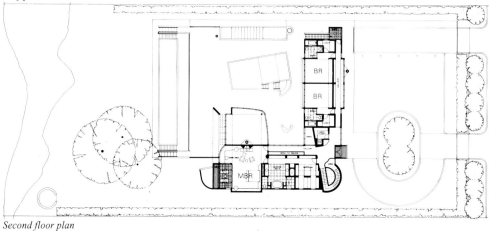
Second floor plan

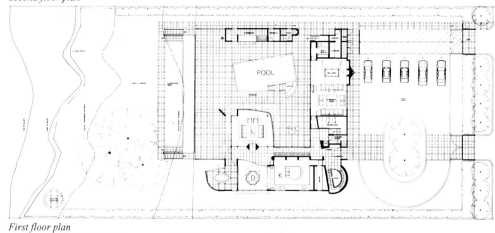
First floor plan

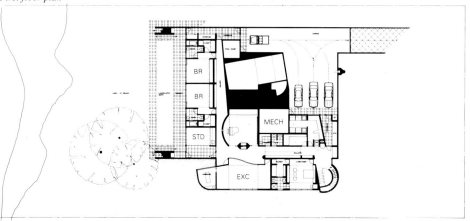
Lower floor plan

△▽ Bird's eye view

Model photos: Jock Pottle/ESTO

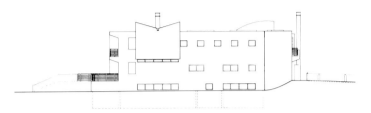

East elevation

South elevation

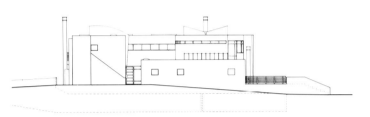

West elevation

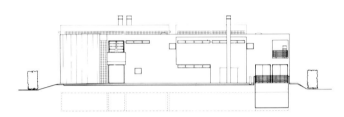

North elevation

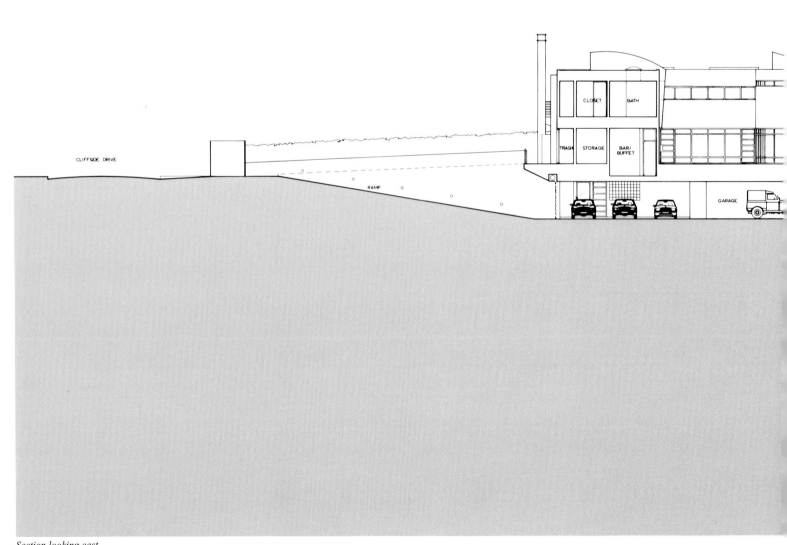

Section looking east

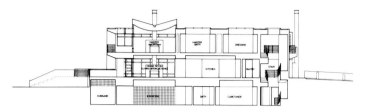
Section looking west

Section looking north

Section looking east

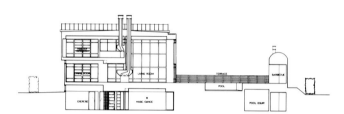
Section looking south

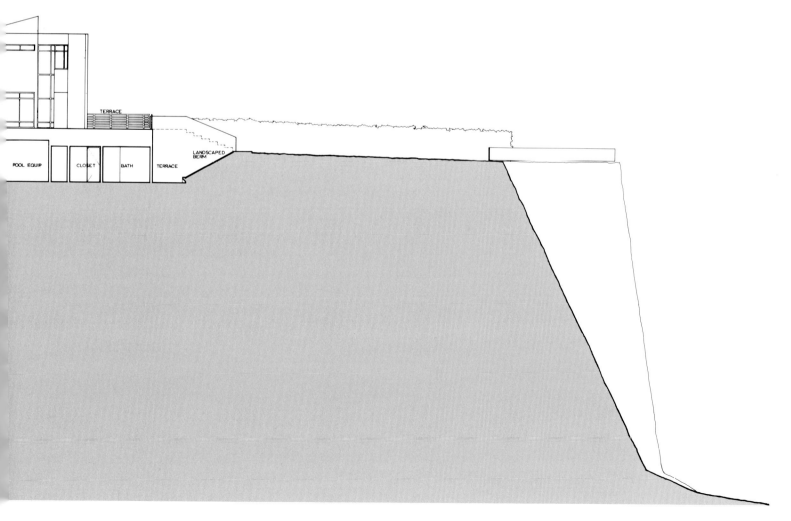

GWATHMEY SIEGEL

HILLTOP RESIDENCE
Austin, Texas, U.S.A.
Design: 1993
Completion: 1996

The Hilltop Residence is located on a wooded eighty-five acre site overlooking downtown Austin and the University of Texas. The program included an independent entertainment area and extensive on-site parking to accommodate large family gatherings and business functions. Although a separation between parents' and children's private spaces was considered desirable, the owners also wanted the children's indoor and outdoor play spaces visually connected with the adults' living areas.

The building is organized around a horizontal spine, with the "family house" to the northwest and the "entertainment house" to the southeast treated as complex, figural objects within the landscape. The curved roof of the indoor lap pool creates a cross-axial boundary between the two zones. At the top of the hill, a man-made plateau was created by building up the eastern portion of the site to maximize views from the house while preserving existing vegetation. The change in level mediates between the service areas (including a staff apartment, mechanical rooms, and a six-car garage) embedded at grade on the arrival side of the house, and the main floor and a series of outdoor terraces reached by way of the elliptical grand staircase in the skylit entry hall.

The house and topography are integrated to transform the landscape, and passage through the "wall" of the house reveals a series of outdoor "rooms" that reiterate interior programmatic events. At the southeastern corner of the house, a sweep of glazed doors opens from the curved two-story entertainment pavilion onto a series of terraced platforms. These platforms overlook downtown Austin and can be tented to become an outdoor room for large parties and gatherings. The pairing of indoor and outdoor spaces continues around the perimeter of the house in a series of smaller pavilions. A double-height glazed breakfast room extends into an outdoor dining terrace. A corner of the double-height living room is carved away to accommodate a screened sitting porch. The spa, exercise room, and children's playroom are pulled away from the frame of the spine, which opens onto another series of terraces leading down to the outdoor swimming pool, changing rooms, and a bicycle path. The interplay between indoor and outdoor spaces is reinforced in section on the third floor. A guest bedroom and a screening room/conference area in the entertainment zone open to a deck that looks into the double-height entertainment room and out over the pool terrace. The curved study off the master bedroom looks down into the living room, screened porch, and terraces below. The structure of the glazed breakfast room extrudes above the roofline to create a private study for the master bedroom.

Stainless steel wall panels, curved lead-coated stainless steel roofs, and broad expanses of glass articulate the volumes of the pavilions as a series of objects collaged to the stucco frame of the spine. The full extent of the house is visible only from the air. From the ground, it is read as layers of building fragments that are integrated into layers of landscape fragments, and can be comprehended only through memory and speculation as one moves from indoors to outdoors and around the site.

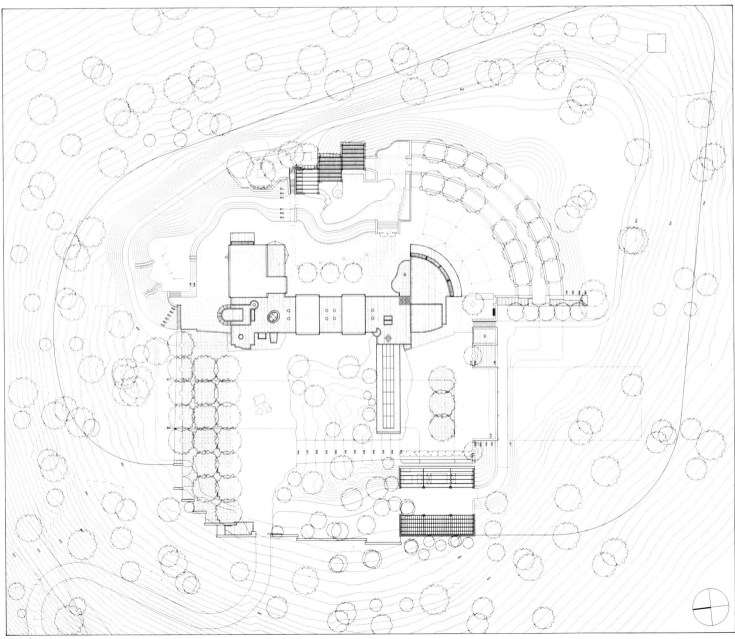

Site plan

テキサス大学とオースチンの市街を見晴らす85エーカーの木々の茂る敷地にある。プログラムには、大家族での集いや仕事上のもてなしのための、独立したエリアと敷地内の広い駐車スペースが含まれる。また、両親と子供の領域の分離も望ましく、施主もまた、大人たちのためのリヴィング・エリアから見える、子供たちの屋内屋外の遊び場をつくることを要望していた。

建物は水平軸の周囲に構成され、北西に「ファミリー・ハウス」、南東には「エンタテイメント・ハウス」が、景観のなかのコンプレックス、形象的なオブジェとして扱われている。室内のラップ・プールの湾曲する屋根は、この2つのゾーンの間の交差軸となる境界をつくりだす。丘の頂上には、人工の台地が、既存の植生を保護しながら、住宅からの眺めを最大限とするために敷地の東部分を積み重ねることによってつくりだされる。レヴェルの変化によって、この建物への到着地点側の地盤に埋め込まれたサーヴィス・エリア(使用人用アパート、機械室、6台収容のガレージが含まれる)と、スカイライトから日差しの入るエントリー・ホールにある長円形の大階段を経ていく主階と一連の戸外テラスとの間を調停している。

住宅と地形は風景を変形するために合体され、住宅の「ウォール」を貫く通路は、内部のプログラム上のイヴェントを反復する一連の戸外の「部屋」を明らかにしていく。建物南東のコーナーには、湾曲する2層の接待のためのパヴィリオンから大きなガラスのドアが段状のプラットフォームへ向けて開いている。これらのオースチン市街を見晴らすプラットフォームは大勢でのパーティーや集いの際には戸外の部屋として使える。内部スペースと戸外スペースの組み合わせは一連の小さなパヴィリオンのなか、この住宅の周辺に沿って続いていく。2層吹抜けのガラス張りの朝食堂が戸外のダイニング・テラスへと広がっている。2層吹抜けのリヴィング・ルームのコーナーはスクリーン付きのポーチをつくるために切り取られている。スパ、体操室、子供の遊戯室はスパインの枠から引き出され、戸外の水泳プール、更衣室、自転車道へと降りていく別のテラスの連なりへと開いている。内部と外部スペースの間の相互作用は、3階の断面で強調されている。接待ゾーンにあるゲスト用寝室と映写室/会議室エリアは2層吹抜けのエンタテイメント・ルームが見え、外のプール・テラスの上に突き出ているデッキに開いている。主寝室の隣にあるカーヴした書斎からは居間、スクリーン付きポーチ、下のテラスが見下せる。ガラス張りの朝食堂の部分は主寝室に隣接する書斎をつくるためにルーフラインから突き出している。

ステンレス・スティールの壁板、湾曲する鉛引きのステンレス・スティール製屋根、広いガラス面が、パヴィリオンをスパインを構成するスタッコ塗りのフレームにコラージュされたオブジェとして分節する。この住宅の全体像は空からしか見えない。地上からは、風景の断片と合体した建物の断片のレイヤーと見えるだけであり、内部から外部へ敷地周辺へと歩いていきながら記憶と沈思を通してのみ理解できるものである。

Architects: Gwathmey Siegel & Associates Architects—Gustav Rosenlof, associate; Juan Miro, project architect; Meta Brunzema, Frank Thaler, Richard Lucas, project team
Consultants: Datum Engineering, Inc., structural; 3D/Engineering, mechanical; Gebhard Sarma Group, civil; H.M.Branston & Partners, lighting; Shen Milsom & Wilke, acoustic/AV

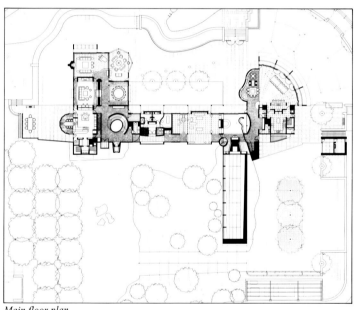
Main floor plan

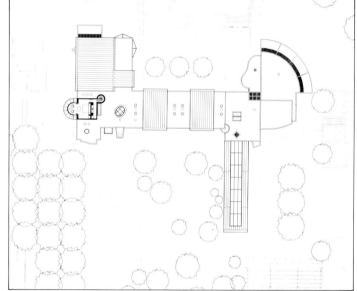
Third floor plan

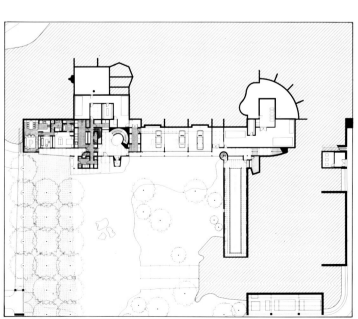
Ground floor plan

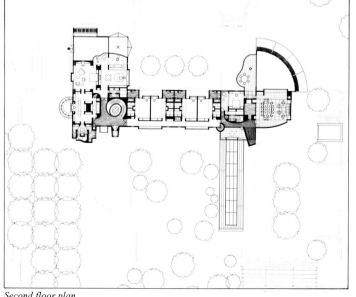
Second floor plan

Model photo: bird's eye view

Section looking north

Section looking east

Section looking south

Section looking south
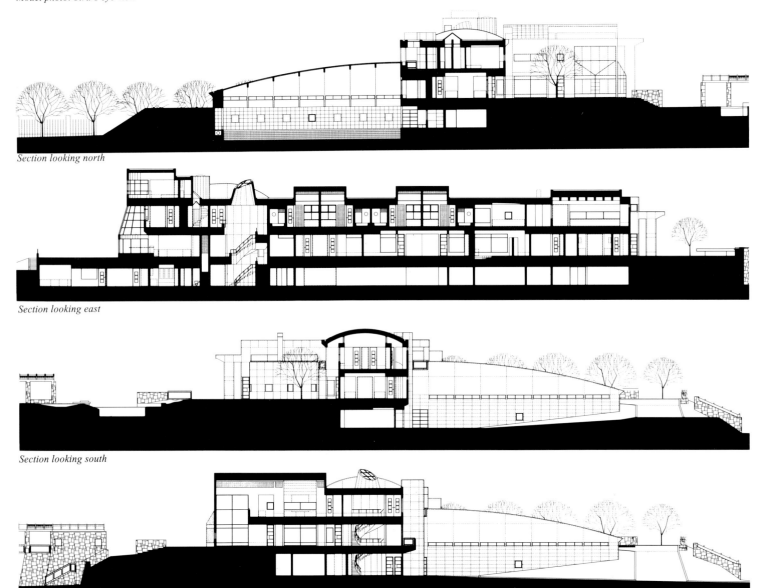

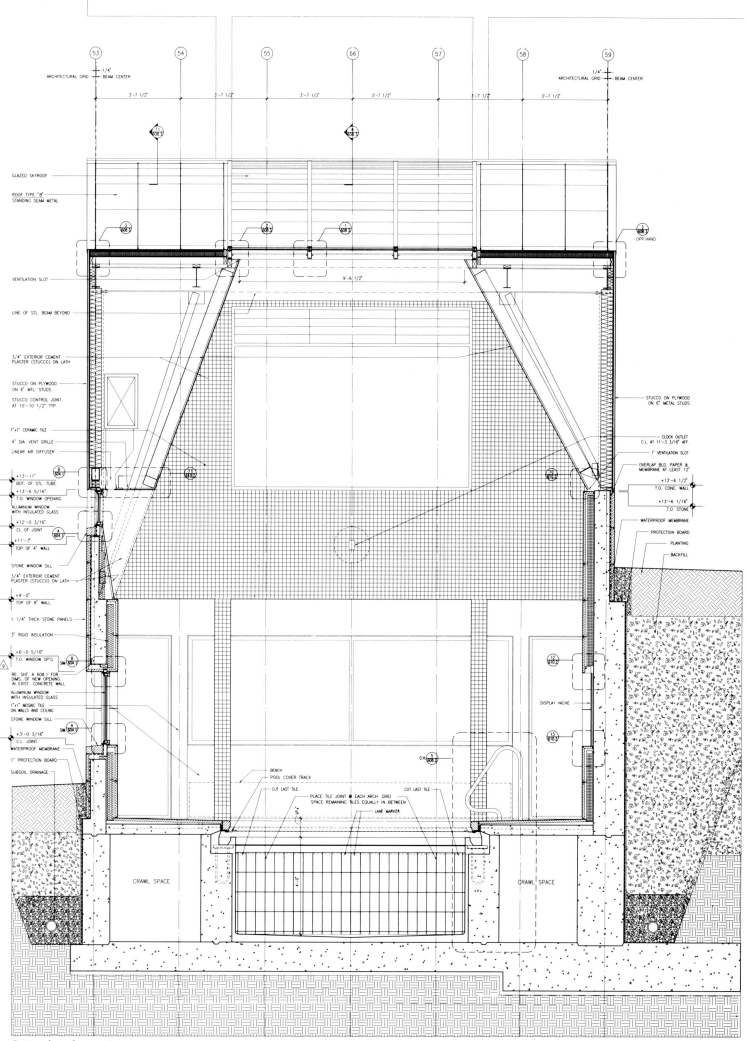

Section through natatorium

GWATHMEY SIEGEL

SAN ONOFRE RESIDENCE
California, U.S.A.
Design: 1993
Completion: 1996

The San Onofre Residence is located on one-and-a-half acres in a quiet residential neighborhood near the top of Malibu Canyon. The two level site suggested a bi-nucleate parti. A three-story curved limestone pavilion, housing the main living spaces, sits on a promontory looking south and east toward Santa Monica, the Pacific Ocean, and the skyline of downtown Los Angeles. A three-story cube containing support space is embedded in the slope behind it, overlooking the canyon to the west.

The support building becomes an object in the land, anchoring and stabilizing the pavilion. The pavilion itself becomes an object on the land, separate, unique and contrapuntal both in its spatial organization and its rendering. Its curved limestone wall can be read as both a found object and a ruin, transforming the experience of the landscape as one moves through it from the ordered programmatic disposition of the support building into the explosion of space and vistas revealed by the pavilion's glazed facade.

An autocourt at entry level leads from the cul-de-sac to an entrance hall that accommodates the vertical circulation. From it, one passes over a bridge, through the wall of the pavilion, and into the double-height living room. Ahead, the panorama of Santa Monica is silhouetted against the ocean and framed by the stainless steel brise-soleil of the south facade. To the west, a window punched into the curve of the pavilion reveals the prospect of the canyon.

The kitchen and the master bedroom above become an object that floats within the space of the pavilion, forming a boundary between the living room and the formal dining area, with its view towards the skyscrapers of downtown Los Angeles. The breakfast room penetrates the screen of the glazed facade and creates an outdoor terrace for the bedroom above. At ground level, the entertainment room becomes a kind of giant "piloti," recessed within the curve of the pavilion to create a shaded terrace that opens onto the southern lawn and leads back to the swimming pool and spa facing the canyon.

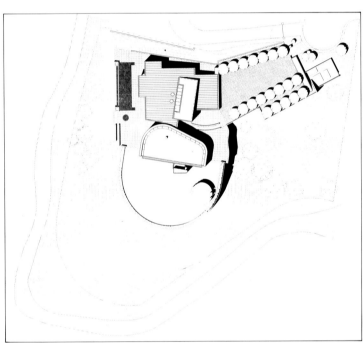
Site plan

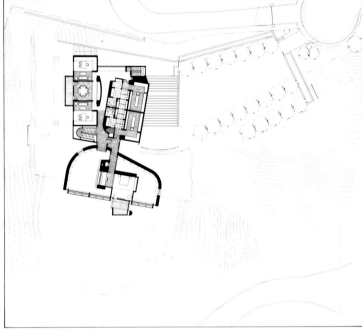
Third floor plan

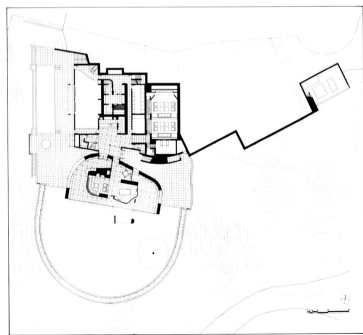
First floor plan

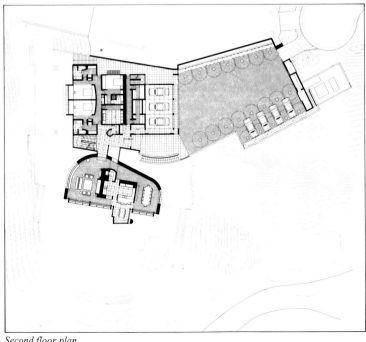
Second floor plan

△East view ▽Northwest view

Model photos: Jock Pottle/ESTO

South elevation

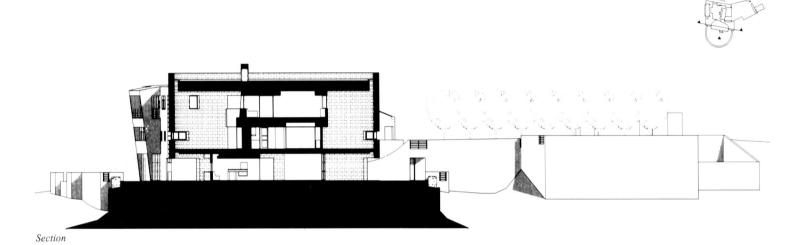
Section

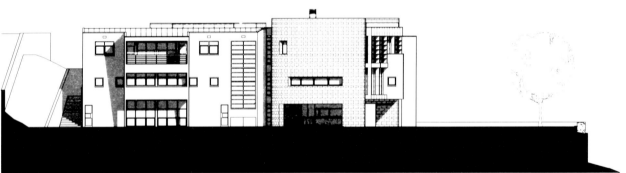
West elevation

Section

マリブ・キャニオンの山頂に近い静かな住宅地の一角，1.5エーカーの敷地である。2つの段差からなる土地からは，2つの核で構成する方法が考えられた。石灰石でできたカーヴする3層のパヴィリオンには，主となるリヴィング・スペースが置かれ，南と東には，サンタモニカ，太平洋，ロサンジェルス市街が見晴らせる。その背後の斜面にはめこまれた，3層のキュービックな棟にはサポート・スペースが入り，西側の渓谷を見下ろしている。

サポート棟は地中のオブジェとなり，パヴィリオンを係留し安定させる。パヴィリオンは地上のオブジェとなる。それは独立し，個性的で，空間の組立および建築表現の両面において対位法を構成する。その石灰石の壁はファウンド・オブジェクトとも廃墟とも見える。規則的な配置をもつサポート棟から，パヴィリオン棟のガラス張りのファサードが展開する空間と視界の広がりのなかへと移動していくにつれて，風景は変貌していく。

入口階にあるオートコートが袋小路から上下方向への動線が始まるエントランス・ホールへと導いていく。そこから，ブリッジを渡り，パヴィリオンの壁を抜け，2層吹抜けのリヴィング・ルームに至る。前方には大洋を背景にしてサンタモニカ市の全景が浮かびあがり，南面を覆うステンレス造のブリーズ・ソレイユが額縁のようにそれを切り取っている。西に向いては，パヴィリオンの曲面壁に穿たれた窓が渓谷の景色を見せてくれる。

上階にあるキッチンと主寝室がパヴィリオン内に浮かぶオブジェとなり，リヴィング・ルームとフォーマルな食堂部分の間の境界をつくる。そこからは，ロサンジェルス市街の高層ビルが見える。朝食室がガラス張りのファサードを貫通して上階の主寝室に続く戸外テラスをつくりだす。地上階では，エンタテイメント・ルームが一種の巨大な"ピロティ"を形成する。ここはパヴィリオンの曲面壁の内側に後退し，影の落ちるテラスとなり，南側には芝生が広がり，渓谷に面した側には水泳プールとスパがある。

サポート棟は左右対称に構成されている。マリブ渓谷を見下ろす，光が燦々と注ぐ周辺部には，地上階に体操室，エントリー・レヴェルに客用寝室，主寝室階の上にオフィス／会議室がある。コアには映写室，資料記録保管室が地上階に，エントリー階のガレージ背後に倉庫とサーヴィス・エリアがある。3階では，オフィスの反対側にある主寝室用化粧室と浴室は，パヴィリオンへと戻っていくブリッジと軸線上で回転している。

オートコートの玉石，湾曲するパヴィリオン，地中にはめ込まれたキューブの湾曲する亜鉛引きの屋根の上に浮かぶオフィスと主寝室用浴室――上から見るこうした形態とテクスチュアの並置は，キュビストの浅浮彫りのようである。この材料によるコラージュは，スタッコ仕上げのサポート棟のファサードを分節するステンレスのパネル壁，そしてパヴィリオンの石灰石の湾曲する壁と対比するステンレスのブリーズ・ソレイユによっても反復される。

Architects: Gwathmey Siegel & Associates Architects—Charles Gwathmey, principal; Gerald Gendreau, associate; Greg Epstein, project architect; Peter Pawlak, Joseph Hsu, project team
Consultants: Severud Associates, structural; The Sullivan Partnership, mechanical; Athans Enterprise, Inc., electrical; Spindler Engineering Corp., civil; Hillmann Dibernardo & Associates, Inc., lighting; Burton & Company, landscape
Contractor: ARYA

West view

South view

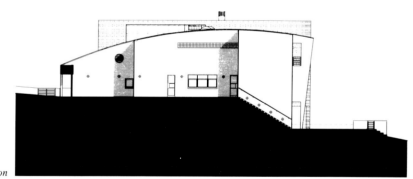
North elevation

Section

ALEXANDER GORLIN

HOUSE OF THE GLASS SPINE
Livingston, New Jersey, U.S.A.
Design: 1995
Construction: 1996–97

This project is concerned with the idea of the house as the intersection of the public and private domain. Two open, L-shaped courts are established, one of arrival and one for the private life of the family, linked together through the glass spine that makes both the entry and engages the garden and pool in the rear. Overlapping and interpenetrating spaces merge inside and outside. Developed in plan and section, this spatial concept gives dual meanings to zones that are simultaneously part of two or more areas. The double height glass spine slices through the two court blocks creating a corridor of deep perspectival space that opens up laterally to the living room and outdoor garden beyond. This glass element serves multiple purposes; at once skylight, circulation spine, a prismatic, transparent wall that defines edges while being a powerful place by itself. Bedrooms occupy the southern wing of the house, with the lower block of communal rooms; kitchen, dining, media; framing the pavilion of the double height living room. Clerestories and balconies ring the upper level of this room making a dynamic space that interlocks with and opens out to the garden and sky. An asymmetrical pattern of windows create a feeling of movement across the view to the pond.

Isometric

Model photo: bird's eye view

このプロジェクトではパブリックとプライヴェート領域の交差として住宅構成を考えている。一つは車寄せ，一つは家族のためのオープンなＬ字型のコートが２つあり，入口と裏手にある庭とプールを結ぶガラス張りのスパインで連結されている。重なり合い，浸透し合うスペースが内部と外部を合体させる。平面と断面に展開されたこの空間についてのコンセプトは，これらの領域に，同時に２つの部分であり，それ以上のエリアであるという二重の意味を与える。２層分の高さをもつガラス張りのスパインは，２つのコート・ブロックを切分し，側面にリヴィング・ルーム，その奥に戸外庭園へと開かれた深い見通しをもつ廊下をつくりだす。このガラス張りの部分は多様な役割を果たす。スカイライトであり，動線のスパインであり，自身が強力な場である一方で境界を形成するプリズムのような透明な壁である。寝室は建物の南側の翼を占め，下の階には，キッチン，ダイニング，メディアなどの共有スペースがあり，２層吹き抜けのリヴィング・ルームを縁取っている。この部屋の上方に巡らされたクリアストーリーとバルコニーが，庭と空と抱き合わされ，開かれたダイナミックな空間をつくりだす。非対称に開けられた窓のパターンが，池に向かって行くような動きを感じさせる。

Architects: Alexander Gorlin Architect—Alexander Gorlin, principal-in-charge; Christian Dickson, project architect; Lavinia Pana, project team
Consultants: Ross Dallano, structural; Sheldon Lazan, mechanical; Paul Siskin, interior design

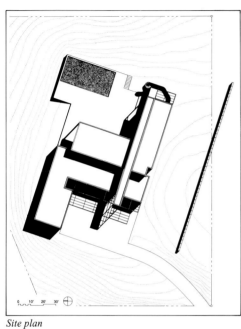
Site plan

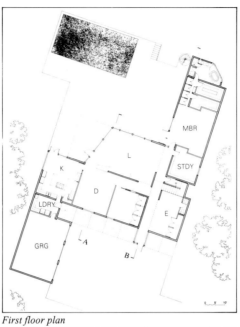
First floor plan

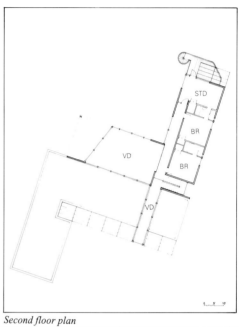
Second floor plan

Northwest view

Unfolded elevation

East view

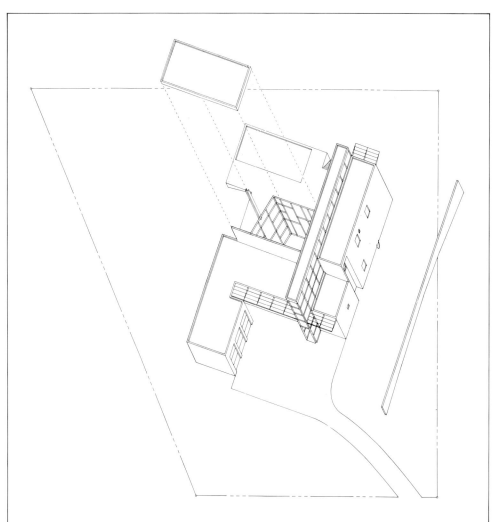
Axonometric

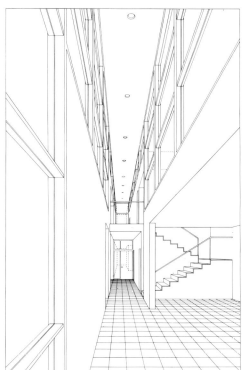
Perspective: entrance

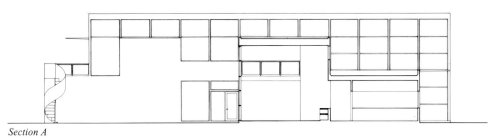
Section A

Section B

GIN + DESIGN WORKSHOP

Ee HOUSE
East Coast Road, Singapore
Design: 1994
Construction: 1994–96

This project has addressed an existing urban fabric, it also addresses the history of its place and the people responsible for that history. The social art of architecture will be taken seriously both in terms of engaging the client in the act of the development process, building and in reconciling the designs with surroundings and precedent. The flexibility and complexity demands the design to deal with the micro function separately. Thus the development to three "Pavilions" connected to a common gallery. Each of this pavilions is clearly defines through its usage and function while still having a dialogue with each other through visual and physical link. The five foot walkway of the paranakan house ties the whole development into family unit.

From the front door in the first pavilion, a major axis follows past the two other pavilions and flows into the courtyard. As if in a ritualistic procession, the habitant is consciously experiencing a series of frames in side and outside, single to double volumes, light to dark and function to defunction

このプロジェクトは，既存の都市ファブリックのみならず，この場所の歴史，その歴史に関わった人々にも語りかけるようなものとした。建築のもつ社会性とクライアントの要望のどちらにも配慮し，周辺環境と融和させる。フレキシビリティの要請とプログラムの複雑さから，各機能空間を細分する必要がある。この結果，コモン・ギャラリーで結ばれた3つの〈パヴィリオン〉という構成が生まれた。各パヴィリオンはその機能が明快に分かれているが，視覚的物理的な繋がりによって対話を交わす。5フィートの通路が全体を家族のユニットへ連結する。

一番目のパヴィリオンの正面ドアから主軸線が延び，残る2つのパヴィリオンを抜けて中庭まで通っている。儀式的な行列のように，住む人は，内と外，単層のヴォリュームと2層のヴォリューム，明と暗，機能空間と機能をもたぬ空間……と，フレームの連なりを意識的に経験する。

Architects: GIN + design workshop—Gin Wah Ang, principal-in-charge
Consultant: K.C. Fong Consultants, structural

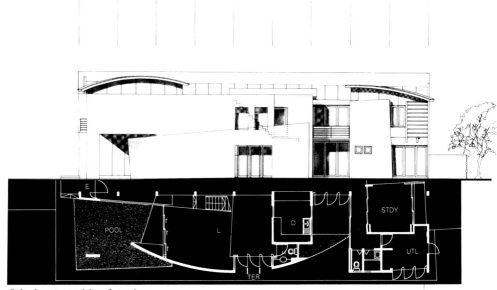
Side elevation and first floor plan

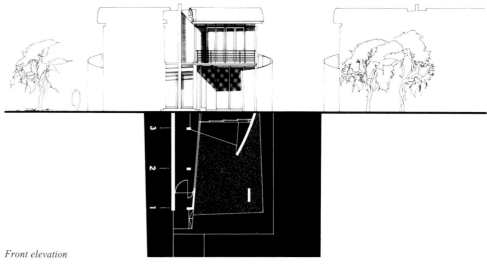
Front elevation

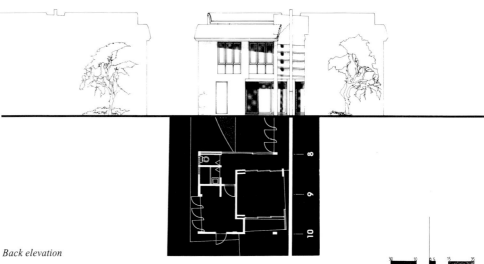
Back elevation

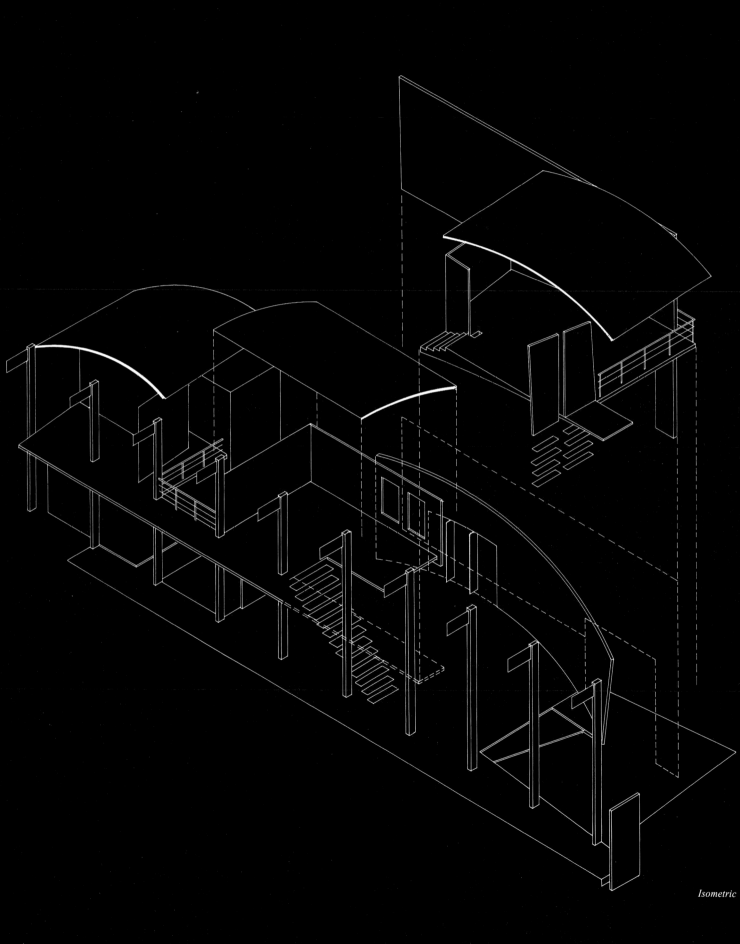

Isometric

HANRAHAN MEYERS

DUPLICATE HOUSE
Bedford, New York, U.S.A.
Design: 1994–96
Construction: 1996–97

Architects: Thomas Hanrahan + Victoria Meyers, Architects—Thomas Hanrahan, Victoria Meyers, principals-in-charge, Lawrence Zeroth, project team
Clients: Dr. Kurt Langsten and Rae Langsten
Consultants: Anthony Webster, P.C., structural; Manny Rubiano, P.C., mechanical; Tse-Yen Chu, interior; Mecili Kulik Williams Assoc., landscape

This project explores ideas of duplication and the manner in which duplicates transform in response to formal, programmatic and site situations. These transformations are diagrammed in this text both sectionally and planimetrically.

The program is for a professional couple, a psychiatrist and a painter, with grown children. The program suggests a preliminary opposition of mind/body that might be resolved within the simplicity of a domestic arrangement. Both people desire to work at the house.

The site is a gently southwesterly sloping, wooded suburban site in Bedford, New York, a suburb of New York City. Like many suburbs in the United States, it can no longer be considered purely a bedroom community, and the inclusion of the workplace within the traditional single family home reflects this growing complexity of these types of towns.

The first duplication involves a sectional idea of an upper building of working and sleeping. The lower construction is a pedestal that is terraced with respect to the slope of the site. The void between these two volumetric plates is the negotiated terrain of living, the space between mind/body and opposite genders.

The second duplication involves a plan opposition between the counseling office and the painting studio. These two volumes, the residue of the upper plate, are situated at opposite sides of an open court.

The third duplication is the positioning of two major masking walls that suggest both identity and disguise. These masks are placed at tight angles, introducing alternative relations between the two workspaces and the inner court and the landscape beyond.

このプロジェクトは，複製という考え，形態，プログラム，敷地条件に対応しての変形を複製していくという手法を追求したものである。これらの変形操作は，断面平面の双方から図式化されている。

プログラムは，精神科医と画家という，専門職をもち，成長期の子供たちのいる夫妻のためのものである。それは，住宅の機能構成の単純さのなかに解消されていくであろう，心と身体の対立を前もって示唆している。二人ともこの家で仕事することを望んでいる。

敷地はニューヨーク市郊外，ベッドフォードにある，木立に包まれ，南西に向いた緩やかな斜面である。アメリカの多くの郊外地のように，そこはもはや純粋なベッドタウンではない。伝統的な独立住宅の中に仕事場が包含されることは，こうしたタイプの町が複雑さを増してきていることの反映である。

一番目のデュプリケーションは，仕事場と眠る場を収めた上層の建物についての断面上の操作に関わるものである。下層の建物は，敷地の斜面に合わせて段になった一種の台座である。この２つのヴォリュームにはさまれたヴォイドはリヴィング，心と身体そして反対の性の間の協定された土地である。

２番目のデュプリケーションは，診療所と絵のスタジオの間の平面上の対比についてのものである。上層の面の残部である２つのヴォリュームは，オープン・コートをはさんで反対側に位置している。

３番目の複製は，アイデンティティと偽装の両方を示唆する大きなマスキング・ウォールの配置である。これらのマスクは，直角に立てられ，２つの仕事場と中庭，その向こうの風景の間の選択的な関係を導入する。

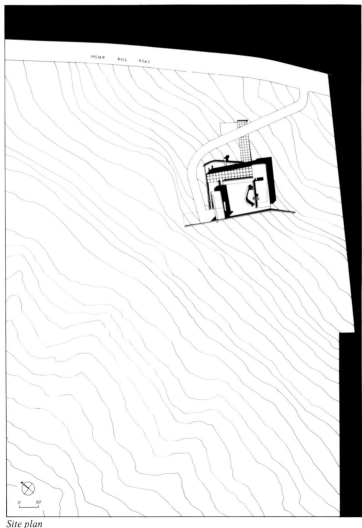

Site plan

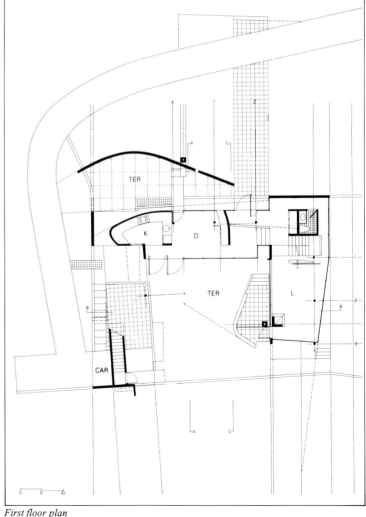

First floor plan

△South view ▽Northwest view

Model photos: Jock Pottle/ESTO

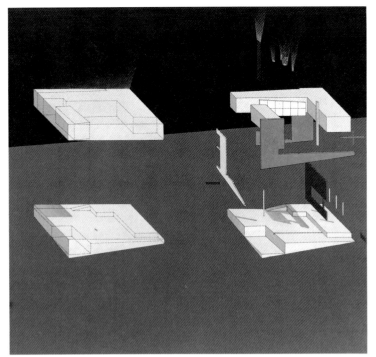
Diagram

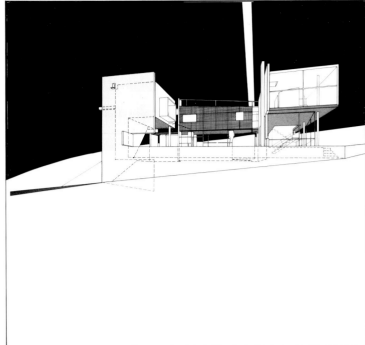
Exterior view

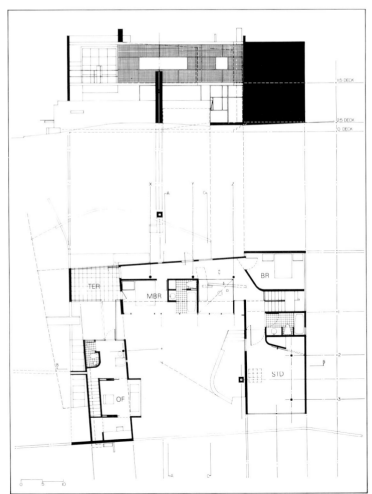
Reflected elevation and second floor plan

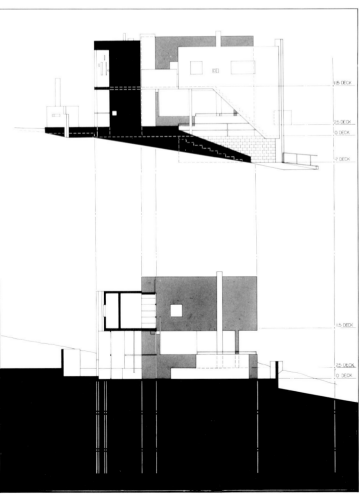
West elevation and section A-A

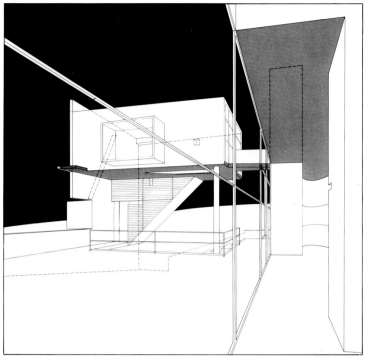
View from entry

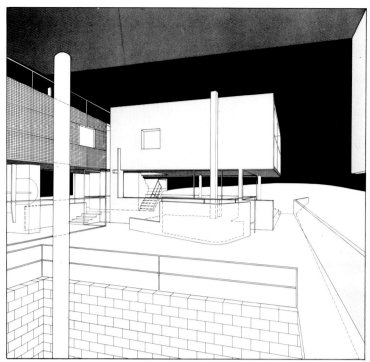
View toward living room

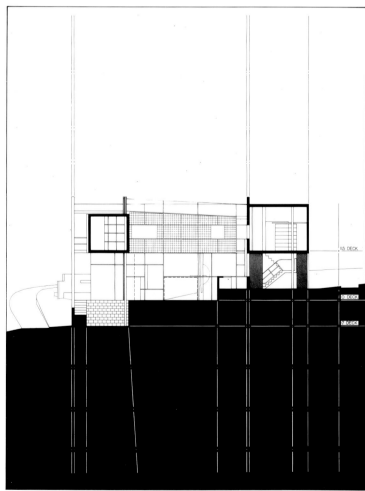
Section B-B

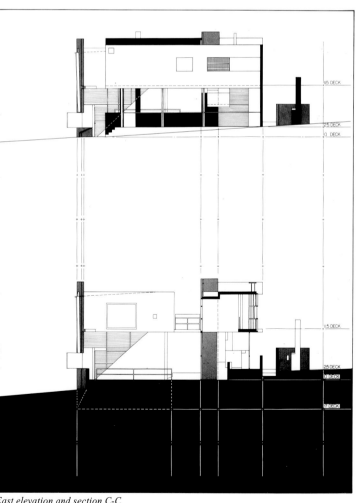
East elevation and section C-C

OSAMU ISHIYAMA

SETAGAYA VILLAGE
Setagaya, Tokyo, Japan
Design: 1995–96
Construction: 1996–

The purpose of this experimental metal structure is threefold: (1) to build a flexible environment which serves primarily as a residence but also houses an architect's studio and a multi-purpose space which serves as a performing/exhibition space; (2) to do in a way that approaches energy self-sufficiency; and (3) to give, in the process, the architect a greater control particularly in the areas of cost analysis and of contracting. To approach self-sufficiency, the architect has developed an energy generating system that uses a windmill as the main source accompanied by auxiliary solar energy collectors. Much of Japan belongs to a monsoon belt resulting in abundance of wind year-round even in the densely populated urban areas. The system takes advantage of this climate. The windmill which had been tested for efficiency and durability in the architect's design studio at the Waseda University has light-weight blades made of wood and operates at minimum wind velocity of 1.8 meters per second with a projected average production of 6 kilo watts per day. Solar batteries supplement it as an auxiliary source, and solar panels augment the water heating capacity. A portion of the water source relies on a well. In the summer, the water is circulated in the shelter's metal wall cavities, and a mist producer is being considered as a part of the cooling system. In the winter, hot air is forced into the cavities to increase heating efficiency. The top of the shelter is covered with sod and a garden to maximize insulation year-round. The result, in all, is a highly energy efficient shelter, and a series of auxiliary systems that supplement the energy source as its notable feature.

Although it is a custom-designed structure, the architect uses, for the most part, readily available industrial materials of known quality and price, enabling him to maintain an accurate and detailed account, thus producing a design that is cost effective. It requires, however, the architect's commitment to produce, in addition to the customary plans, sections, and elevations, more drawings, in great details, showing how the parts are put together. During this process, the architect comes in a direct contact with product manufacturers and sub-contractors who provide information and advice, giving him, consequently, the confidence to act as a general contractor and experiment in the supervision and the management of the construction. The result is a substan-

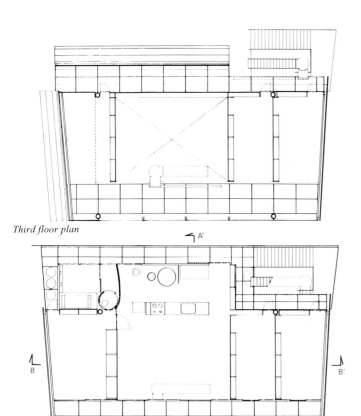

Third floor plan

Second floor plan

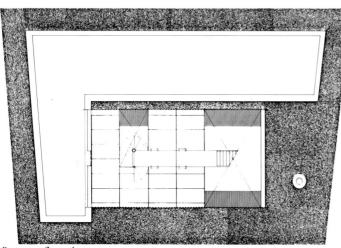

Basement floor plan

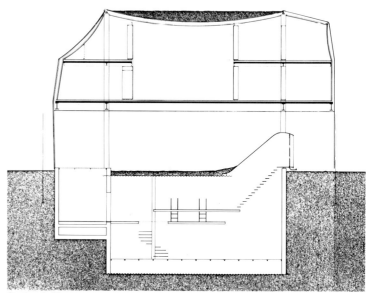

Section B-B'

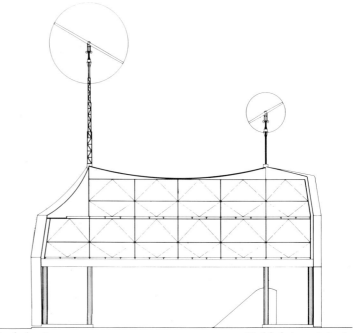

South elevation

Model photo: east view ▷

tial saving in the overall cost, and a building practice fundamentally different from that of the Japanese norm.

The primary function of this shelter is to house a family. It incorporates effective interior partitions to increase space efficiency by freeing rooms and making them adaptable to variety of uses. Currently, a traditional wooden house with a family occupies the site. The metal shelter is built above the house not interfering with the life below. The family moves up when the new living quarter is complete. The vacated house is demolished and the ground is excavated to bury a corrugated metal pipe 6 meters in diameter that is planned to house the architect's underground studio. The ground level above then is enclosed as a large multi-purpose space. As the family grows and the life style changes, the living quarter transforms accordingly. In fact the whole environment continues to evolve reflecting the dynamics of the life it contains.
Osamu Ishiyama

この金属製シェルター建設では三つの試みがなされる。1）できるかぎりのエネルギー自給自足を目ざす。2）全部品のコストコントロールを可能なかぎり行い，設計施工の形に近づける。3）住宅ではあるが，住むだけの機能に限定しない。工房になったり，小劇場になったり，ギャラリーになったりする。

エネルギー自給自足のためには，私の研究室で性能実験，耐久性実験等を続けてきた小型風車を主に，太陽電池，太陽温水器などを従にシステムを組んだ。日本列島はモンスーン地帯に属し，大都市においても常に良い風が吹いている。その風のエネルギーを住宅に供給する試みである。プロペラは木製，軽量である。1.8mの風から反応を始める。年平均6kwの電力を獲得する予定だ。不足分は太陽電池で，温水供給の一部を温水器に頼る。水供給の一部を井戸水に頼るが，夏期の冷房はシェルター全体に水を巡回させ，一部を噴霧することが考えられている。

冬期の暖房も同様で，金属シェルターの中空部分に温風を循環させ，暖房効率を上げる試みがなされる。金属シェルターの頂部には土が盛られ，草花が植えられ断熱性能を上げる。高性能なエネルギー循環を旨とするシェルターが構想されているのだ。各種装置のメンテナンス，あるいは部品の取換えのための補助装置がデザインの特色の一つになっている。

金属シェルターの全体を工業化された部品の集合とすることで，コストコントロールを建築家の手許に引寄せることが可能なようにする。一品生産でありながら，その部品設計の水準を高め，それぞれの部品の値段がキチンと誰にもわかりやすい内容にするためである。

これは現実には製作する図面の形式に反映される。建築の全体像を示す図面，つまり平面図や断面図，立面図の他に精緻な各種部品図を製作することによって，施工の分野を主体的に再構成し得るように努力する。

そのことによって，全体を施工するマネジメントを建築家自身の手で行う。部品メーカーの力とサブコンの力を借りながら，結果として施工にゼネコンを使わぬ実験をする。それは大幅なコストダウンを計ることにつながるだろう。

この金属性シェルターの主機能は住居であるが，高性能の可動間仕切をセットすることによって，固定されたプランから自由になれるようにする。そのことで，様々な生活のスタイルがこの金属シェルターを介して可能なように考える。

現在，敷地には伝統的な木造建築が建てられている。そこでは生活がなされている。建設はこの木造住宅をそのままにしながら，木造住宅の上でなされる。金属シェルターがほぼ出来上った段階で生活の場は木造住宅から上に移される。

次に古い木造住宅が取り壊されて，土地が掘られる。地下に直径6mのコルゲートパイプが埋設される。金属製の工業化されたトンネル状の空間が地下に作られ，そこはアトリエ，工房機能が想定されている。次に地上部分，つまり1階が，ガランとして何にでも使用できる場所として作られる。

おそらく，その時期には，第一段階で建設された金属シェルター部の改装や生活の変化に対応するための工夫がなされるであろう。

つまり，この住居は未完であり続け，変化し続けるだろう。ここでなされる生活の姿に対応しながら。
（石山修武）

North view

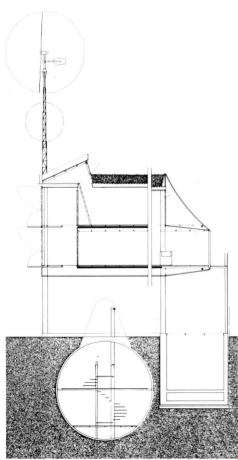

Section A-A'

計画：世田谷村／東京都世田谷区
用途：住居・スタジオ／家族：特定多数
建築設計：石山修武研究室
　担当／石山修武，松野勉，高木正三郎
構造設計：梅沢良三
設備設計：川合健二
敷地面積：410.50m²／第二種住専
建築面積：162.80m²
延床面積：445.10m²
建築規模：地上3階地下1階，最高高さ10m
主体構造：鉄骨，亜鉛メッキ鉄板皮膜およびアルミ
外部仕上：亜鉛メッキ鉄板およびアルミ
内部仕上：すべて可動パネル
特記事項：風力発電，太陽光発電，井戸給水

△ Overall view ▽ Bird's eye view

Model photos: Y. Takase

YOSHIHIKO IIDA

J VILLA GUEST HOUSE
Yamanakako, Yamanashi, Japan
Design: 1995
Construction: 1996

This is a guest house attached to a vacation house that is a log house. It is a one room addition built half underground at the end of the deck of the existing house. The deck rises in a stepping formation over the addition and becomes its roof forming a large terrace useful for a gathering. There is a barbecue pit on one side. The terrace functions also as an amphitheater.

Inside, the room opens on one side in its full length toward the woods, and the rest is all concrete walls cast in place with folded plates as moldings. The opening glaze is made of LCD glass and the degree of translucency controls the privacy. The roughness of the concrete wall compliments the polished smoothness of glass, metal and stone.
Yoshihiko Iida

別荘のゲストハウスである。

既存のログハウスの庭に半分埋設された一室空間である。屋根上はログハウスのバルコニーから延びるデッキが階段状にせり上がり，広大なテラスを形成する。片隅にバーベキューのための炉がもうけられ，多人数のパーティなどに対応し，またアンフィシアターとしても機能する。

室内は，森に向かって幅いっぱいに切り取られた横長の開口部以外，折板を型枠に打たれたリブ状のコンクリートで覆われる。開口部には液晶ガラスが用いられ，適宜半透明にすることでプライバシーを確保している。

コンクリートの荒々しさと，ガラス，金属，石の繊細さが同時にあるような空間をイメージした。
（飯田善彦）

Model photo:bird's eye view

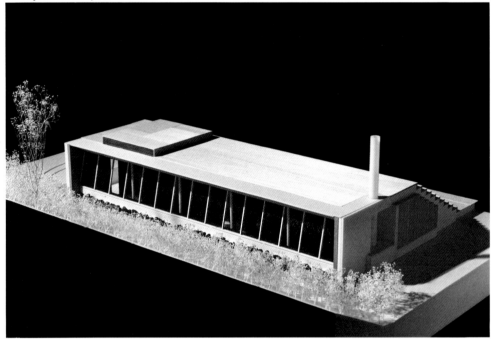
Southeast view

計画：J山荘ゲストハウス／山梨県山中湖
用途：別荘
建築主：K. INTERNATIONAL
建築設計：飯田善彦建築工房
　　　　　担当／飯田善彦，小原賢一
構造設計：構造企画研究所
施工：梶原工業所
敷地面積：1190.49m²／国立公園第2種特別地域
建築面積：81.51m²
延床面積：76.05m²
建築規模：地上1階，最高高さ2.6m
主体構造：鉄筋コンクリート造
外部仕上：外壁／唐松縁甲板型枠 コンクリート打放し，
　　　　　テラス／米杉防腐注入材スノコ貼り キシラデコール塗装
内部仕上：床／黒大理石貼 水磨仕上　壁／黒御影石貼 割肌仕上
　　　　　天井／折板型枠 コンクリート打放し

Interior

Model photos: Y. Takase

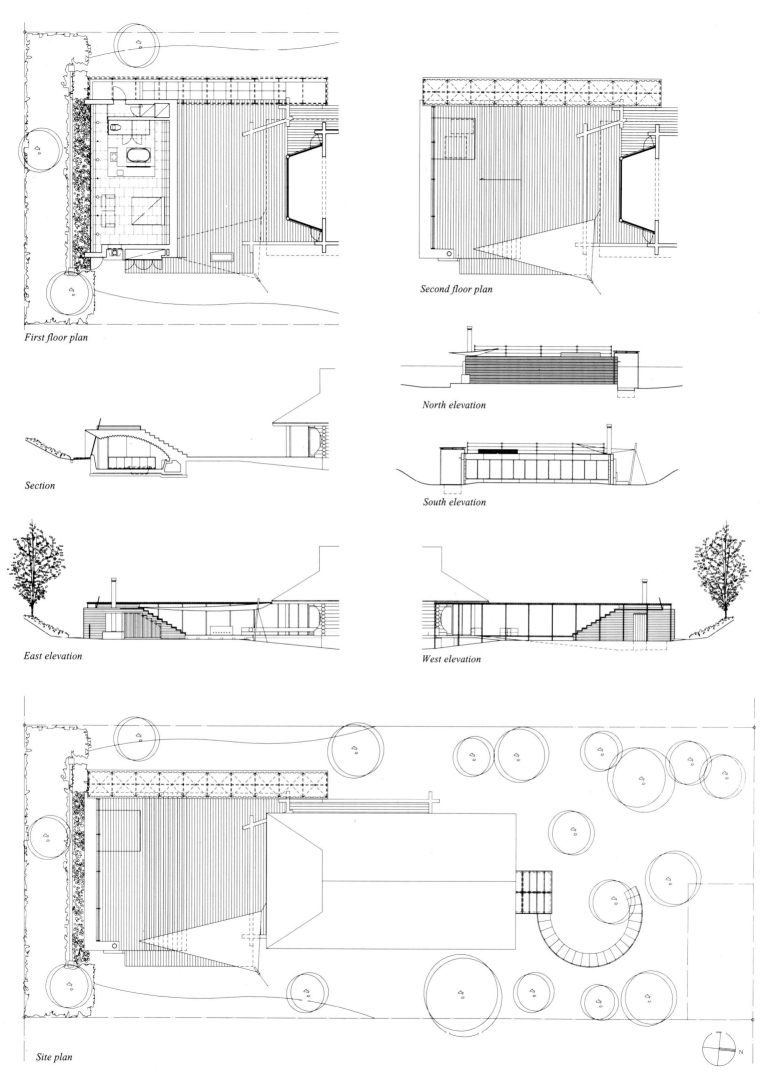

TOSHIAKI ISHIDA

T²
Itabashi-ku, Tokyo, Japan
Design: 1995-96

都心では貴重な公園に面した十字路の角地に計画地はある。都心に近く交通の利便性が良いことから周辺では一戸建てから中層マンションへの建て替えが進んでいる。こうした背景から建築のプログラムは1階にオフィスと駐車場，2階にアパート，3〜5階はオーナーの2世帯住居という複合した用途になっている。複合化したヴォリュームにシステムを備えたカーテンウォールで被膜した上で，内部の機能に応じてグラフィカルな壁面に還元すること。オープンスペースに動線を重ね立体的に経路化することで各々の用途を接続するとともにヴォリュームを空洞化し風や光，情報を提供することで空間の均質化を図ること。これらが都市に対してできるかぎり建築を開こうとした建築意図である。

（石田敏明）

The site occupies a corner in an intersection, but has a view toward a park which provides a rare glimpse of natural landscape in an urban situation. Being in close proximity to the city center, some single-family houses in the neighborhood have already been converted into apartment buildings. In this context the program asked for a mixed-use building on this site consisting of office spaces and a garage on the ground level, apartments on the second level, and the client's family quarters on the 3rd through 5th levels that were to accommodate two households. The design challenge included visual articulation of volumes with different functional requirements wrapped in a coherent skin, three dimensional layering of a circulation pattern with a series of open spaces serving as a connector of different functional elements, and transforming of some volumes into void in order to allow penetration of natural influences, like wind and light, as well as artificial influences culminating at the end in one harmonious whole. In essence the intention of this architectural exercise was to liberate a building in a dense urban situation from its self confinement and allow it to start a dialogue with its surroundings.
Toshiaki Ishida

計画：T²／東京都板橋区
用途：共同住宅＋事務所
建築主：今関富郎
建築設計：石田敏明建築設計事務所
　　　　　担当／石田敏明，石黒由紀，森田隆広
構造設計：テクトニックコンサルタンツ　担当／阿部透
設備設計：山崎設備設計事務所　担当／山崎克己
　　　　　川口設備研究所　担当／川口洋輔
敷地面積：172.76m²／住居地域
建築面積：119.90m²／建蔽率69％（許容70％）
延床面積：445.25m²／容積率257％（許容300％）
建築規模：地上5階，最高高さ15m
主体構造：鉄骨造

Model photo: Y. Takase

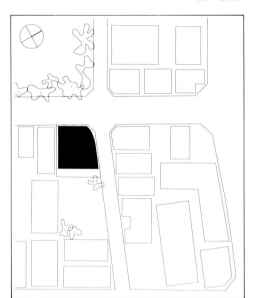
Site plan

Third floor plan

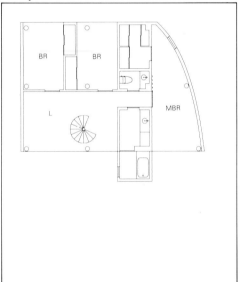
5th floor plan

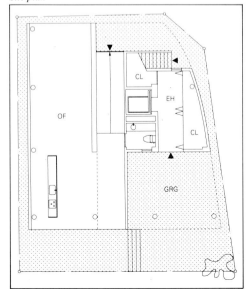
First floor plan

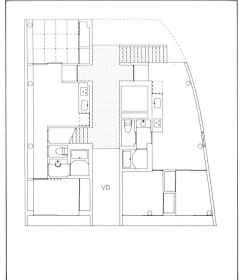
Second floor plan

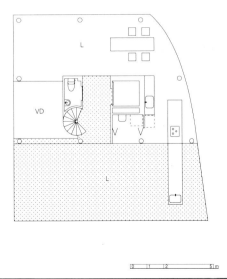
4th floor plan

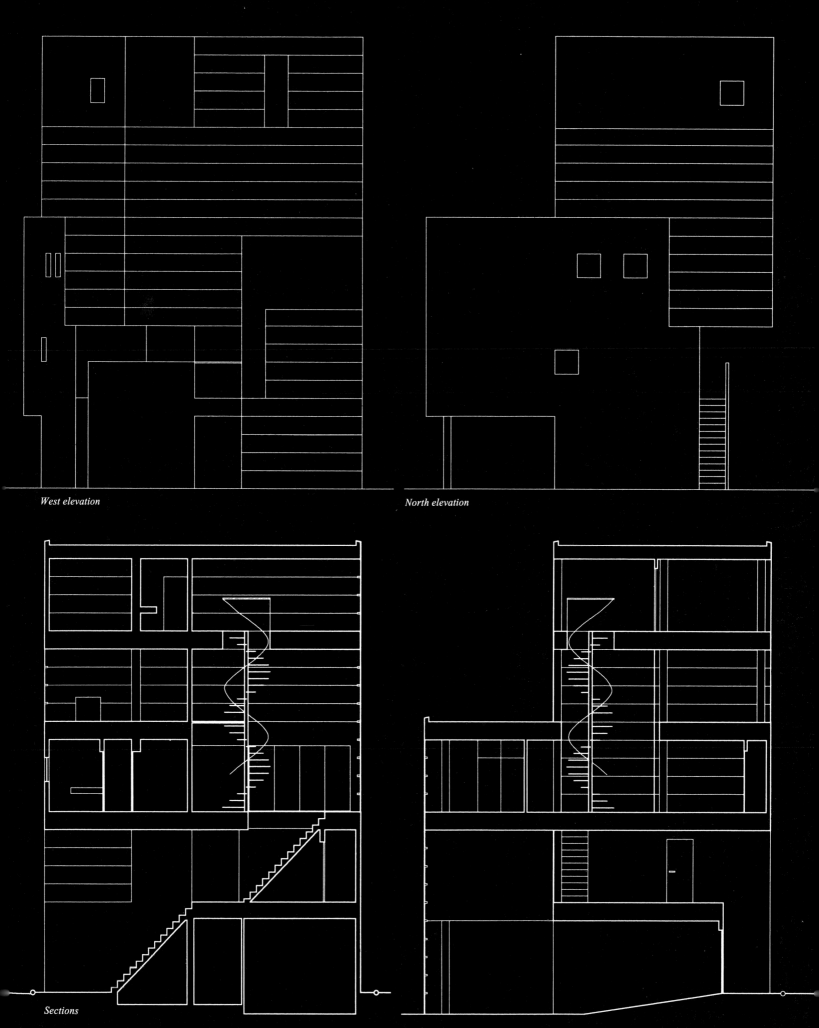

JIM JENNINGS

VISITING ARTIST SUITES
Geyserville, California, U.S.A.
Design: 1991
Construction: 1998

Site
The crest of an open, rolling hillside of oak trees and native grasses. The site is part of a large tract of land devoted to commissioned outdoor sculpture.

Program
The suites for visiting artists to stay while working at the ranch. Accommodations are to be simple and reclusive, yet accessible to studios and other facilities on the property.

Solution
The building is made from the simple act of connecting two sides of a hill by cutting through it. Into this cut is placed the armature of a perceptual telescope, which is defined by its properties in section.

The site is sliced by two seemingly parallel walls, the convergence of which focuses on a distant sculpture, and divergence of which opens in the direction of a small lake. The ground between the walls slopes upwards toward the point of convergence and slopes downward in the diverging direction. Likewise, shifts in floor planes cause different dimensions and spatial proportions to occur in each portion of the plan. This opposite shifting of horizontal and vertical planes throughout the section of the building accentuates the perspectival phenomena of elongation and foreshortening of space.

Unlike the refracting telescope, in which viewing toward the divergent direction of the instrument causes distant objects to appear larger and closer, the perceptual instrument acts in reverse. The perceived elongation of the converging space causes the distant object to appear larger and closer. In this way, architecture may make a mute contribution to the dialogue between art, artist, and site.

敷地：カシや草が生え，やわらかにうねる，明るい丘の斜面。野外彫刻を展示するための広大な区域の一画。

プログラム：ここで仕事をする間，アーティストが滞在するための2組のスイート。簡素で隔絶されてはいるが，この広大な領域内にあるスタジオや他の施設へも行きやすいこと。

解答：丘の両側面を貫いて連結するという簡単な方法から建物を構成する。この切り通しのなかに，望遠鏡ともいうべき甲冑をはめ込む。

切り通しになった敷地には，一見すると平行しているように見えるが，その延長線の一端は遠くに置かれている彫刻に向かって収束して行き，一端は小さな湖に向かって広がって行く2枚の壁を立てる。壁の間の地面は，収束点方向に上がって行き，外へ広がって行く方向に向かって下がって行く。同様に床面の変化は，平面の各所で，ディメンションやプロポーションの変化をつくりだす。建物全体にわたる水平垂直面の逆方向への変化は，空間の奥行きを引き伸ばしたり，縮めたりして，遠近感を強調する。

無限大方向に向けて見ることによって，遠くの物体を大きく近づけて見せる屈折望遠鏡とは違って，この知覚の道具は逆に作用する。収束して行く空間の知覚的な伸張が遠くの物体を大きく近づけて見せるのである。この方法によって建築は，アート，アーティスト，敷地との間の対話に無言のうちに貢献する。

Architects: Jim Jennings Arkhitekture—Jim Jennings, principal-in-charge; Cheri Fraser, Tim Perks, design team; May Sung, Les Taylor, Vincent Chew, modelmakers
Clients: Steven and Nancy Oliver

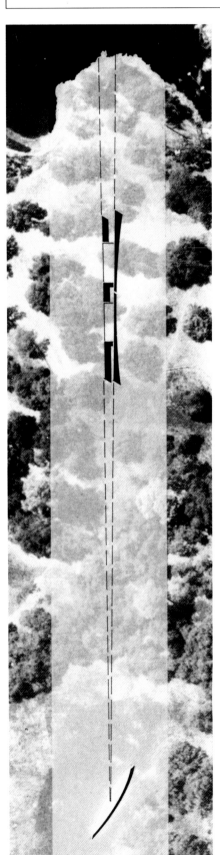

Site plan

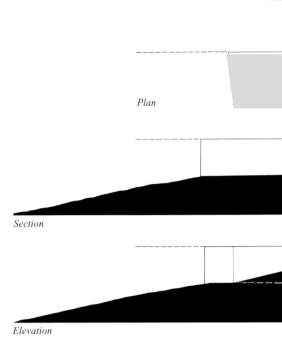

Plan

Section

Elevation

Model photos

Courtyard perspective

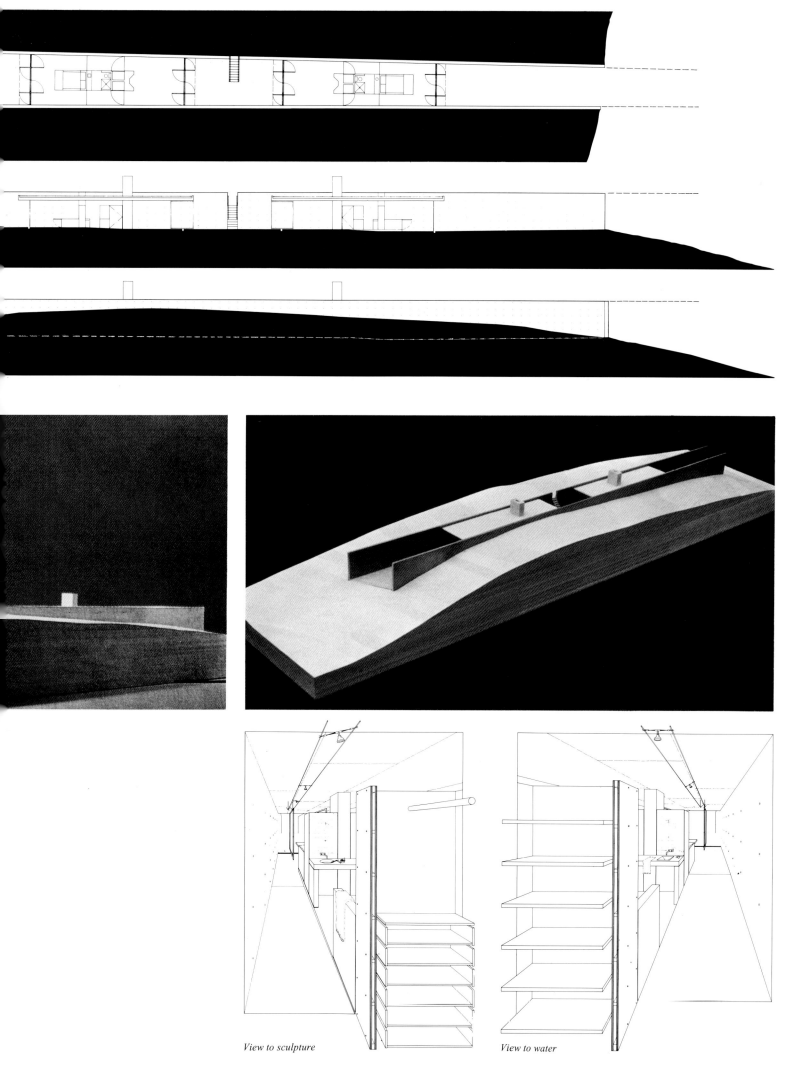

View to sculpture   *View to water*

GUDMUNDUR JONSSON

THE WALL
(A Summerhouse in Grímsnes)
Grímsnes, Iceland
Design: 1995–96
Construction: 1996

Perspective

The walls are embracing the lava ravine making a shelter from the road and the prevailing winds. They act as a simple organizer making the two independent zones, the zone of privacy and the public zone. Between those walls, the icelandic lava nature and the view towards the mountain Ingolfsfjall is embraced. The prevailance of the walls is only agitated by the curved formations of the living room and the bathroom units formed in a dark glossy plywood as a contrast to the concrete walls. In cold evenings the steam from the hot-spring basin surrounds the living room creating a mysterious and foggy mood expressing the icelandic mythology.

壁は，道路と卓越風から守られたシェルターをつくりだすように，溶岩流の谷を包んでいる。これらの壁は，パブリックとプライヴェートという2つの独立した領域を構成する単純なオーガナイザーとして働く。これらの壁の間に，アイスランドの特長である溶岩質の大地とインゴルフスヤール山に向かう眺めが抱き取られている。壁の優位性を乱しているのは，リヴィングの湾曲する形と，コンクリートの壁とは対比的に艶のある濃い合板でつくられたバス・ユニットだけである。寒い夜には，リヴィングを囲む温泉の水盤から立ち昇る湯気が，アイスランドの神話を物語る神秘的で霧につつまれた雰囲気をつくりだす。

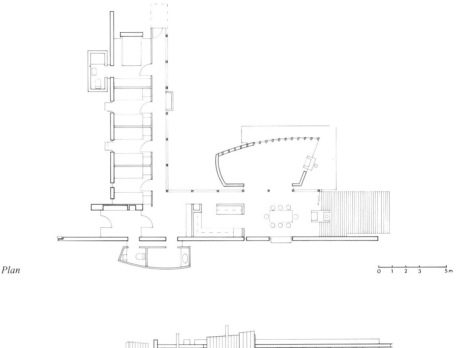
Plan

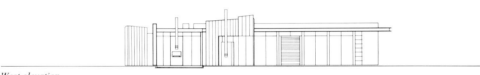
West elevation

Section

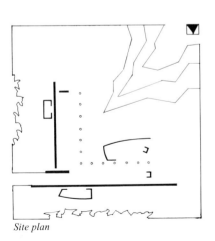
Site plan

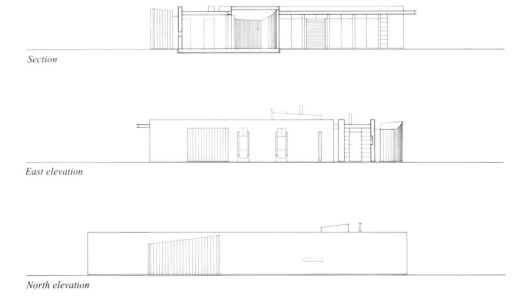
East elevation

North elevation

South elevation

Architects: Gudmundur Jonsson; Alice Sturt, Gunvor Thorsen, project team
Client: Jóna Gróa Sigurdardóttir

GUDMUNDUR JONSSON

THE ELEVATING INTERSECTION
(A Summerhouse in Hamarøy)
Hamarøy, Norway
Design: 1995–96
Construction: 1997

Architects: Gudmundur Jonsson; Alice Sturt, Gunvor Thorsen, project team; Robert Sannes, perspective
Client: Signe Winther Lohre

Hamarøy is a beautiful island north of the arctic circle facing the dramatic and majestic mountain range of Lofoten towards west. The site is a curved shelf on the major hill at this part of the vicinity. The shelf marks significant differences in the landscape view in each direction. At the ground level the view is restricted towards north and south. To the west the beautiful view towards the spectacular mountain range is blocked by four meter high peak.

This summer house acts as a elevating bridge at the intersection of the different views of this variable landscape.

The staircase element elevates the visitor to the breathtaking view in the funnel-formed living room, acting as a summary of all movements in the house. In the evening the midnight sun and the following stars are experienced through the elevated part of the glazed front of the living room forming the mysterious silhouette of the mountain range in the horizon.

ハマロイは北極圏の北にある美しい島で、西に向けて威風堂々としたロフォテンの山並みが広がっている。敷地はこの山並みに近い大きな丘の上に広がる、湾曲した岩棚である。敷地からは方位によって際だって異なる景色が望める。地上からの眺めは北と南に限られている。壮大な山並みに向かう西側の美しい眺めは4mの高さの頂に遮られている。

この夏の家は、変化に富む風景が繰り広げている多彩な眺望の交差点にかかる高架橋としての役割を任じている。

階段室が来訪者を、じょうご形をしたリヴィング・ルームから見える、息を呑むような眺望へと引き上げてくれる。ここは内部のすべての動きを要約する場所として働く。夕方になると、高く持ち上げられたリヴィングのガラス面から、地平線に横たわる山並みの神秘的なシルエット、真夜中の太陽や星星を見ることができる。

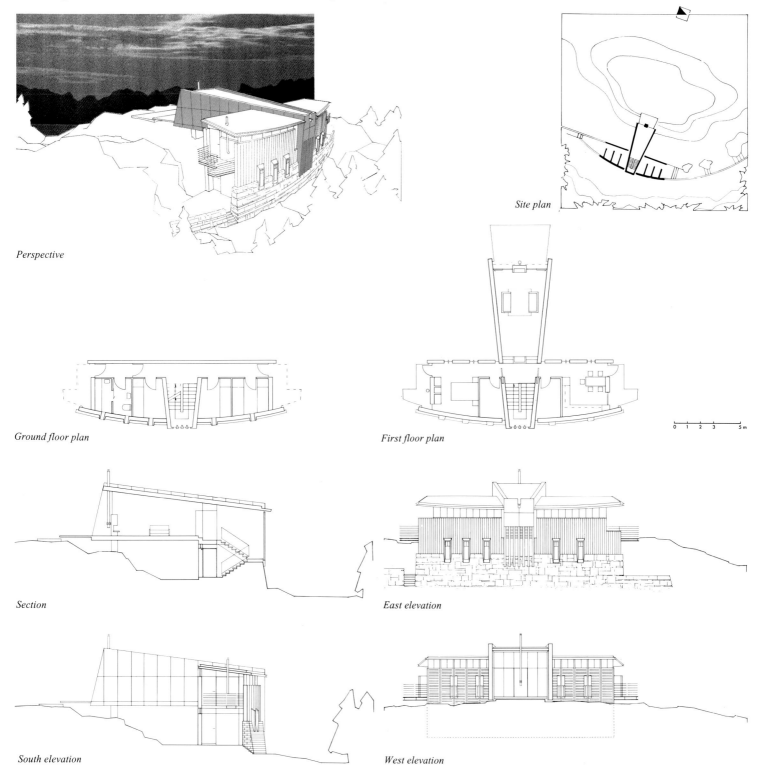

Perspective

Site plan

Ground floor plan

First floor plan

Section

East elevation

South elevation

West elevation

ANN M. PENDLETON-JULLIAN

BIOCLIMATIC HOUSE FOR TENERIFE
The Canary Islands, Spain
Design: 1995
Construction: 1996–97

This project for a bioclimatic house in Tenerife approaches the construction of space in the landscape from three facets: bioclimatically, spatially and metaphysically. It attempts to integrate certain physical forces of the site into the space of the house. These forces—the wind, the angle of the winter sun, the view to the volcano from which the island was formed, and the zenith of the path of the constellation cancer—create a series of vectors which operate consistently at an angle of forty five degrees relative to the east-west axis of the site and relative to the ground. Therefore, the initial study for the house began to explore the possibility of engaging the diagonal through a series of cubes which were modeled integral with their own axonometric projections of themselves. These cubes when brought together in series engage the site through these physical forces and the phenomena associated with them.

The house is a simple box floating off of the ground and oriented east-west. It is formed of four spatial units, two of which unfold their south faces upward to provide the optimum orientation for the photovoltaic awnings during the winter months. These awnings shield the house from the strong southern sun and, like the brim of a hat, arriving to 1.5 meters off of the main living space, they collapse the view of the landscape into a horizontal space which parallels the horizon line of the sea. The north face of the eastern most spatial unit unfolds in plan to create a wind scoop for the north-easterly winds. The western most unit unfolds out and upward to frame a view of the volcano Mount Teide.

The four units form one continuous space which is a tube of wind and light. On the eastern end of this tube is the porch through which the wind enters. The western face of the building is a series of baffles which modulate the draw for the air flow and play with the changing conditions of light. As layers of vertically sliding sun filters and glass closure, they can be configured to pull air through at the lower main living level during the day or at the upper sleeping level during the night. Or both levels simultaneously. The sun filters open or veil the view, and cut and pattern the light in a similar manner. The interior of the house is a very open space allowing for the movement and passage of air and light. Sliding panels can be configured to separate off spaces for privacy or to shield specific areas creating small microclimates and still pockets within the larger space.

The upper sleeping level—another tube nesting within the larger tubal space—reinforces the east-west equinoctial orientation of the house. Vertical elements and their edges, such as the barbecue's chimney or edge of the wind scoop, create marks in space—referents for the migration of the rising sun relative to the equinoctial line. On the western face of the building, sun filters create a prism for the setting sun's light. These vertical and horizontal louvered panels can be overlapped in various configurations fracturing and banding the light—changing its density from thin to thick. On the equinoxes the light from the setting sun will penetrate this face, cover the entire length of the house and then disappear. Adjacent to the entry, a third tube of space penetrates the main tubal volume vertically allowing light into the work space below the house and framing the zenith of the rise of Cancer—the constellation for which the Tropic, on which this house sits, is named.

Materials for the house are wood and concrete. Glulaminated wood structural components and treated plywood panel sheathing. A second roof in concrete, supported by six concrete columns and the canted northeastern wall, is placed over the wood box of the house to protect the volume below from the heat of the sun.

An instrument—scientific or musical—for the phenomena and conditions of the landscape, embracing the issue of bioclimatic in its broadest sense. Disturbing the site as little as possible while celebrating its space.

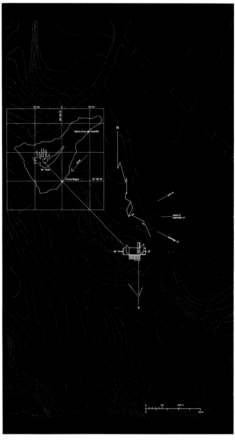

カナリア諸島、テネリフェ島に、生物気候学を応用した家を建てるという計画である。生物気候学、空間、哲学という3つの面から考えて、自然風景のなかに空間を構築する。敷地に存在する自然力を住宅空間のなかに統合しようと試みた。これらの力が——風、冬の日差しの角度、この島を形成した火山の眺め、黄道帯の星座軌道の天頂など——敷地の東西軸と地盤に対して45度の角度によって効率的に作用する一連のベクトルをつくりだす。従って、まず、対角線を、自らのアクソノメトリックと統合するようにデザインした一連の立方体によって結合する可能性についてスタディを始めた。これらの立方体は、鎖のようにつながると、自然力やそれに関連する現象によって敷地と合体する。

建物は地盤面を離れて浮かび、東西に方位を向けたシンプルな箱である。4つの空間ユニットから成り、そのうちの2つは、光電流装置となっている日除けが、冬期に最適な方位を向けられるように南面が上に開かれる。これらの日除けは強い南の日差しを遮り、帽子のつばのように、主要なリヴィング・スペースから1.5m離れ、景色を、海の水平線に平行する水平な空間のなかへたたみこむ。東側の最も広いスペース・ユニットの北面は、北東風を掬い取るように平面を拡げている。西側ユニットはテイデ火山の眺めを枠取るように外側に向けて上に開く。

4つのユニットは風と光のチューブである一つの連続空間をつくる。チューブの東端は風の入るポーチである。家の西面は、空気の流れを調節し、変化する光と遊ぶバッフルを連ねている。上下にスライドするサン・フィルターとガラスの囲いを重ねてあり、昼間は下のメイン・リヴィングに、夜は上のスリーピング階に空気の流れを引き込むように構成できる。あるいはまた2つの階に、同時に送り込むこともできる。サン・フィルターは眺めを見せ、あるいは遮り、同様に、光を遮り、あるいはパターン化する。家の内部は非常に開放的で、人も空気も光も自由に動き、浸透する。スライディング・パネルは、プライヴァシーの欲しいときはスペースを区分することもでき、特定のエリアを囲んで微気候に包まれた小さな場所、広い場所のなかの静かなポケットをつくることもできる。

上の寝室階——大きなチューブのなかに巣ごもった別のチューブなのだが——、天球赤道の走る東西に向いたこの家の方位を強調している。バーベキュー用の炉の煙突とかウィンド・スクープの端部といった垂直要素やそのエッジは、空間のなかの標識であり、天球赤道線と対応する朝日の移動を指示する。建物の西面では、サン・フィルターは日差しのプリズムとなる。これらの垂直水平のルーヴァーの付いたパネルは、幾通りにも重ねることができ、光をさまざまに束ね砕き、その厚さ薄さを変化させる。春分秋分には、陽光はこの面から差し込み、家の全長を浸して消えていく。エントリーに隣接して3番目のチューブがメイン・チューブのなかに垂直に侵入し、家の下の仕事場に光を差し込ませ、天頂に昇った蟹座——この住宅の建つ場所である南回帰線の星座に名付けられた——を枠取る。

この住宅に使われている材料は木とコンクリートである。集成木材の構造部材に合板パネル被覆。6本のコンクリート柱と北東側の傾斜壁で支持された下の屋根はコンクリートで、木造の箱形の家の上を覆い、その下のヴォリュームを太陽熱から保護する。

広い意味で生物気候学的な問題を抱き込んだ、この風景のもつ現象や状況に対する科学的あるいは音楽的な、楽器である。敷地に手をつけるのは最小限におさえながら、豊かな空間をつくりたいと考えた。

Architects: Ann M. Pendleton-Jullian, Architect; Les Norford, Civil Engineer, Robert Matthew Noblett, Todd Thiel, project team
Client: Istituto Tecnologico y de Energias Renovables

Model photo: northwest view

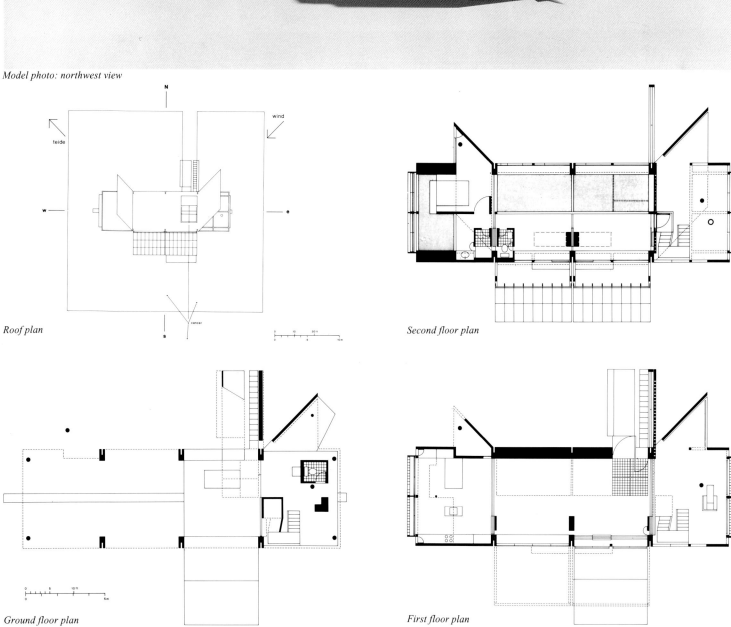

Roof plan

Second floor plan

Ground floor plan

First floor plan

75

Southwest view

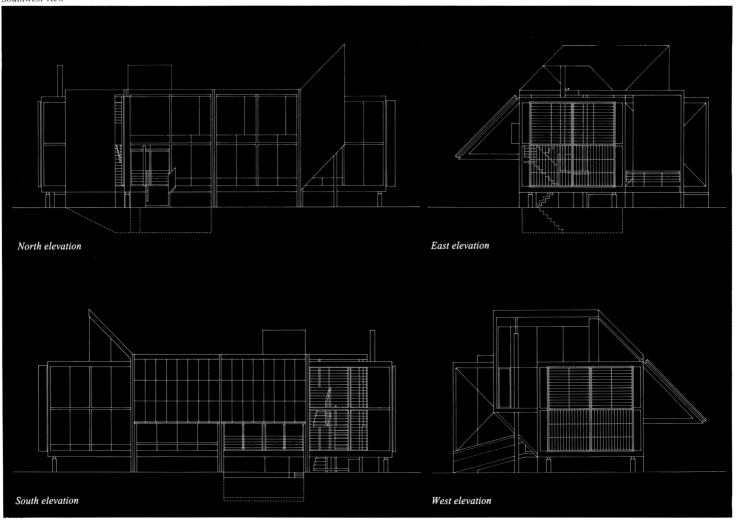

North elevation

East elevation

South elevation

West elevation

Bird's eye view

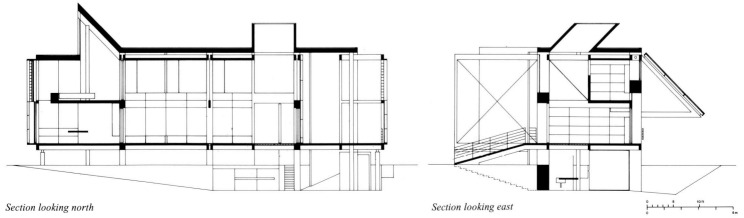

Section looking north

Section looking east

WARO KISHI

HOUSE IN HIGASHINADA
Kobe, Hyogo, Japan
Design: 1995–96
Construction: 1996

The house is planned for the Higashinada district of Kobe. The clients, a mother and a daughter, asked that the house be a place where one would continuously sense the presence of the other, and not a place where one's privacy is always protected.

The site, 70 sq. m. with 4.25 m. street front is not, by any standard, considered spacious. Yet the very restricted site looks towards a park on north across a street. So the design began with the relationship between the park and the site as the key element to explore. The resulting rectangular concrete box of 16 m. in length and 3.6 m in width, built to the edges of the site, holds a tall courtyard on its south-west corner occupying about 1/4 of the entire volume. The rest of the volume is occupies by three levels of living spaces off set in the middle by a stair well in a split level fashion. There are no internal doors in the house as a response to the clients' wish that they may not wish to see each other all the time but wish to be able to sense the existence of the other. This resulted in a vertical spatial continuity at the stair well and the courtyard. In fact the whole house was conceived as one room fragmented visually by various level changes but spaciously continuous whole.

The ceiling height of lower floors were intentionally kept very low so that it could take the maximum height on the 3rd level where the family usually socialize. This space has a generous gentle stairs that leads to the roof terrace on the south. On entire north wall is glazed and opens upward turning the room into well ventilated, semi-outdoor space. "How to keep in touch with the nature in the dense urban situation" and "how to maintain a close contact with the neighboring park on high above 3rd level off the ground" were the issue addressed here.
Waro Kishi

神戸市東灘区に計画中の住宅である。クライアントは母＋娘という二人家族であり、それぞれのプライバシーを確固として守るというよりはむしろお互いの気配を常に感じながら生活できるような家でありたい、というのが要望だった。

決して広いとはいえない70m²の敷地、4.25mという間口、という厳しい敷地形状ではあるものの、北側道路を隔てた向かい側は大都市内では貴重な緑である公園があるため、この公園との関係を鍵に設計をスタートした。敷地一杯に設定した間口3.6m、奥行16mのコンクリートのボックスの南西隅、約1/4を中庭とし、残った部分を3層のスキップフロアの構成とする。二人の家族がお互いに姿は見えないが、それぞれの気配が感じられる空間、という依頼に対する解答として、水廻り以外にドアは無く、階段室と中庭が建物を垂直に繋ぎ、全体を一つの大きなワンルームではあるものの視線は通らないような、立体的な空間を計画した。

さらに1階、2階は通常の階高よりも低めに押さえ、逆に家族が集う場である3階のダイニング・ルームは可能な限り天井高を高くとり、3.9mの高さとした。その天井高の高い空間は南側では緩やかな階段で結ばれたテラスや中庭の吹抜けに面し、また北側の開口は建物の幅一杯が上方に開く形式とする。北側を開放することで3階は公園に面した半屋外の空間へと変化し、風は南から北へとぬけてゆく。大都市の中で自然に接しながら暮らすこと——地上から離れた3階にいても北側の公園の緑を直接感じる方法はないか、と考えたことの結果である。(岸和郎)

計画：東灘の家／兵庫県神戸市東灘区
用途：専用住宅／母＋娘1人
建築設計：岸和郎＋K. ASSOCIATES　担当／三上裕美子
構造設計：都市デザイン研究所
敷地面積：71.61m²／第2種住居専用地域
建築面積：42.76m²／建蔽率59.72％（許容60％）
延床面積：127.96m²／容積率178.70％（許容200％）
建築規模：地上3階、地下1階、最高高さ9.95m
主体構造：鉄筋コンクリート造
主要仕上：コンクリート打放し

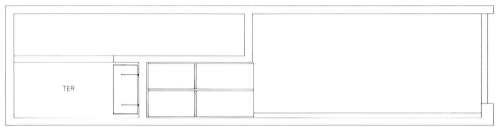
Roof plan

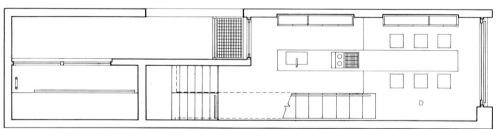
Third floor plan

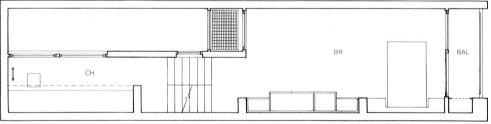
Second floor plan

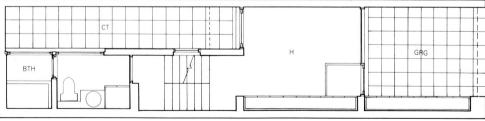
First floor plan

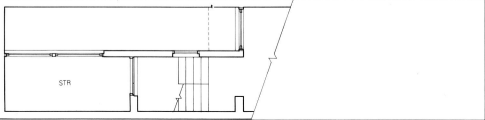
Basement floor plan

Site plan

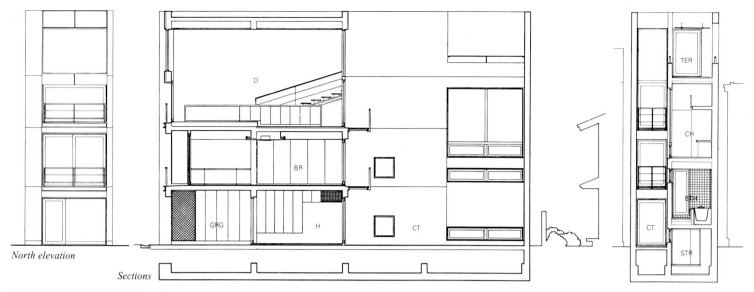

North elevation

Sections

Sectional model Model photo: H. Ueda

View from dining room

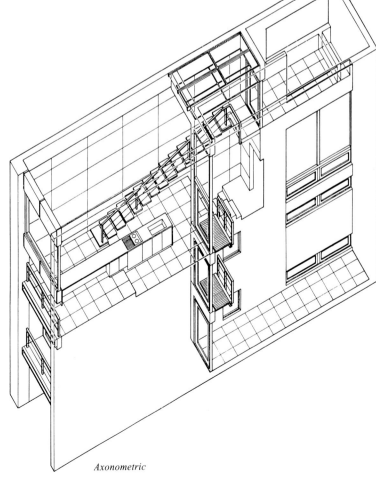

Axonometric

View from terrace

ATSUSHI KITAGAWARA

C HOUSE
Nagano, Nagano, Japan
Design: 1995
Construction: 1996

The climate of the northern region of Shinshu where this house is to be built unveils its true nature in the winter: the air gives off a silvery glow as the particles of ice drift; everything disappears under the veil of snow; nothing seems discernible; everything ceases. Such is the image of northern Shinshu. It is naturally a deception. Life abounds below, yet only the spirit roams above in a seeming transparency and clarity—resembling an aspect in Japanese culture. C House is like that. It is a simple rectangular box—its corners slit open to reveal fragments of life inside. But it is all walls on four sides.... plain white walls.   *Atsushi Kitagawara*

信州の北部の自然環境は冬期にその特徴が表われる。まず空気が氷の微粒子となって白く輝き，地表に存在するものはすべて雪に覆われ消えてゆく。何も見えず何も存在しない。それが北信ゾーンのイメージだ。ただ，何も見えず何も存在しないように見えるが，実は生々しいものが隠蔽された表面的な透明感が空間を支配している。これは日本的な文化の一面でもある。C邸の場合，単純な直方体の四隅を切り欠いて，そこに日常生活の断面を見せながら，東西南北の各々のファサードは白い寡黙な壁だけが立つ。
（北川原温）

計画：C邸／長野県長野市
用途：専用住宅／夫婦＋子供1人
建築設計：北川原温建築都市研究所
　　　　　担当／北川原温，下吹越武人
構造設計：関田構造設計事務所
敷地面積：280.14m²／第一種住居専用地域
建築面積：110.77m²／建蔽率39.5%（許容40%）
延床面積：237.71m²／容積率58.9%（許容60%）
建築規模：地上2階，地下1階，最高高さ6.920m
主体構造：鉄筋コンクリート造
外部仕上：RC打放シ，RC打放シ抜目地ノ上VP

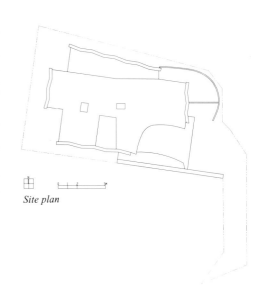
Site plan

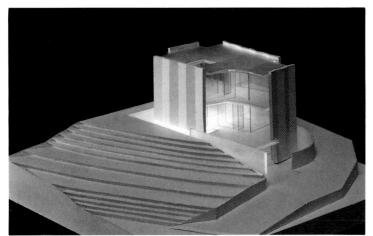
Model photo: H. Ueda

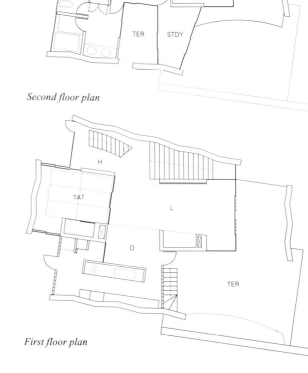
Second floor plan

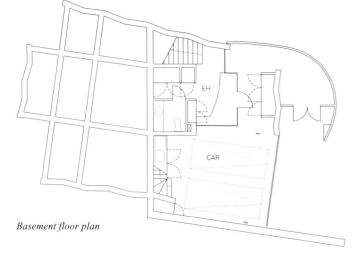
Basement floor plan

First floor plan

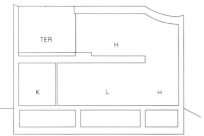
Sections

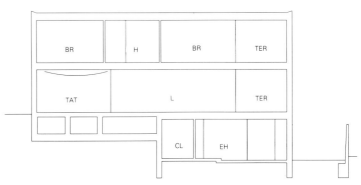

RICARDO LEGORRETA

CASA OFFER
Haifa, Israel
Design: 1995–

Architects: Legorreta Arquitectos—Ricardo Legorreta, Victor Legorreta, Noe Castro; Jorge Tena Urbina, Jorge Covarrubias, design team; Isaac Broid & Partners, executive architect

Model photo: southwest view

Northwest view

The client of this house is a young entrepreneur couple who is moving to Israel. The site has a strong character as it is located by the sea at the top of a cliff, north of Tel Aviv. The soil consists of dark red sand with spectacular views to the sea.

The aim is to have a house that adapts to the surroundings and the climate. Family life is created around a central blue courtyard which can be flooded and converted into a fountain. This patio will give a fresh interior environment to the very rough surroundings. The design includes a system to open the windows electrically so that there is a really an interaction between interior and exterior when the weather conditions permit it.

It is intended to take advantage of the dramatic views but also to frame them. From the entrance there is a special window through which the patio, living room and the sea can be seen. At the end of the courtyard there is a large living room that has both views: to the sea and patio.

Each of the spaces of the house have a different character: the family room related to the pool, the dining room with cylindrical shape, the children's room, each one with a special patio and the main bedroom located at the second floor in order to have the best views. In this second floor there is also a small studio from which it is possible to get out to the roof and get advantage of the flat area.

The color of the exterior walls will be in different tones of oxide so it plays with the walls and volumes.

The result is an abstract composition of walls, towers that will blend in a landscape with the red sand and series of olive trees.

Model photos: Lourdes Legorreta

クライアントは，イスラエルに転居することになっている若い企業家夫妻。敷地はテルアヴィヴの北に位置する，海岸に面した絶壁の頂上という強い特長を持つ場所である。土壌は暗赤色の砂地で，前方には素晴らしい海の景色が広がっている。

周囲の気候風土に適した住宅をつくることを主眼とした。家族の生活は，水を張って噴水にすることもできるブルーのセントラル・コートを囲んで繰り広げられる。このパティオは荒涼とした周辺風土のなかに，みずみずしい屋内環境を提供するだろう。天気のよいときは，屋内と屋外が直接交流しあうように，電動で窓を開閉できるシステムを導入している。

素晴らしい景色を広々と見せると同時に，絵のように枠取ることも考えた。エントランスからは，特別にデザインした窓を通して，パティオ，リヴィング・ルーム，海までが見える。また，コートヤードの端にある広いリヴィング・ルームからは海とパティオの両方が見える。

内部空間の性格は，それぞれに異なっている。プールと結ばれたファミリー・ルーム，円筒形のダイニング・ルーム，専用パティオの付いた子供部屋，家中で一番見晴らしの良い2階の主寝室。2階には屋上に出られる小スタジオもあり，屋上の平坦に広がるエリアを自由に使える。

外壁はさまざまなトーンにするつもりなので，壁面や建物のヴォリュームとこれらの色彩が戯れ合うだろう。

そして最後に，壁面とタワーの抽象的構成からなる住宅が，赤い砂とオリーヴの林が広がる風景に溶け込んでいく。

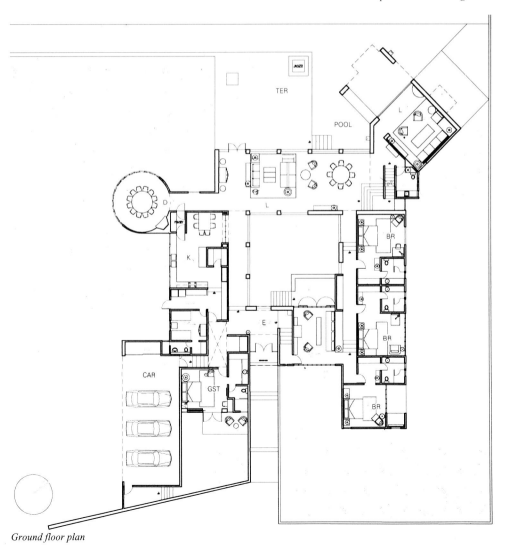

Ground floor plan

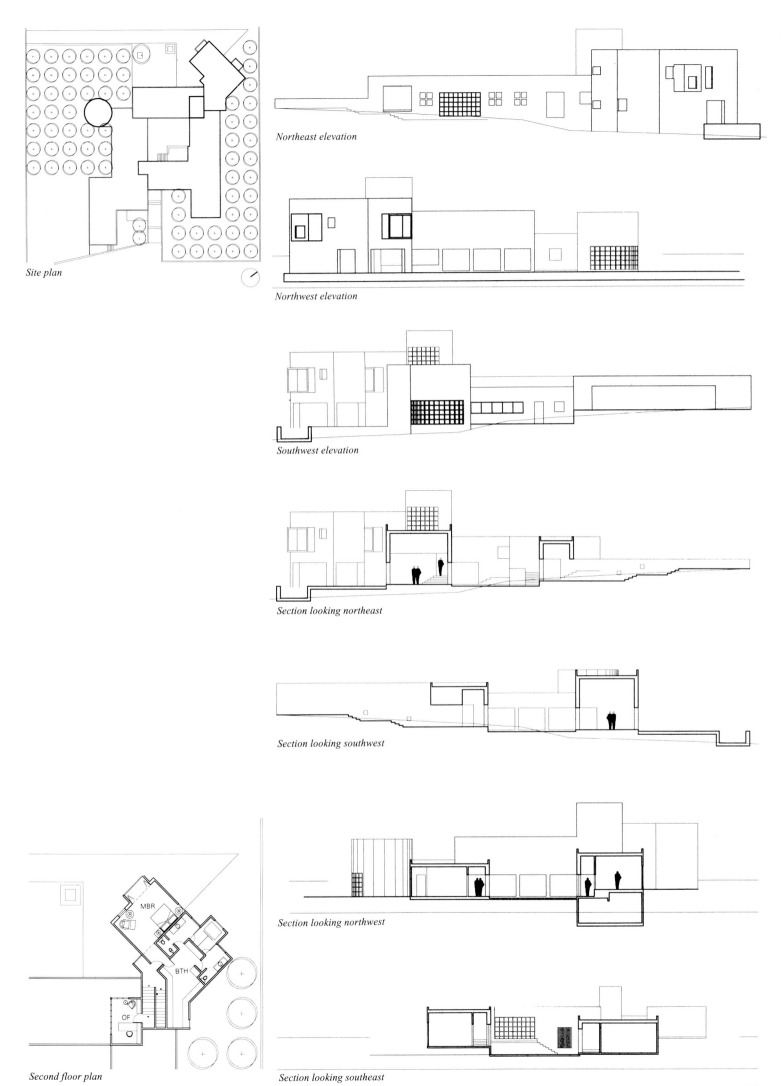

Site plan

Northeast elevation

Northwest elevation

Southwest elevation

Section looking northeast

Section looking southwest

Second floor plan

Section looking northwest

Section looking southeast

83

MARK MACK

RITENOUR HOUSE
Malibu, California, U.S.A.
Design: 1995
Construction: 1996

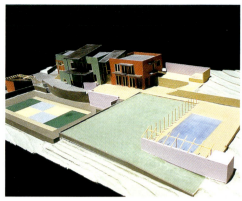

Model photos: bird's eye view

On the hills of Malibu overlooking the shore, this house is built on an existing structure and tennis court. These restraints called for a new organization of the whole site in regards to entry and landscaping. Two new wings (3000 sq.ft.) embrace the old structure (3000 sq.ft.), and tie all the structures (existing and new) together as a new and consistent building.

Two colors of stucco accentuate the forms and create a playful relationship between the parts. A pool and open fireplace towards the back of the property extend the living parts of the house into the landscape.

The entry court meets a curving patio which establishes a *piano nobile fresco* as a new transition between the raised floors of the house and the sunken tennis court. The landscape design reinforces the new orientation of the house with a continuous row of palms from the front to the back of the property. Facing the street, the house expresses the variety and playfulness of the new form.

海岸を見晴らすマリブの丘の上にある敷地。この家は既存建物とテニス・コートの上に建てられる。これらの制約によって，エントリーとランドスケーピングに関して，敷地全体の再構成が必要となる。2つのウィングを増築し（3,000sq.ft.），元の建物（3,000sq.ft.）を囲み，新しい統一体を構成するように連結する。

二色のスタッコが建築形態を引き立て，各部分のあいだに陽気な関係をつくりだす。敷地の背面に向いたプールと暖炉がリヴィング・スペースを景色のなかへと広げている。

エントリー・コートは湾曲したパティオに接し，このパティオは，住宅の高く持ち上げられた床面と低い位置にあるテニス・コートのあいだの，新たな移行ゾーンとして＜ピアノ・ノビーレ・フレスコ＞を構成する。造園では，敷地正面から背面へ椰子の並木をつくり，この住宅の新しい方位を強調した。通りに面しては，新しい形態構成は変化に富んだ楽しい表情を見せている。

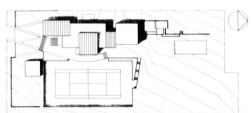

Architects: Mack Architects—Mark Mack, principal; Frances Moore, Robert Flock, Tim Sakamoto, Gloria Lee, Michael Dax, Arden Young
Clients: Lee and Carmen Ritenour
Consultants: Parker-Resnick, structural; Mia Lehrer, landscape
General contractor: Archetype

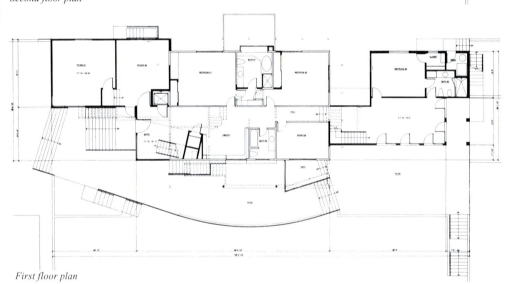

Second floor plan

First floor plan

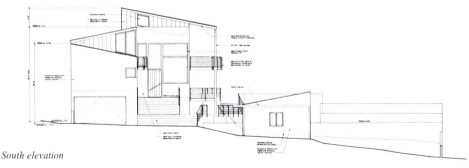

South elevation

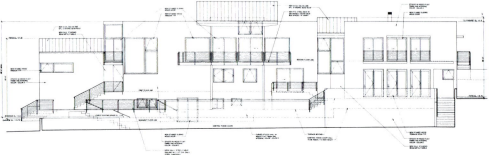

MARK MACK

HOUSE IN TAOS
New Mexico, Mexico
Design: 1995

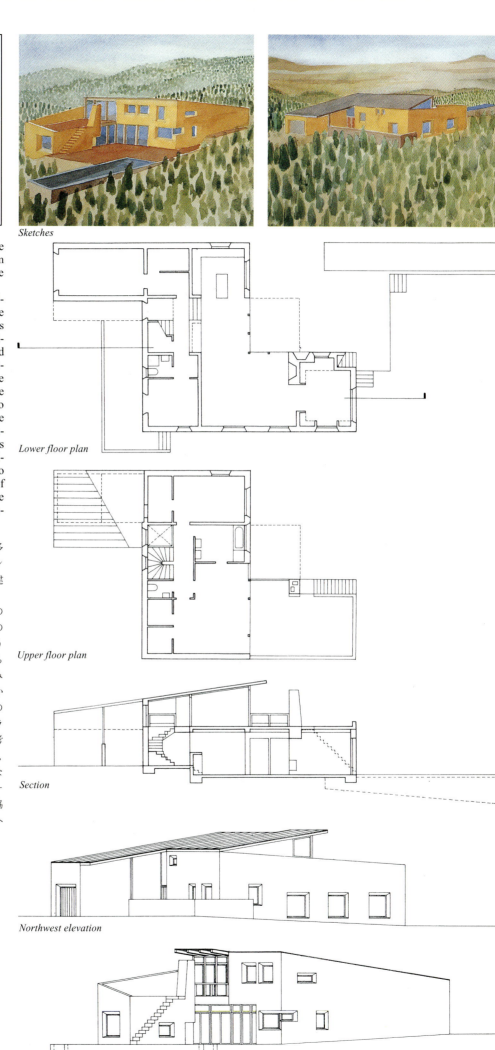

Sketches

Lower floor plan

Upper floor plan

Section

Northwest elevation

Southeast elevation

A home for a psychiatrist and his family in the comforting environment of the American Indian culture as an alternative to the highly active urban life of Vienna.

On the high elevation desert of the Taos Valley the house carves out a place for itself on the ridge of a pine forested hill. The house conforms to the restraints of a long narrow site and the advantage of views to all sides. Low flung and close to the ground, built from earth (adobe), accessible only from a narrow road, the house reaches from the front to the back following the form of the ridge. Emulating the Indian Pueblo tradition, the form and organization of the house reflects the outdoor lifestyle and the sheltered interior. Thick walls and chambered window edges exaggerate the earth enclosure and create a traditional yet modern appearance. Large terraces to the south and the west enhance the orientation of the house towards the pool. A sleeping terrace off the upper story master bedroom and an exterior stair extends the ground level to the sky.

精神科医とその家族のための住宅。ウィーンでの多忙な都市生活に代わる，アメリカン・インディアン文化の伝統をもつ，やすらぎのある環境のなかに建てる。

タオス渓谷の砂漠高地の上，マツの生い茂る丘の尾根を切り開いた敷地である。建物は細長い敷地の制約に合わせるとともに，四方に広がる眺望という地の利を生かしている。土（アドベ）によってつくられ，大地に近く，低く投げだされ，細い道からのみアクセスできる建物は，尾根の形に沿って，前面から背面へと延びている。プエブロ・インディアンの伝統を手本にした，建物の形と構成は，戸外でのライフスタイルと，覆い囲まれた内部ということを考えたものである。厚い壁と面取りをした窓の縁は，土の被膜を大きくみせ，伝統的ではあるがモダンな外観である。南と西に設置された広いテラスがプールに向いた方位を強調する。上の階にある主寝室脇のスリーピング・テラスと外部階段が地上階を空へ向かって広げる。

Architects: Mack Architects—Mark Mack, principal; Michael Dax
Client: Michael Leodolter

RICHARD MEIER

RACHOFSKY HOUSE II
Dallas, Texas, U.S.A.
Design: 1991–96
Construction: 1993–97

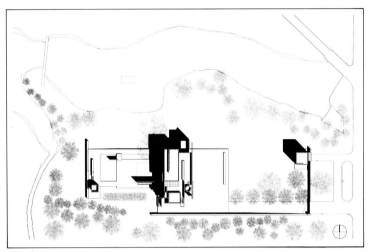
Site plan

Architects: Richard Meier & Partners—Richard Meier, Thomas Phifer, design team; Donald Cox, project architect; Raphael Justewicz, Jeff King, Gil Rampy, Thomas Savory, collaborators; Daniel Heuberger, model maker
Consultants: Ove Arup & Partners, structural; John Altieri Consulting Engineers, mechanical; Armstrong-Berger, Inc., landscape; Fisher, Marantz, Renfo, Stone, Inc., lighting
General contractor: Thos. S. Byrne, Inc.

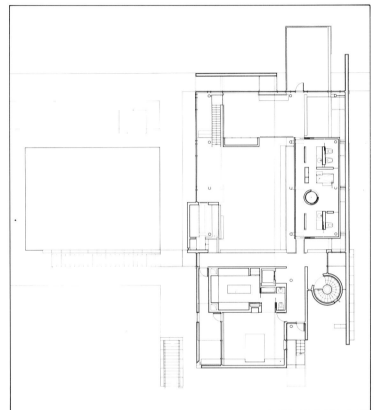
Third floor plan

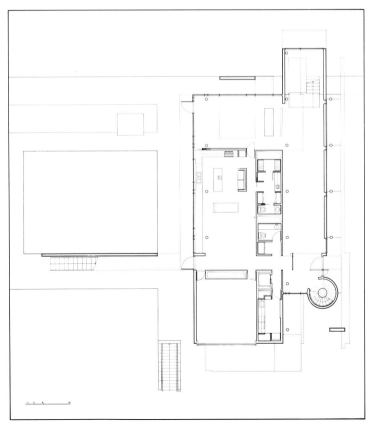
Ground floor plan

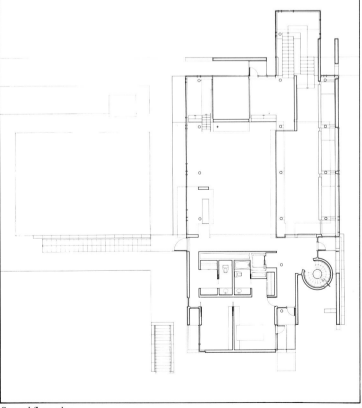
Second floor plan

Rachofsky House II is both a continuation and departure from the by now thirty year history of Richard Meier houses: a clean geometric volume wedded to its surroundings by views from the inside. What is new, however, is the attenuated physical separation of the house from the earth, effected here by a black granite podium extending from the apex of the sloped driveway to a sculpted pool terrace on the house's rear face.

At the entry, a wall and an art gallery stand as a protective layer from a major thoroughfare to the subsequent space which fronts the main residence. The main structure is comprised of three elemental parts. A cubic solid houses the private and service areas. The remaining primary element is a suspended vertical plane which serves as a buffer between public and private zones. The living room on the second level commands a view of the sculpted podium and the landscape to the west. Also located on the second level are the library and guest bathrooms. The third level houses the master suite including bedroom, wardrobe, and bath, as well as a small study and exercises area which open to the living room below.

Raised one meter above the ground, the podium, underscores and deepens the relationship between the house and the green world. It is difficult to view the Rachofsky House as anything but a finely machined object, yet the abstraction of the Texas earth into a composition of black stone and water allows one to fully appreciate the formal elegance and complexity of the architecture, independent of its relationship to the "natural" realm. It is a gesture at once bold and diplomatic, to simultaneously interpret the ground and acknowledge its primacy.

ラチョフスキー邸IIは，マイヤーのここ30年間の住宅作品の歴史──内部からの眺めによって周辺環境と融合した，明晰な幾何学形態をもつヴォリューム──に続くものであると同時に，新たな展開でもある。何が新しい展開かといえば，地上からの分離感が物理的に希薄になっていることで，ここでは，坂道のドライヴウェイの先端から住宅背面のプールの彫り込まれたテラスまで広がっている黒御影のポディウムがその役割を果たしている。

エントリーには，一枚の壁とアート・ギャラリーが，それに続く主屋に面したスペースを主要通路から保護するレイヤーとして立っている。主屋は3つの基本的部分で構成されている。キューブはプライヴェートおよびサーヴィス関係の部屋を収める。残る主要エレメントは吊された垂直面で，パブリックとプライヴェート領域の間の緩衝装置として働く。2階のリヴィングからは彫り込まれたポディウムと西側の風景が見渡せる。書斎とゲスト用浴室も2階にある。3階は寝室・ワードローブ・浴室から成る主寝室スイートで，小さな書斎と，下のリヴィングに向かって開いた体操室が付いている。

地盤面より1m高いポディウムは，住宅と緑の世界の結びつきを強調し深める。ラチョフスキー邸を，洗練されたマシン・オブジェ以外の何物かと見ることは難しい。しかし，テキサスの大地を黒い石と水の構成へと抽象化したことによって，＜自然＞界と独立した関係を結ぶこの建築の優美な形態と多彩さを存分に味わえる。それは，大胆であり如才なくもあり，同時にこの土地を理解し，それを優先した表現なのだ。

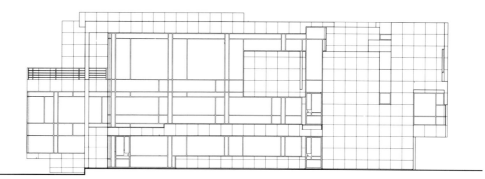
West elevation

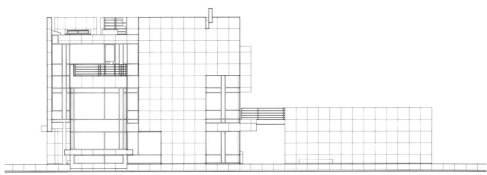
North elevation

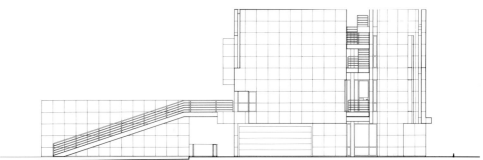
South elevation

East elevation

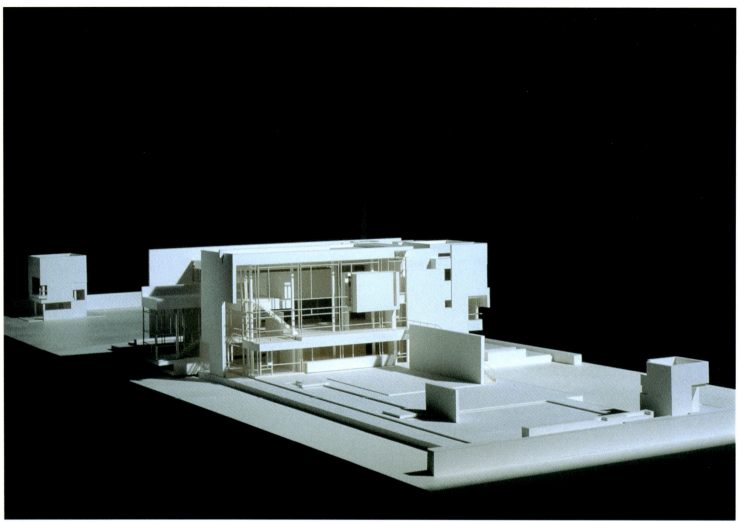
Model photo: overall view

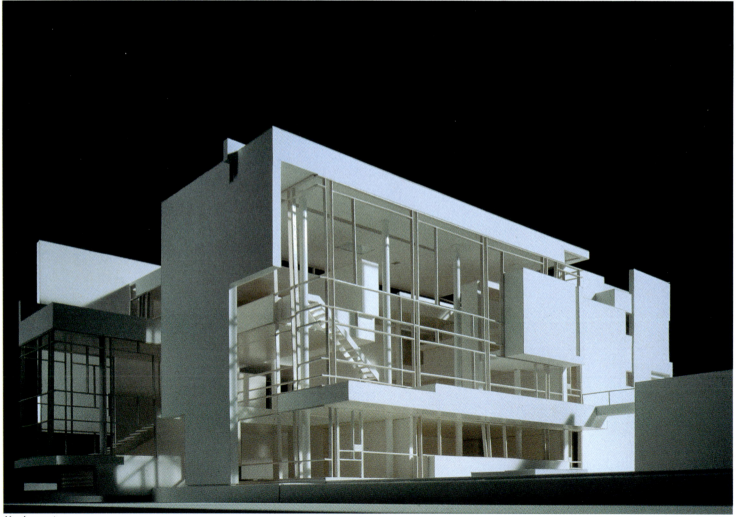
Northwest view

Model photo: Esto Photographics

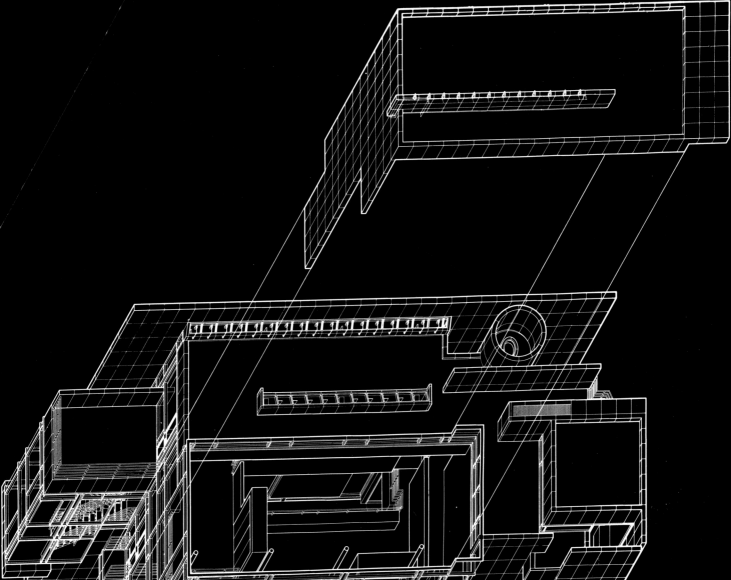

MECANOO

DUTCH AMBASSADOR'S RESIDENCE
Copenhagen, Denmark
Design: 1993–95
Construction: 1996–97

Architects: Mecanoo Architekten—Francine Houben, project architect; Chris de Weyer, Aart Fransen, Theo Kupers, Gerrit Schilder, Carlo Bevers, Jan Bekkering, Katja van Dalen, project team
Client: Dutch Ministry of Foreign Affairs
Consultants: ABT, Delft, structural; Ketel, Delft, mechanical; local partners in cooperation with Dissing & Weitling architektfirma, Denmark

The residence for the Dutch ambassador is situated on the Hambros Allé in the residence quarter Gentofte Kommune in Copenhagen. The Hambros Allé was designed as an avenue with a view to the Sont of the Ollegard. Its beautiful linden trees and the special views at both ends have given the Hambros Allé the status of "protected cityscape."

In the same building line as the other villas, the residence is situated in a large garden and is accessible by a driveway. The garden is mostly surrounded by an existing hedge but on the street side no screen has been raised so the villa makes an open impression here. The garden was designed in close harmony with the villa. The lawns functions as a base in which the different elements have each found their own place. The villa is the central element around which the other elements are grouped: bamboo; a leaf garden; a slightly elevated terrace; a sun room with its own terrace; a water section full of lilies and the driveway. All elements are in direct interaction with one another because they seem to, as it were, shift into each other. Viewed from the villa, along the various sight axes, the interplay of these elements creates a unique atmosphere in each direction. Since the facades are mostly glass there is a continued sense of space from within the villa.

The residence is of course lived in but also functions as the backdrop numerous receptions and dinners. In the spatial layout of the villa this purpose has been taken into consideration and as a result the ground floor made more spacious.

The interior of the ground floor is characterized by its white walls with short sliding panels, which do not run floor to ceiling. These relatively low panels and their composition create a continuous spatial experience. This experience is further enhanced by the open connection with the garden through the glass partition. The toilet block and kitchen have been used as separate architectural volumes in this design method. They have been partially shifted into the hall as "boxes" and are thus the center of the villa, a position which is underlined by the deadlight. The staff rooms form a separate domain within the residence and in the same way the private rooms of the ambassador and his family can be seen as a house within the house. In this house the family room functions as an intermediary space between the bedrooms and the gardens.

The permanent sunscreens around the upper part of the building are composed of thin copper tubes. These as well as the glass and wooden panels, are characteristic features of the facades. The eye-catching roof surfaces are made of copper with folded seams, a material which acquires a beautiful patina over time. The large deadlight over the entrance hall breaks the monotony of

Site plan

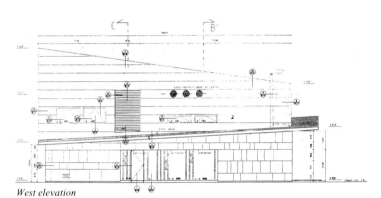
West elevation

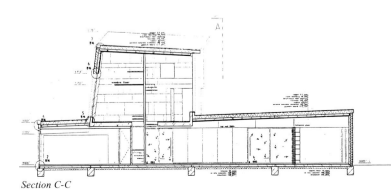
South elevation

Section C-C

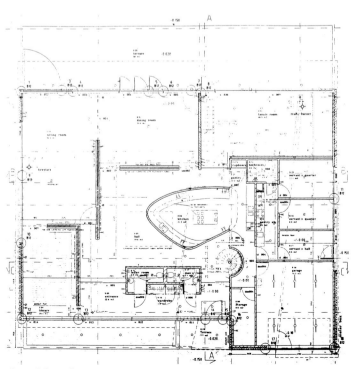
Ground floor plan

the roof and provides natural light for the hall. The partitions are composed of different types of colorless glass, varying from completely transparent to opaline.

The palette of materials used both for the exterior and the interior of the villa has been carefully assembled from natural materials like copper, wood, plaster and glass. With colors being applied sparingly, the use of natural materials and their contrasts define the color scheme of the villa. This range of natural colors as well as the composition of volumes and surfaces will give the residence the appropriate elegant appearance.

オランダ大使公邸はコペンハーゲンの住宅街，ハムブロース通りにある。この通りは終端にオアゴーの入江が見える並木道としてデザインされている。その美しい菩提樹の並木と，両端に望める見事な眺望によって，市の〈美観保全地区〉に指定されている。

建物は，他の邸宅と壁面線を揃えて広い庭園内に立ち，玄関までドライヴウェイが続いている。庭園の大半は元からある生け垣で囲まれているが，道路側にはスクリーンを立てていないので，開放感がある。庭園は建物と緊密に調和するようにデザインした。芝生は，その上で異なったエレメントがそれぞれの場を見つけられる基壇の役割を果たしている。このヴィラはその周囲に他のエレメント——竹林，葉の庭，少し高くなっているテラス，テラス付きサンルーム，ユリの群生する水盤とドライヴウェイ——を集めた，中心となるエレメントである。これらのエレメントはすべて，互いに直接的な影響関係にある。というのは，それらは，いわば，互いに場所を交換しあっているからである。視線の通るさまざまな軸線に沿ってヴィラから眺めると，これらのエレメントの相互作用は各方向に独特の雰囲気をかもしだしている。ファサードは大半がガラスなので，ヴィラ内部から連続していくように感じられる。

ここには，もちろん人が住むのだが，頻繁に開かれるレセプションや夕食会の背景としての役割もある。平面構成にはこの目的を配慮したために，1階は広々とした空間となった。

1階のインテリアは白い壁と，天井には達しない低いスライディング・パネルに特徴がある。これらのかなり低いパネルとその配置は，空間を連続したものとして感じさせる。この感覚は，ガラスの間仕切りを通した庭園との開放的なつながりによってさらに強められる。洗面所ブロックと厨房は，この設計方法のなかでは別の建築的ヴォリュームとして扱われている。これらは，部分的に〈箱〉としてホールへと転換し，ヴィラの中心，明かり取りが強調する位置を占めることになる。スタッフ・ルームはこの住宅内での別の領域を構成し，同様に，大使とその家族の私室も家のなかの家と見なした。この家のなかではファミリー・ルームが寝室と庭園のあいだに位置する中間ゾーンとなる。

建物の上層を包む恒久的な日除けは銅製の薄いチューブでつくられている。これらは，ガラスと木のパネルとともにファサードを特徴あるものにしている。人目を引く屋根は銅製で，年を経ると美しい緑青を帯びるだろう。エントランス・ホールの上を覆う大きな明かり取りは，屋根の単調さを破り，ホールに自然光を落とす。間仕切りは，完全に透明なものから乳白色まで，異なったタイプの色無しガラスを使う。

内外部とも，銅，木，プラスター，ガラスなどの自然材料を注意深く組み合わせた。色彩は抑制して使われているが，自然の材料を使い，その材料間の対比がこの建物のカラー・スキームを決定した。こうした自然の色調とヴォリュームと面の構成によって，大使公邸にふさわしい優雅さが生まれるだろう。

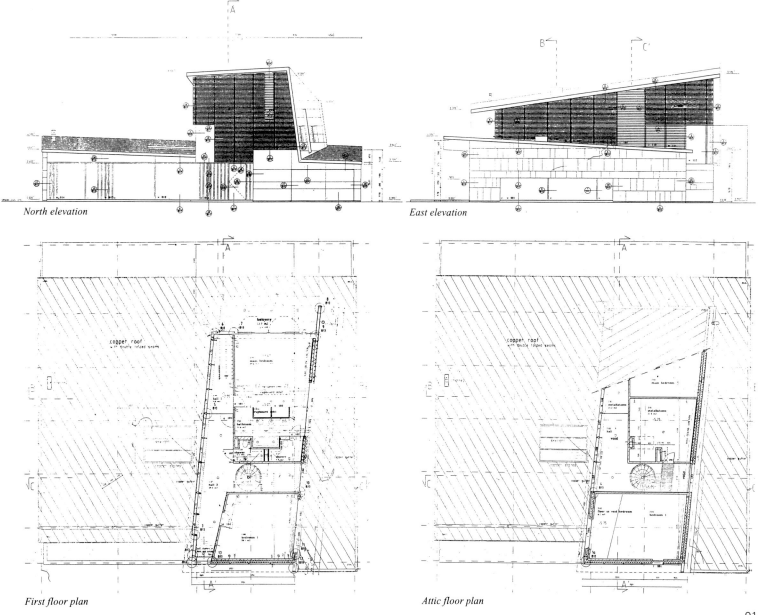

North elevation

East elevation

First floor plan

Attic floor plan

TORU MURAKAMI

HOUSE IN IMABARI
Imabari, Ehime, Japan
Design: 1995
Construction: 1996

This building is planned in the center of the city. It is situated just off the main route that leads south from the city hall. The ground floor consists of a retail store and the storage. The 2nd and the 3rd floors constitute a typical urban residence the clients and their family...a young couple, who also own the retail below. The house is perceived as rooms in a box. The movable glass partitions make rooms. They open to make the entire floor one room, or close off part of the floor to be a room. The glass enclosed terrace is a flexible transitional space. In good weather it could be the alternative living room. It could be opened up to be a garden. No space is definitive any more. The boundaries become fuzzy. A room could be out door or indoor. The air flow in and out of the space freely. The transparent elevator shaft penetrates the center of the floor, and the whole space gives an impression of floating. The stainless louvers cast delicate shadows. The light, wind and other natural elements affect the colorless static space. The modern family demands individuality yet its life style is fluid. It seeks neutrality and maximum flexibility. Freer and more flexible architecture is a device that embraces it.
Toru Murakami

市街地の中心部での計画。市役所からまっすぐ南へ向かう国道から、一本だけ裏に入った通りに面した場所に位置する。1階が店舗(倉庫)、2・3階が典型的な都市型住宅となっている。クライアントは店舗のオーナーである若夫婦とその家族である。

　この住宅は各部屋が一つの大きな箱の中にある。ガラスの仕切を開けると一室空間となり、個々の部屋は消失する。必要なところだけ区切ることもできる。ガラスで覆われたテラスは多様な使い方を可能にする中間領域となる。気候のよい時期は、第二の居間にすればよい。庭が必要になれば、ガラスを開放できる。透明なエレベーターシャフトがこの場の中央を貫く。そこはもはや内でもなく、外でもない。つくられる空間もよりファジーになってゆく。外の空気が内の空気と一体となり、空間が宙に浮く。ステンレスのルーバーは繊細な影を落とす。無彩色で静的な空間に、光・風といった自然要素が作用する。現代社会における家族というゲマインシャフトの繋がりは、個を優先しながら、その暮らし方は流動的である。生活の場は、ニュートラルでオールマイティなものが求められる。より可変的で、自由な場をつくる、建築はそれを覆う装置となる。　(村上徹)

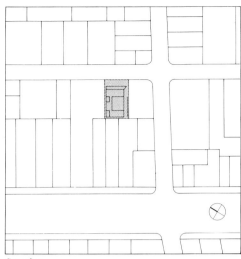

Site plan

計画：今治の家／愛媛県今治市
用途：住宅＋店舗／夫婦＋子供2人＋祖父
建築設計：村上徹建築設計事務所
　　　　担当／村上徹、谷本幸、馬立歳久　協力／高田憲一郎
構造設計：カナイ建築構造事務所
敷地面積：235m²／近隣商業地域
建築面積：141m²／建蔽率60%(許容80%)
延床面積：384m²／容積率163%(許容300%)
建築規模：地上3階、最高高さ10.2m
主体構造：鉄筋コンクリート造＋鉄骨造
外部仕上：合板型枠コンクリート打放し、アルミ押し出し成型板
内部仕上：木、アルミ押し出し成型板、ガラス、他

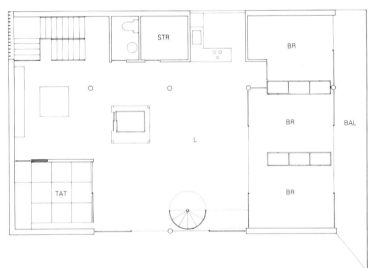

Second floor plan

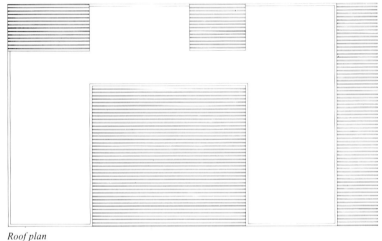

Roof plan

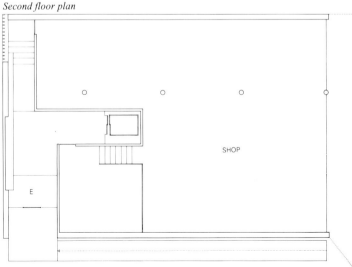

First floor plan

Third floor plan

East view   Model photo: Y. Takase

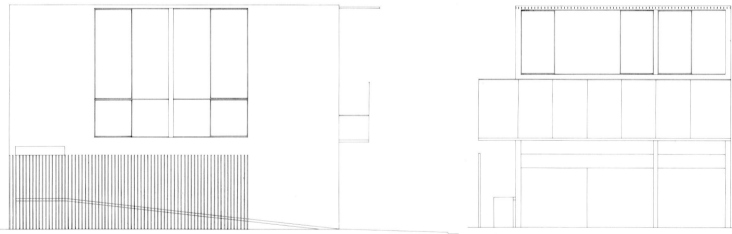
South elevation   *East elevation*

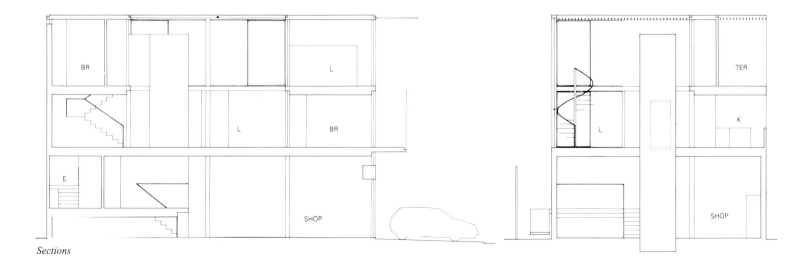
Sections

TAREK NAGA

THE SCANDARS RESIDENCE
Quattameyya Heights, New Cairo, Egypt
Design: 1995–
Construction: 1996–97

Site
"New Cairo" is a newly designed district of The Greater Cairo Metropolitan Area, falling directly to the east of the existing boundary of the city. New Cairo is comprised of several developments, mostly residential and recreational in nature.

The site area is approximately 6000 square meters with variable elevations from +273 to +285 meters above sea level. The general area is part of the plateau that is at the edge of the Great Eastern Desert that stretches from the Nile Valley to the Red Sea. Unlike most populated and urbanized parts of Egypt which are flat plains, the site is hilly desert terrain.

Since ancient times, Egyptians have, for the most part, confined themselves to the Nile Valley. However, recent sociological and economic developments have created a shift towards urbanizing farther stretches of the desert surrounding the Valley. Put in an historical perspective, this paradigm shift is extremely significant. It truly reflects a new era in the urban development of Cairo.

Within this context, this project is in the vanguard. The surroundings of the site are, for the most part, stretches of desert hills to the east, south, west and northwest. Except for in the north, the desert terrain is interrupted by ribbon of asphalt, The Ring Road, and by another housing development across from it. The Old City, downtown, and the more distant Pyramids lie to the west and northwest. The immediate views from the residence's site will be the golf course and the artificial ponds within it. The prevailing wind blows from the northeast.

Program & design philosophy
The Scandars area a family of four: the parents and their two young daughters. Both parents are professionals with strong background and involvement in the visual and media arts. Their very independent and different sensibilities and vision for their residence represented a challenging polarity. The identity of their residence had to reflect both their common and individual emphases. In the pioneering spirit of leaving Metropolitan Cairo and being in the vanguard of appropriating the desert, this project violates the predictability of "single-family house" typology. Given its unique settings, both physical and sociological, two major questions arose. How does the house inhabit the desert? How will the family inhabit the space within this context?

The Apex, The Plateau and The Bowl
The actual plot has three distinct features: 1. The Apex (the highest point at elevation +285) 2. The Plateau (a generally flat plane of median elevation +280) 3. The Bowl (a steep concave slope descending to elevation +273).

Programmatically, the different quarters of the house had to correspond and interact with the physical features of the land and respond to the phenomenological forces impacting on the site.

Southwest elevation

は北東から吹き寄せる。

プログラム／コンセプト：
クライアントは，夫妻と娘2人の4人家族である。夫妻とも有力な地盤をもつ専門職につき，視覚芸術に深く関わっている。住宅に対する，二人の非常に独自で異なった感覚と夢は，両極性に対する挑戦となった。この住宅には，彼らの共通のまた異なった力説点を反映させなければならない。カイロ都市圏を離れ，砂漠に適応する前衛となるというパイオニア精神によって，このプロジェクトは，一戸建て住宅のタイポロジーのもつ予測性を破壊してしまう。このユニークな条件から，物理的社会的な二つの大きな問題が生まれた——この住宅をどのように砂漠に定着させるか，そして，このコンテクストのなかに広がる空間に，一家はどのように定住することになるか。

頂上・台地・窪地：
敷地には3つの異なった地形がある。1.頂上（海抜285mの最高部）2.台地（海抜平均285mのほぼ平坦な場所）3.窪地（海抜273mまで降りて行く急傾斜の凹面部）。

異なった機能をもつ各ゾーンの配置は，この地形に合わせ，この土地を満たしている現象的な力に応答させなければならない。客を迎えるゾーン，住宅の中心ゾーン，子供の領域，主寝室などの各ゾーンが，螺旋状に地形に従って構成されている。

Architects: Tarek Naga/Naga Studio Architecture—Tarek Naga, principal-in-charge; Khaled Naga, Charlie Hodder, Idris Samad, project team
Clients: Mr. and Mrs. Cherine Scandars

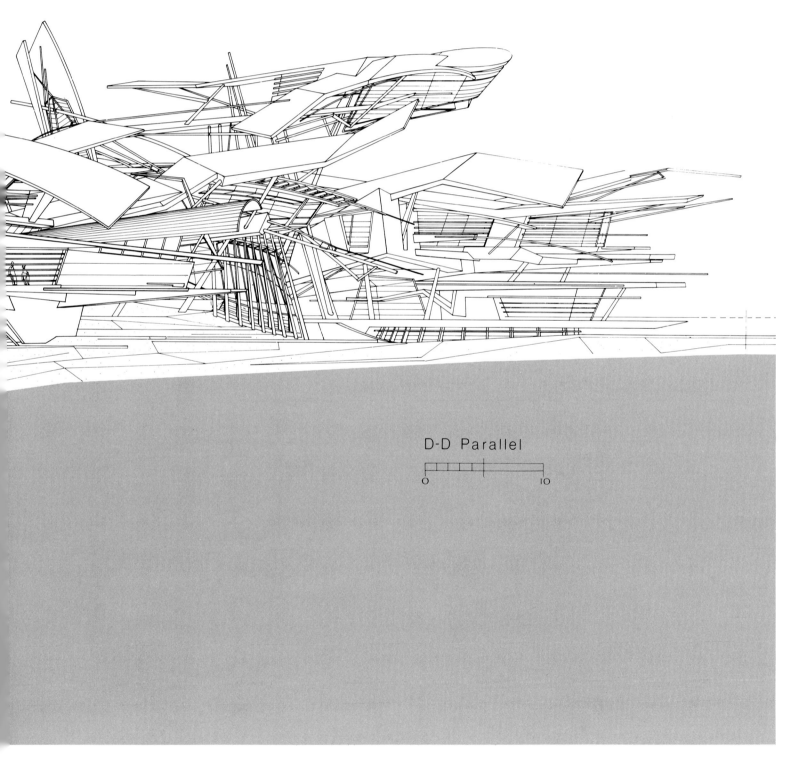

D-D Parallel

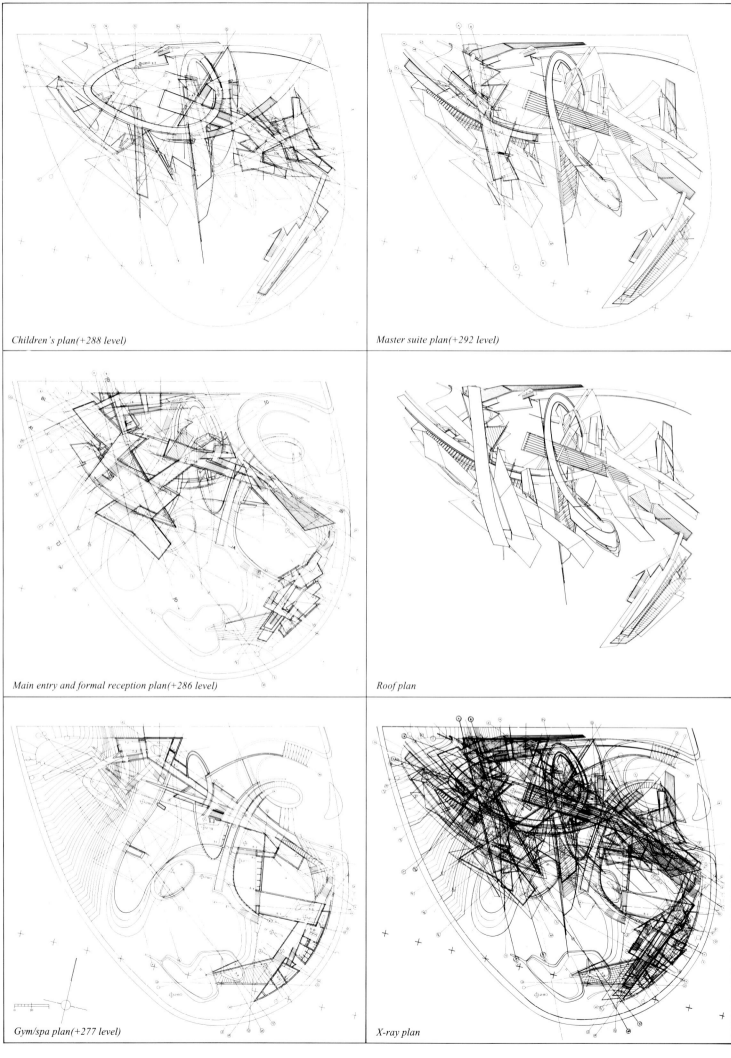

Children's plan (+288 level)

Master suite plan (+292 level)

Main entry and formal reception plan (+286 level)

Roof plan

Gym/spa plan (+277 level)

X-ray plan

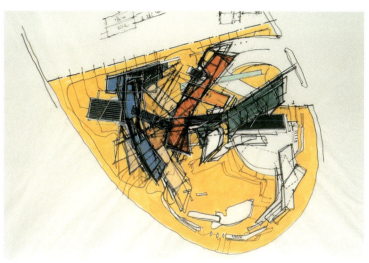

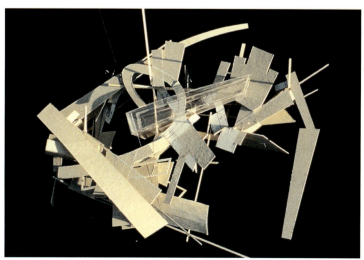

Study models and sketches

TAEG NISHIMOTO

KIM-RYDER HOUSE
Byebrook, Connecticut, U.S.A.
Design: 1995-96

The house is located on a gently sloping hill with a river along its western edge. The surrounding trees provide a colorful backdrop that changes throughout the year. The basic configuration of the house stretches along the river, which amplifies the perception of the spatial openness of the site.

The house is essentially a single volume enveloped by horizontally banded transparent/translucent glazing with programmed spaces, such as kitchen, two bedrooms, fireplace, and library given the articulated volumes and devices inside. Also, a cylindrical volume, made of vertical translucent glass, contains the bathroom and closet.

Within and along the volume of the entire house, the circulation is conditioned in such a way that as one moves horizontally as well as vertically through the house one is provided with a layered and continuous perception of different places without always articulating the space itself.

The horizontally patterned glass walls of the exterior envelope contain jalousie louvers, made of various colored glass, for ventilation. The combination of translucency and transparency and the composed pattern of the colored-glass louvers makes the constantly changing light effect inside of the house as well as the view towards outside, an inherent condition. The bathroom cylinder also contribute to the effect of light at night, when the whole volume is lit from inside.

This project is an effort to create a specific relationship between the figurative quality of circulating through the house and the space-defining volume of the glass wall. In other words, it is a research in the relationship between the phenomenal aspect of the building and the temporal dimension of living/experience inside.
Taeg Nishimoto

Site plan

Architects: Taeg Nishimoto + Allied Architects—Taeg Nishimoto, principal; Thiery Landis, Stephan Roovers (computer operation), assistants
Consultants: Kim & Associates, structural and mechanical

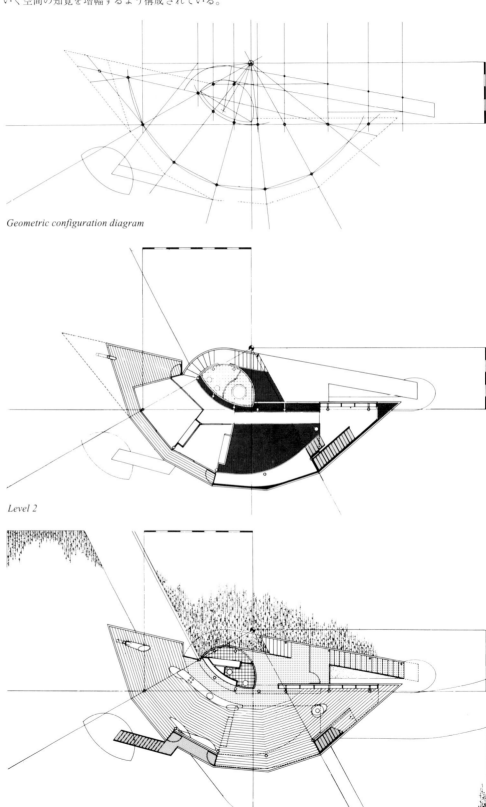

Geometric configuration diagram

Level 2

Level 1

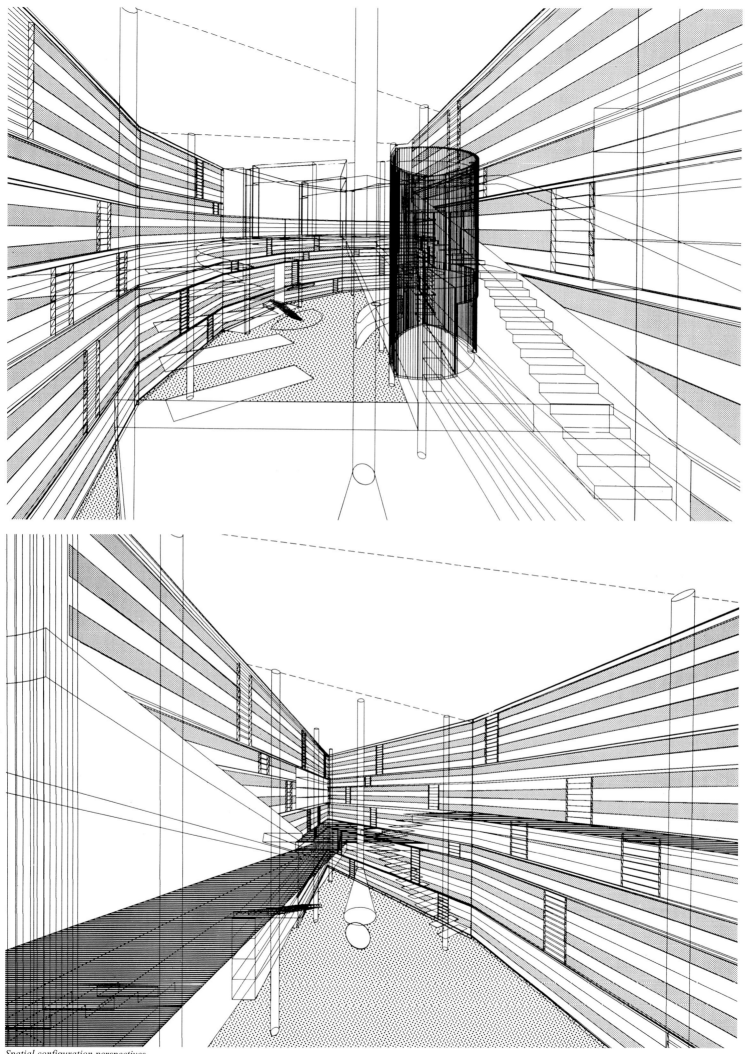
Spatial configuration perspectives

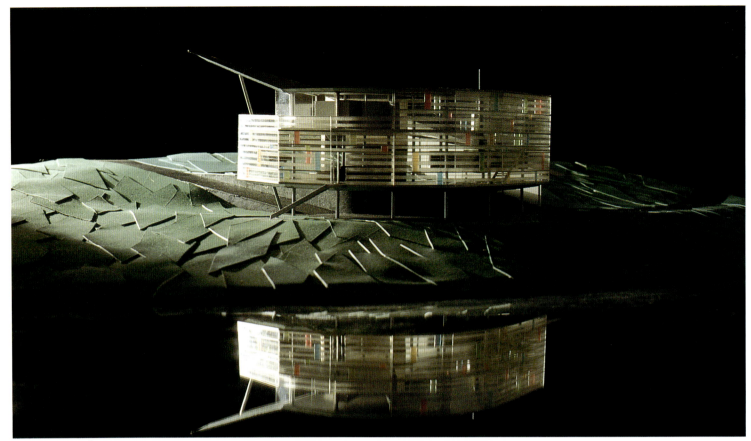
Model photo: southwest view

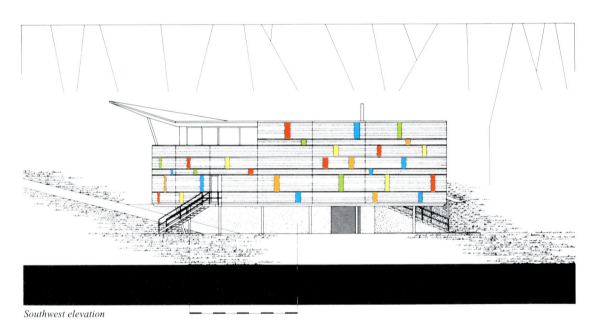
Southwest elevation

Southeast view   *Section behind the glass wall*

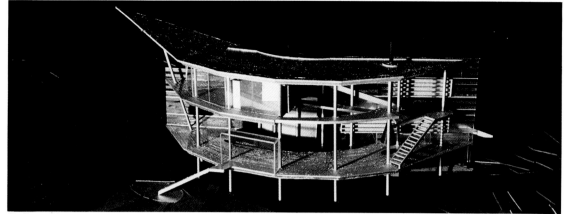
Bird's eye view

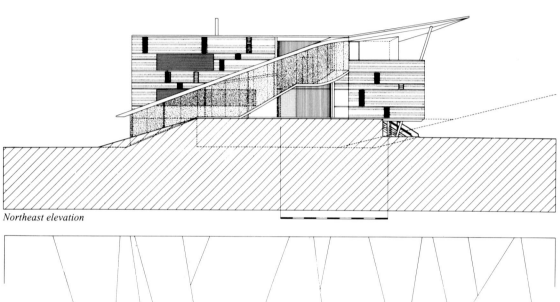
Northeast elevation

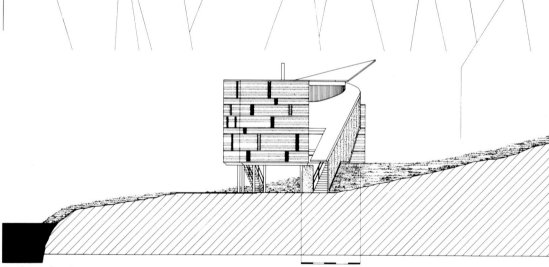
Southeast elevation

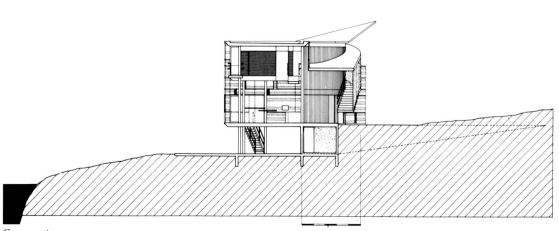
Cross section

EDWARD R. NILES

McKAY RESIDENCE
Malibu, California, U.S.A.
Design: 1994–96

Site
Uphill site overlooking the Pacific Ocean.
Program
A private residence and studio for a video producer in Malibu.
Concept
A series of geometric orders responding to program, site and separation from nature. The specific forms reflect internal program and site options connected by a linkage of glass cubes. The plan orientation responds to view, penetration of sun to uphill landscape. The penetration of sunlight was critical, through the structure to maintain the natural growth of uphill landscape materials.

The concept of the separation from nature allows the man-made as well as natural world to exist as clear and independent realms.

敷地：太平洋を見晴らす丘の上。
プログラム：マリブに住むヴィデオ・プロデューサーのための，住宅兼スタジオ。
コンセプト：プログラム，敷地，自然からの分離という条件に対応する幾何学的形態の連なり。内部の機能配置と敷地条件からガラスのキューブを連ねた。平面の方位は，眺望と丘の上の風景への陽光の差し方を考慮して決めている。丘の上の風景を構成している植物の成長を妨げないために，建物を抜けて日差しが浸透することが重要である。

自然との分離というコンセプトは，人工の世界と自然界が明快な，独立した領土として存在することを認めることである。

Architects: Edward R. Niles FAIA—Edward R. Niles, principal-in-charge; Liba Niles McCarthy, James Corcorad, project team
Client: Heather McKay
Consultants: Dimitry Vergun, structural; American Energy, mechanical

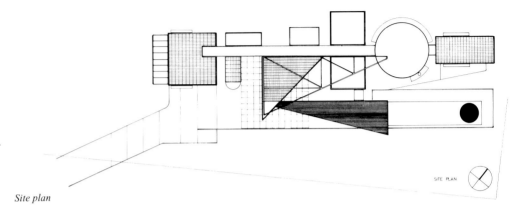
Site plan

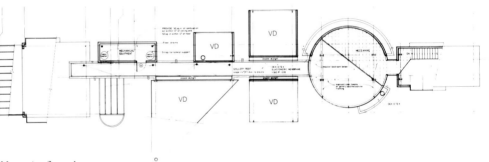
Mezzanine floor plan

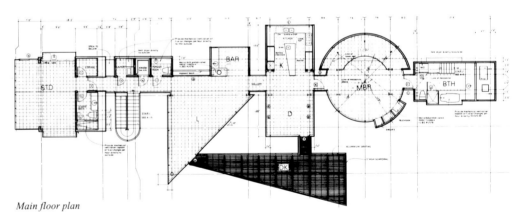
Main floor plan

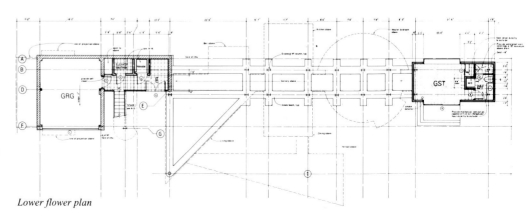
Lower flower plan

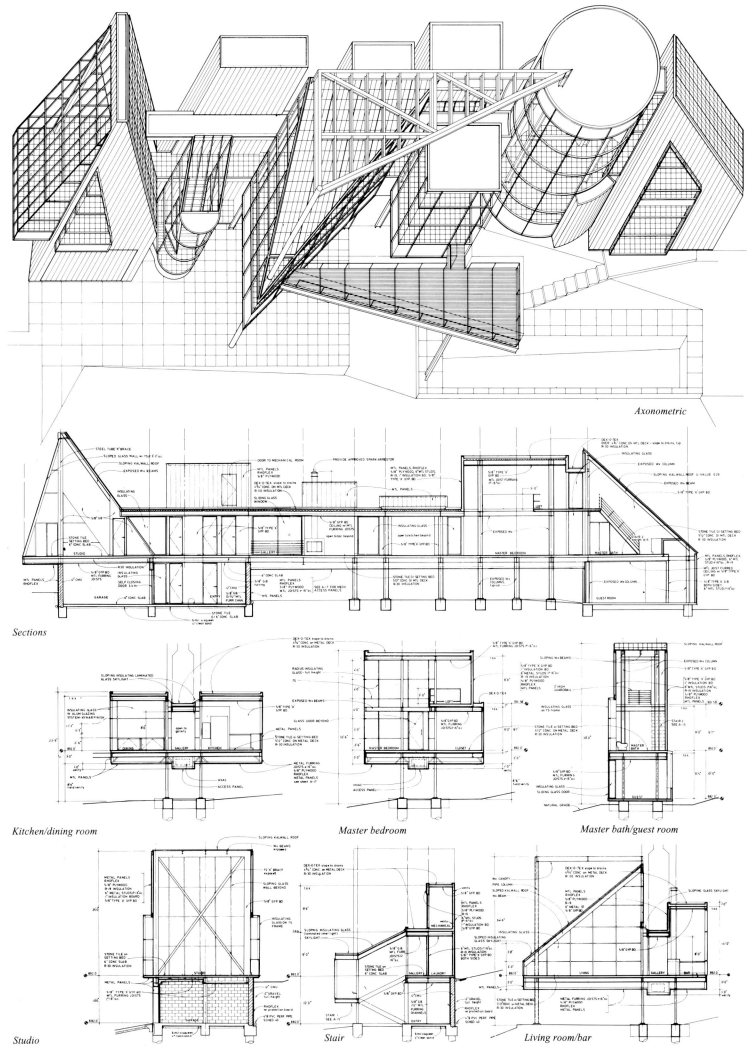

Axonometric

Sections

Kitchen/dining room *Master bedroom* *Master bath/guest room*

Studio *Stair* *Living room/bar*

PLESKOW + RAEL

AVNET HOUSE
Topanga, California, U.S.A.
Design: 1995

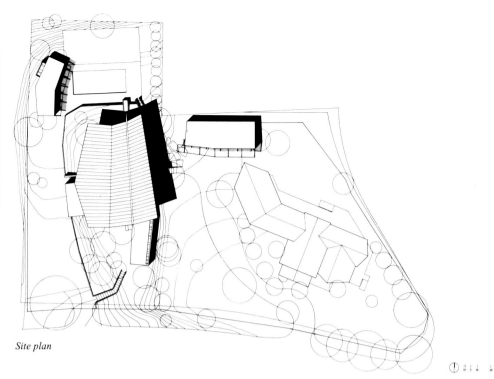
Site plan

The project is a new house to be built on property adjacent to the client's existing home. Initially, it will serve as a place of sport and recreation for the family, later to be converted into a three bedroom house. A pool house and garage flank each side of the house.

The body of the house bends and deflects to preserve all existing trees. The folded form of the roof diverts rain water to a cistern for reuse. An operable screen wall shields the west side of the house from the setting sun while allowing mountain views to be maintained through sliding screens when open. When closed, the screens provide a sheltered extension of the interior spaces. Entrances from each side of the house are aligned along an east-west cross-axis connecting the existing house to the lower play yard.

A gym/living room, playroom/dining room and wet area/kitchen are situated on the main level of the house, separated from guest quarters by a bending storage wall. An indoor/outdoor art studio is located atop the stone faced form of the guest quarters. A bridge spans across the gym to a screened veranda.

クライアントが現在住んでいる住宅に隣接する敷地に新しく計画された住宅である。最初は，一家のスポーツやレクリエーションの場とするはずであったが，後に3寝室住宅に変更された。家の両側をプール・ハウスとガレージが挟んでいる。

既存の樹木を全部残すために，建物は屈曲している。折り版屋根が雨水を再利用のために水槽へ導く。開閉できるスクリーン・ウォールが西側に付き，陽を遮る一方，開ければ山の眺めを楽しめる。閉めると，このスクリーンは，内部に囲まれた空間を増やしてくれる。家の両側にあるエントランスは，既存住宅を下の運動場へと結んでいる東西軸に沿って整列している。

ジム／リヴィング，プレイルーム／食堂，ウエット・エリア／キッチンは，湾曲した収納壁によってゲスト・クォーターと分けられ，この家の主階に置かれている。石貼りのゲスト・クォーターの頂上に屋内／屋外のアート・スタジオが乗っている。ジムを横切ってスクリーンを巡らしたヴェランダへブリッジが渡されている。

Architects: Pleskow + Rael—Anthony Pleskow, Tom Rael, principals-in-charge; Tami Nguyen, model
Client: Jon and Barbara Avnet
Consultants: Gordon Polon, structural; Mel Bilow, mechanical; Ray Moses, electrical

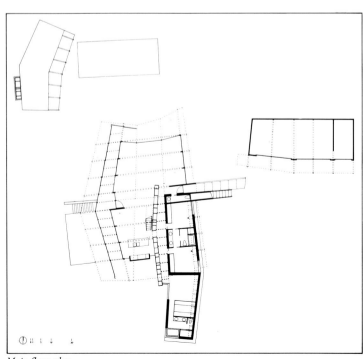
Main floor plan

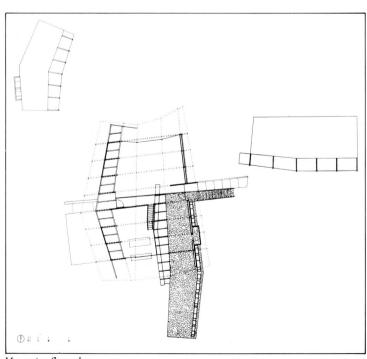
Mezzanine floor plan

Model photo: southeast view

East elevation

South elevation

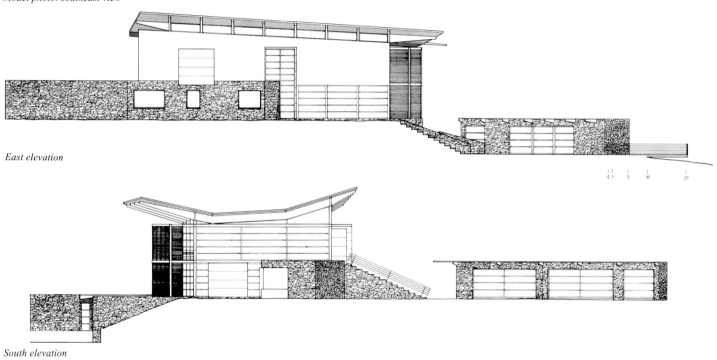

North elevation

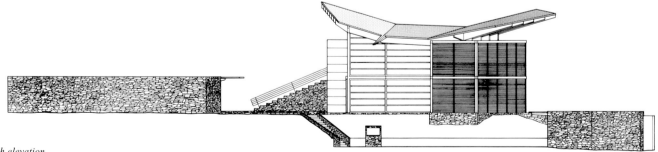

West elevation

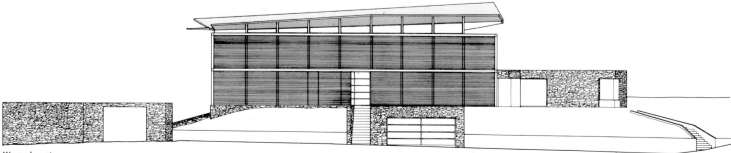

SCOTT PARKER

POIRIER RESIDENCE
Topanga Canyon, California,
U.S.A.
Design: 1994–95
Construction: 1996–97

View from driveway approach

Initially, the architect for this project was to be John Lautner. After years of working with John as a contractor, my client had decided that he wanted John to do the house. Tragically, however, John passed away the day that my client was going to give him the retainer to start work. My client called me for several days after John's death and said, "well, if I can't have John, I've decided I'd like you to design my house." It was then that we began work.

The project has been a collaboration from the first telephone conversation, I would discuss ideas I had and my client would answer by referencing his experiences with both John's and Frank Lloyd Wright's work. The early discussions established the goals of the design, 1) to open up to the exterior as much as possible in order to take advantage of the privacy inherent in the properties location and to maximize views, especially to the rock formations that surround the site, 2) to make the project a showplace for the various trades that the client specializes in, 3) to create an open feeling interior to breakdown any sense of an inhibiting enclosure.

With these goals in mind, I created a reference grid that served to locate the project in a greater framework as established by the conventions of surveying already on the site. These lines became the form generators for the house and served as a constant reference in order to keep the collaboration from becoming a random assemblage of ideas.

The final design attempts to use the reference grid as a guide to bring the project goals to a final architectural form.

Spatial experience
[Entry] The entry is located on the dark side of the house and is completely isolated from the views that the main house frames. [Living area] This area of the house is the organizer of the house. All the major visual experience are accessible here, through several frameless glass windows, views to the canyon and to the major rock formations are framed. [Kitchen] The kitchen is open to the living area and is seen as an integral part of that space. [Terrace] This is the major public terrace, which the living area spills out toward. [Private view terrace] This area is accessed from the living area through a cut in the hillside four feet below the living area elevation. The terrace itself is located beneath a canopy of trees that provide needed shade and create a sense of privacy. [Master bedroom] A semi-private area that has a loft like feel. At the two ends are, respectively, the bedroom itself and opposite, the terrace. The major view is to the hillside while the bed is located in order to shield it from direct morning sun.

Poirier Residence
Topanga Canyon, CA
Project 1994-1995
Construction 1996

Bird's eye view

最初，このプロジェクトの建築家はジョン・ロートナーになるはずであった。建設業者としてロートナーと何年も仕事を共にしてきたクライアントは，ジョンに自分の家を設計してもらうことにした。しかし，悲しいことに，仕事を始めてもらうための予約料を渡そうとしたその日に，ジョンは世を去ってしまった。ロートナーの死の数日後，クライアントは私に電話をかけてきた。「ジョンがもういないのだとしたら，君に私の家を設計してほしい」。そして，私たちは仕事を始めた。

このプロジェクトは，電話での最初の会話から一つの協同作業であった。私は自分のアイディアを話し，私のクライアントは，ジョンとフランク・ロイド・ライトとの仕事の経験を参考にして答えた。初期のディスカッションにより，デザインの目標が決められた。1.プライヴァシーが保てるという敷地の性格を利用して，戸外にできるだけ開かれ，眺めを最大限楽しめる——特に敷地を囲む岩の配置——ものにすること。2.クライアントの専門とするさまざまな事業を目にできる場とする。3.どのような意味でも抑制された囲みというような感覚を打破した，開放的なインテリアとする。

こうした目標を念頭において，既に現場での調査による取り決めによって策定されていた大きな枠組みのなかにこのプロジェクトを位置づける働きをする参照グリッドを作成した。これらのグリッドは，この家のための形態生成装置となり，アイディアのランダムな組み合わせに協力しつづけるための定常的な参照点として働く。

最終案はこの参照グリッドを，最終的な建築形態へ導くガイドとして使う試みから生まれた。

＜空間体験＞
[エントリー]エントリーはこの家の暗い側に位置し，主屋が枠取っている眺めから完全に孤立している。
[リヴィング・エリア]ここはこの住宅のオーガナイザーである。主要な視覚的経験へはすべてここから出発する。いくつもの枠のないガラス窓から，渓谷や大きな岩が広がる景色が見える。[キッチン]リヴィングに開かれ，リヴィングに統合された空間と考えている。[テラス]ここはリヴィング・エリアがこぼれ出て行く最も広いパブリックなテラスである。[プライヴェート・ヴュー・テラス]ここには，リヴィング・エリアの下4フィートの丘の斜面に掘り抜かれた抜け道から出られる。テラスは日陰を落とし，プライヴァシーを与えてくれる木々のつくるキャノピーの下にある。[主寝室]ロフトのような感じのセミ・プライヴェートなエリアである。一端が寝室，反対側の一端がテラスである。ベッドは朝の直射日光からは遮られる位置にあり，丘の斜面が見える。

View from terrace

View from living area toward kitchen

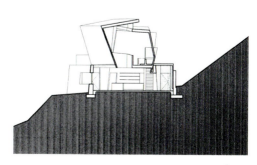

Architects: Scott Parker Design—Scott Parker, principal-in-charge; Dianne Parker, project team
Client: Robin Poirier
Consultants: Ingrid Stinchcomb, structural; Brent Stinchcomb, mechanical; Tom Hester/Tom Hester Studio, computer

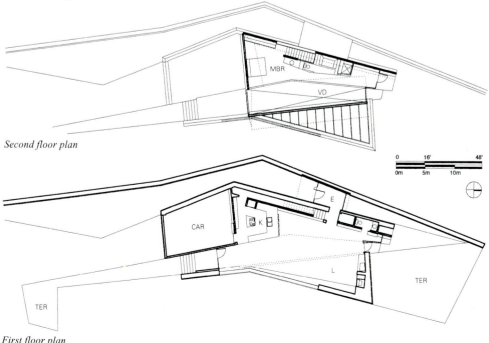

Second floor plan

First floor plan

SHAFER ARCHITECTS

RESIDENCE
Salt Lake County, Utah, U.S.A.
Design: 1993–95
Construction: 1995–

Site: The site is located at the mouth of the Little Cottonwood Canyon at the beginning of a scenic, canyon road which ascends to the Alta and Snowbird ski resorts. At the base of the Wasatch Mountain range, the site offers spectacular panoramic views up and down the canyon.

Program: A 6400-square-foot three-story single-family residence which must eventually accommodate "single," "married" and "family" stages of life while continually providing an intriguing living experience between the interior and exterior.

Design solution: The design has been consciously stratified, both sectionally and geologically in order to heighten one's understanding of "place," either within the carved sub-terranean environment of thick walls and slot windows, or on the exposed "shelf" of the living room. The upper floor turns it back on the panoramic world, both concealing and securing its inhabitant in the privacy of the office and master bedroom suite.

The "Pavilion" positions itself to embrace the panoramic views north to the Great Salt Lake, Antelope Island and Salt Lake City. Easterly views up Little Cottonwood Canyon reveal vibrant and rugged mountain vistas. The "shelf" provides an expansive and limitless base for the "Pavilion," spatially contained only by the form of its floating roof.

The "Box," on the other hand, has been designed for semi-private spaces such as the kitchen and dining room on the first level and personal and professional privacy on the Upper level offering localized and framed views "up" the mountain. Offering localized and framed views up the mountain, this upper level suite in direct response to the "individual" in both scale and detail, providing the secluded and tranquil area of the house. In contrast to the transparency of the "Pavilion," the more residential enclosure system of the "Box" is of cedar cladding with operable wood windows and doors.

The "Parterre" accommodates the programmatic requirement of an exterior living space for personal lounging and entertaining. A bi-level cedar deck provides for both winter and summer activities. Additional outdoor "rooms" have been developed within the interstitial spaces between the three components and the excavated "shelf." Formal entry requires ascension through a carved-out space between "Box" and "Pavilion."

The profile and mass remains intentionally "horizontal" and low, contributing to a minimalist "bulk," burying nearly half of the living space below grade. This effort enables a particularly large volume to "appear" smaller and offers the user an opportunity to experience both the concealed and exposed environments within the house. Circulation through the house is noticeably effortless when moving "with" the mountain yet becomes consciously more difficult when one moves against the natural grade, either descending or ascending sectionally.

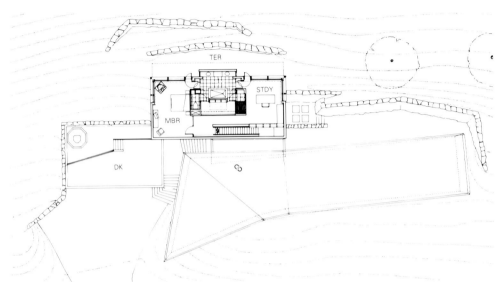
Third floor plan

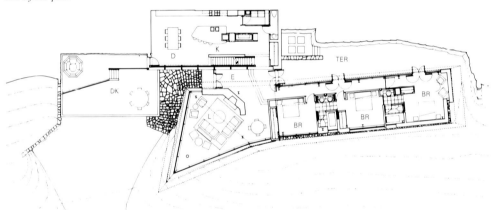
Second floor plan

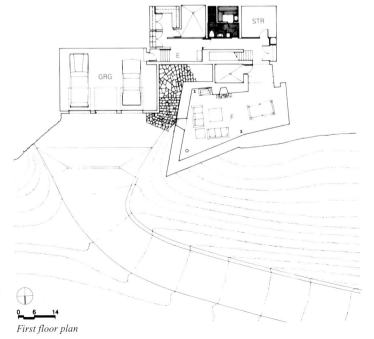
First floor plan

る，小さく枠取られた眺めを与えるようにデザインした。この限定された眺めをもつ上階の部屋は，スケール，ディテールの両面で＜個人＞に対応したものであり，他とは離れた，静かなエリアとなっている。＜パヴィリオン＞の透明性とは対照的に，＜ボックス＞のより住宅らしい外壁は，開閉できる木の窓と扉の付いた，シーダー材の被覆である。

＜パルテール＞は，一人でくつろいだり，楽しむための戸外リヴィングという要求に対応したものである。2つのレヴェルをもつシーダー材のデッキは，冬にも夏にも使える。3つの構成要素と掘り込まれた＜岩棚＞のあいだの切れ目にある空間にも，こうした戸外の＜部屋＞がつくられている。フォーマル・エントリーは，＜ボックス＞と＜パヴィリオン＞のあいだに切り取られた空間を通って上っていかなければならない。

建物の輪郭とマッスは意図的に水平に低く構成し，リヴィング・スペースの半分近くを地盤下に埋めて，ミニマリストの＜大きさ＞をつくるに預かっている。こうした努力によって，かなり大きなヴォリュームでありながら，＜見える＞部分は小さな建物で，かつ，住む人が隠れた環境と外に開いた環境の両方を楽しむことができるものとなった。全体のサーキュレーションは，山と＜一緒に＞動いて行くときは，極めて楽であるが，自然の地盤に逆らって動く際は，上りも下りも意識的に厳しくしてある。

Architects: Shafer Architects.—Tom Shafer, principal-in-charge; David Strandberg, Michael Wilkinson, project architects; Paul Audrain, John Bertram, Josephine Kippert, project team
Consultants: Allen and Bailey Engineers, structural; Design Build, mechanical; Eckhoff, Watson & Preator, civil; Agra Earth & Environmental, geotechnical
General contractor: Lowell Construction

Model photo: northeast view

Northwest view

Section

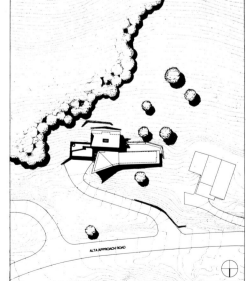
Site plan

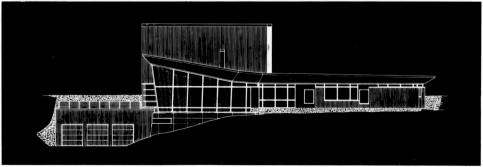
North elevation

SOTTSASS ASSOCIATI

PROJECT FOR RESIDENTIAL COMMUNITY IN PRE-FABRICATED STEEL ELEMENTS
Design: 1995

The project is part of a larger research promoted and financed by the European Economic Community that has involved more than twenty architectural and engineering offices from various member countries of the EEC.

The researche's theme, entitled "The application of steel in urban habitat," is centered on the study of new possibilities for the use of steel in the urban environment. The aspect proposed and developed by Sottsass Associati was that relative to temporary architecture.

The project is based on individuating some typical situations that represent "The ideal environment" for the utilization of temporary architecture, such as suburban squares, urban and natural parks, various kinds of fairs and festivals, abandoned industrial areas, areas struck by natural disasters, etc. Furthermore it identifies two fundamentals structural systems, the development and combination of which allows the possibility to obtain a series of prefabricated building typologies in steel that is able to satisfy the requirements of the identified urban environments.

The first structural solution, called "volumetric" is based on the concept of small inhabitable units, completely furnished and equipped, sized to fit on the classic European industrial containers so that they can be easily and rapidly shipped with any large means of cargo transport.

Once arrived on site and connected to the electric, water and sewer networks these small living units become operative. This solution also allows, through simple welding practices, the possibility to assembling together on site the single volumetric units thus providing the possibility to obtain ample covered areas. With this structural type various single-volume, inhabitable typologies were conceived and designed such as a small house, a patio, an office, a bus stop, a news-stand, a shop, a police station as well as other, pluri-volumetric structures for large public spaces like a covered market and a grand multi-use hall.

The second structural solution, defined as "elemental," is based instead on the site assembly of a series of prefabricated components such as flooring, panels, columns, trusses and roofing, etc. This solution is suitable for obtaining larger volumes with layouts and configurations that are more flexible than those achieved through the volumetric solution. The structural type was used to design other, more spacious and articulated, typologies compared to the preceding ones such as a series of single family houses, a restaurant and a series of multi-use halls to be utilized as civic centters, museums, auditoriums, etc.

Finally, in order to both spotlight the project's potential and to give an overall, comprehensive view of the result, the individual units, designed separately, were placed in the context of a small urban plan thus forming a residential community complete with the necessary infrastructure and services.

9. *Element for open air market*

15. *House 2*

1. *Shop*

7. *Police station*

16. *House 3*

て単一のヴォリュームへとひとつに集めることができるので，覆われた広いエリアをつくることができる。この構造タイプによって，さまざまな単体ヴォリューム，居住可能なタイポロジーが，小住宅，パティオ，オフィス，バス停，ニュース・スタンド，店，交番，さらには，屋根付きの市場，広い多目的ホールのような，大きな公共空間のための多容積の構造体として考え設計された。

二番目の構造的解決案は，〈エレメンタル〉として定義され，前者とは違って，現場での組立を，床，パネル，柱，トラス，屋根などとして一連のプレファブ部材によって行うものである。この方法だと，容積的な案によるものより，大きさも配置構成もフレキシブルに対応できる。この構造システムは，一番目のものに較べ，戸建住宅の連なり，レストラン，市民センター，美術館，オーディトリアムなどに使える多目的ホール，といった，広く，分節されたタイポロジーをもつデザインに使われる。

最後に，このプロジェクトの保持する潜在力と，この成果全体を理解しやすくするために，別々に設計された個々のユニットを小スケールの都市計画のコンテクストのなかに配置して，必要なインフラおよびサーヴィス設備によって完結する住宅コミュニティを形成してみた。

Architects: Sottsass Associati—Ettore Sottsass, Marco Zanini, Mike Ryan; Milco Carboni, co-ordination; Oliver Layseca, Gianluigi Mutti, Neven Zoricic, collaborators; C.S.M. Roma, project manager; C.R.E.A. Roma, engineering assistant
Client: European Economic Community

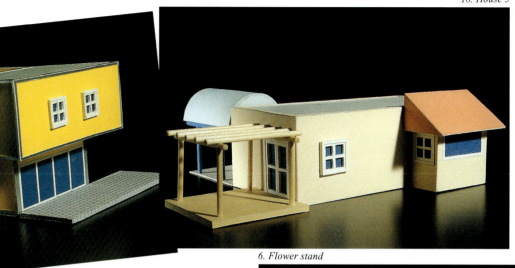

18. House 5

6. Flower stand

Site plan

1 SHOP
2 PATIO
3 OUTSIDE GARDEN FOR PUBLIC SPACE
4 MULTI-USE HALL
5 NEWSSTAND
6 FLOWER STAND
7 POLICE STATION
8 OFFICE
9 OPEN AIR MARKET
10 BUS STOP
11 MUSEUM
12 PUB
13 GARAGE
14 HOUSE 1
15 HOUSE 2
16 HOUSE 3
17 HOUSE 4
18 HOUSE 5

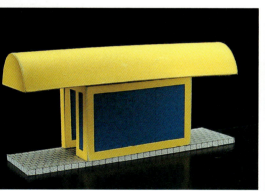

10. Bus stop

4. Multi-use hall

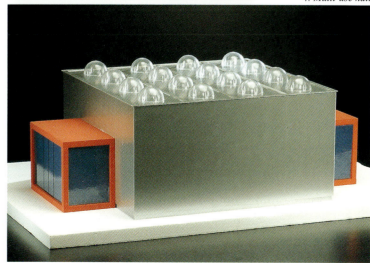

Model photos: Ugo Colombo

Overall view

SOTTSASS ASSOCIATI

JASMINE HILL
Singapore
Design: 1995
Construction: 1996

Master plan
The project is organized with respect to the "Good Class Bungalow" development classification requirements for Singapore, including the side by side lot divisions, minimum set-backs, maximum footprint, and minimum lot size. The project consists of six luxury homes (between 600 –730 m²), each with its own private entrance drive, gate, and pool, to be built on 1400 m² –1600 m² size lots distributed along a central spine street directly off Pierce Road. Due to the natural contour line of the site, the street is located on a mid-level between the upper and lower rows of homes. In this way, the houses are vertically as well as horizontally distanced from each other to maximize privacy. Each houses accessed by a small private road leading up or down to the entry level. The homes are integrated into a fabric of gardens and porticos, courtyards and terraces, creating vistas and privacy, and the luxury of space. Between the homes, the existing trees and landscaping provide a natural privacy screen.

Landscaping
As the project maintains the existing contours of the land, (the site is naturally steep at the upper tier, and flat at the lower tier), the landscaping, as an integral part of the project, is kept natural and casual, utilizing the existing trees as much as possible. Apart from the numerous site-walls and enclosed gardens the site is planted with indigenous plantings and trees; grouped for shade and privacy.

Homes
The houses have been designed individually and each home is different from the next, creating a varied and sophisticated development. All houses include a two or three car carport, a service entry and service quarters, and a large kitchen and pantry area connected to a formal dining area with an attached private courtyard or patio. The living rooms are usually double height, with an attached library niche and open out onto the pool terrace, garden, or balcony allowing for expansion to the outdoors. They are generally situated towards the south, south/east. The upper levels include three or four bedrooms with private baths, including a very large master bedroom suite.

Materials
The project is designed for standard concrete and block or brick construction technique. The exterior (walls and roof) is clad in ceramic tiles, asphalt shingles or natural stone. Windows are custom designed with wood or anodized aluminum frames and insulated glass. Site walls and terraces are finished in concrete or terrazzo.
Interior materials proposed include ceramic tile or wood floors throughout, imported Italian tiling in kitchens and bathrooms and selected walls, and custom designed stairways and railings.

全体計画：横並びの区画割り，最小限のセットバック，最大限の建坪，最小限の敷地面積を含め，シンガポールのための「グッド・グラス・バンガロー」開発の区分要求を尊重している。6棟の高級住宅（600〜730sq.m.），各戸に専用のエントランス・ドライヴ，門，プールが付き，ピアース・ロードから直接分岐する中央軸道路に沿って並ぶ，1,400〜1,600sq.m.の区画に建設する。敷地のもつ自然の起伏により，道路は上方の住宅の列と下方の列の間，中間レヴェルを走ることになる。この結果，各住宅は垂直方向にも水平方向にも距離をとることができ，プライヴァシーが守られる。各戸へはエントリー・レヴェルから上がり，または下がって行く細い私道から入る。庭園，ポルティコ，コートヤード，テラスのファブリックのなかに統合された住宅には，眺望，プライヴァシー，豊かさを備えた空間が生まれる。各住戸のあいだに立つ既存の木々やランドスケーピングが自然の目隠しを構成する。

ランドスケーピング：敷地の自然の起伏を保持するために（上の部分は急斜面，下の部分は平坦である），このプロジェクトの不可欠な部分であるランドスケーピングは，既存の樹木をできるだけ残して，自然でカジュアルなものとした。いくつもの敷地を囲む塀や囲まれた庭園は別として，原産の植物や木を，日影をつくりプライヴァシーを守るように，まとまりをつくって植える。

住宅：各住戸は隣とは異なるように，個別に設計し，多彩で洗練された開発計画をつくりだす。各戸には2〜3台収容のカーポート，サーヴィス・エントリー，サーヴィス・クォーター，中庭やパティオの付いたフォーマルな食堂とつながった広い厨房とパントリーがある。リヴィング・ルームはたいてい2層吹き抜けで，書斎のあるニッチが付き，リヴィングを戸外へと広げてくれるプール・テラスや庭やバルコニーに面している。これらのスペースは一般に南か南／東向きである。上階には専用の浴室の付いた寝室が3〜4室，それに広い主寝室スイートが配置される。

材料：規格のコンクリートとブロック，あるいは煉瓦造の工法を使うように設計した。外観（壁と屋根）はセラミック・タイル，アスファルト・シングル，自然石。窓は特注の木または酸化被膜アルミ枠に断熱ガラス。敷地を囲む塀とテラスはコンクリートまたはテラゾー。内部は，全体をセラミック・タイルか木の床，厨房と浴室，一部の壁にはイタリア製のタイル，階段と手摺には特注デザインを提案した。

Architects: Sottsass Associati—Ettore Sottsass, Johanna Grawunder; Federica Barbiero, project architect; Design Metabolist - Singapore, local architect

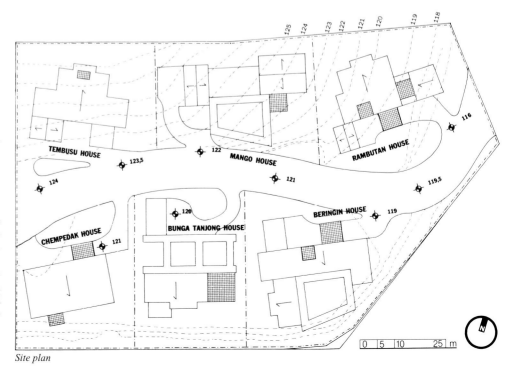

Site plan

Sketches

Model photos: Santi Caleca

SOTTSASS ASSOCIATI

CASA VAN IMPE
St. Lievens Houtem, Belgium
Design: 1995
Construction: 1995–96

The project consists of a 710-meter-square single family home for a contemporary art dealer and his family fronting on a canal on a large lot located on the main street of a small village in central Belgium.

The project was conceived as a home, Art Gallery/Studio, sculpture garden and a physiotherapy studio, and is developed as a central volume, clad in large blue panels; from which spaces, terraces, balconies are carved out. Three blocks in black and white stone extend out from the main block and face onto the canal. An arched volume clad in ribbed stainless steel contains the garage, kitchen and physiotherapy studio.

The house at the grand level is bisected by a large galleria space with guest suites and the gallery office to the east and the entertaining spaces of double volume (living room, dining, etc.) to the west. The first floor contains the master suite.

現代美術の画商とその家族のための住宅。ベルギー中央部の小さな村の大通りに面した広い敷地。710sq.m.の建物は運河に面している。住宅，アート・ギャラリー／スタジオ，彫刻庭園，物理療法スタジオで構成され，大きな青いパネルで包まれた中央のヴォリュームから各空間，テラス，バルコニーが刻みだされている。メインのブロックから黒と白の石で包まれた3つのブロックが突きだし，運河に向いている。畝模様の付いたステンレス・スティールで被覆されたアーチ形のヴォリュームには，ガレージ，キッチン，物理療法スタジオが置かれている。

建物は主階のところで，広いギャラリー・スペースによって二分され，ギャラリー・スペースの東側にはゲスト・スイートとギャラリー・オフィス，西側には2層のエンタテイニング・スペース（リビング・ルーム，ダイニングなど）がある。1階に主寝室スイートが置かれている。

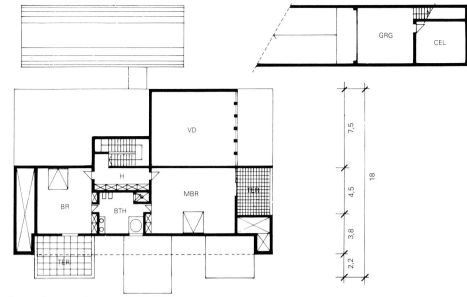

First floor and garage plan

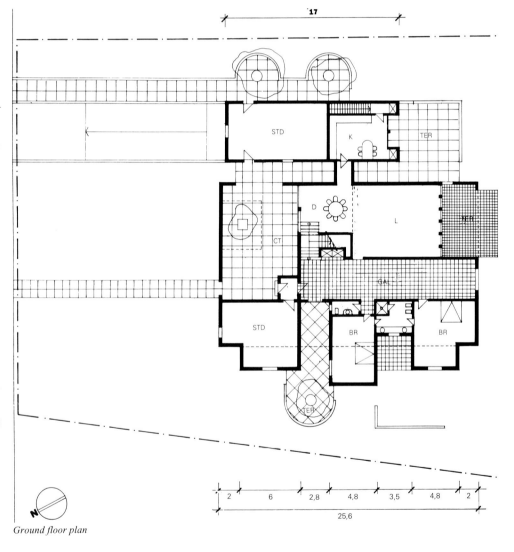

Ground floor plan

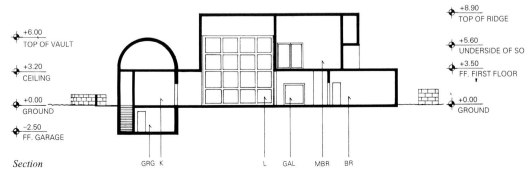

Section

Architects: Sottsass Associati—Ettore Sottsass, Johanna Grawunder; Gianluigi Mutti, project architect; Ron Herremans, local architect
Client: Hedwick Van Impe

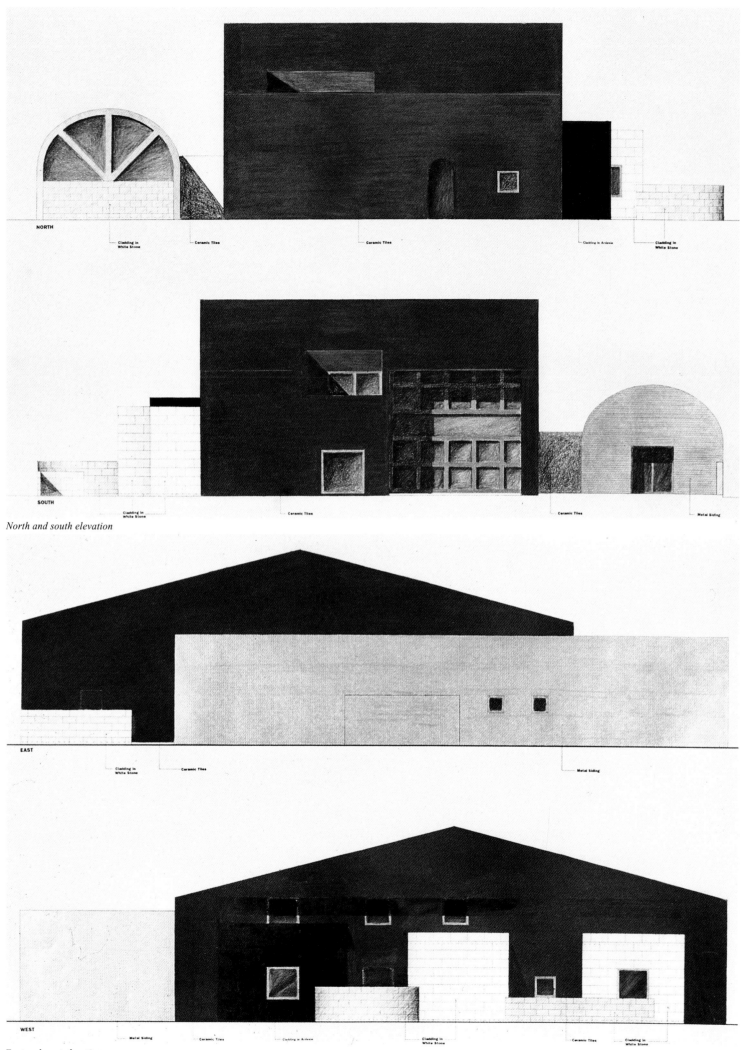

North and south elevation

East and west elevation

Model photo: north view

Southeast view

West view

Model photos: Santi Caleca

HIRO SHUDO

MATSUNAGA HOUSE
Yabakei-cho, Oita, Japan
Design: 1995
Construction: 1996

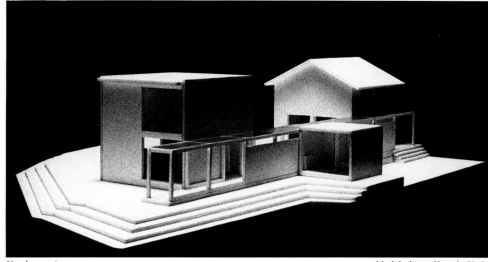

Northeast view *Model photo: Hiroshi Ueda*

The site is located in northern Oita. The view toward east reveals a famous point of interest, Ao-No-Domon right below and along the calm water of Sangoku River. The client had two design requirements: #1 to use materials saved from an old house built about 100 years ago. #2 to provide a gallery space for his artist wife.

The house consists of two district parts. The public half of the house which includes the gallery was placed close to the road on west side of the lot and was to incorporate the materials from the old house and built in a a traditional Japanese style. The private half where the daily life takes place occupies the east end of the lot, and will be built with new materials in a manner in contrast to its counter part. The two structures are connected by a long covered walkway. And somewhere in the middle of the walkway at a spot where the evening view toward the east most revealing, there will be an out house facility.
Hiro Shudo

敷地は大分県の北部にあり，東方には眼下に名所・青の洞門にそって静かに山国川がある。この住宅の場合，オーナーの要求は次の2点である。まず百年ほど前に建てられた昔の家の材料をできれば使用したいこと，アーティストである夫人のギャラリーが欲しいことである。

建物はまずギャラリーのあるパブリックな部分を道路に面した西側に，日常生活するプライベートな部分を奥の東側に配置することとした。パブリックな部分は出来るだけ古材を使用することに心がけデザインも日本的なものとし，奥のプライベートな部分は新たな材料でデザインもそれとは対照的なものとした。対比された2つの立体は，細長い通路によって結ばれ，その中間の一番夕景の美しい場所にユーティリティが置かれた。 （首藤廣剛）

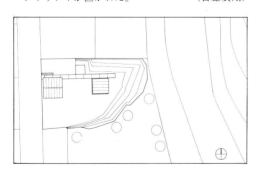

計画：松永邸／大分県耶馬溪町
用途：専用住宅／夫婦＋子供1人
建築主：松永忠
建築設計：首藤廣剛／アルカイック　担当／首藤廣剛、坂本達哉
構造設計：常廣構造設計事務所　担当／常廣俊治
敷地面積：861.44m²／都市計画区域外
建築面積：103.52m²
延床面積：156.05m²
建築規模：地上2階，最高高さ5.86m
主体構造：木造＋補強コンクリートブロック造
特記事項：西側建物の2階部分は江戸末期に建てられた木造を移築。

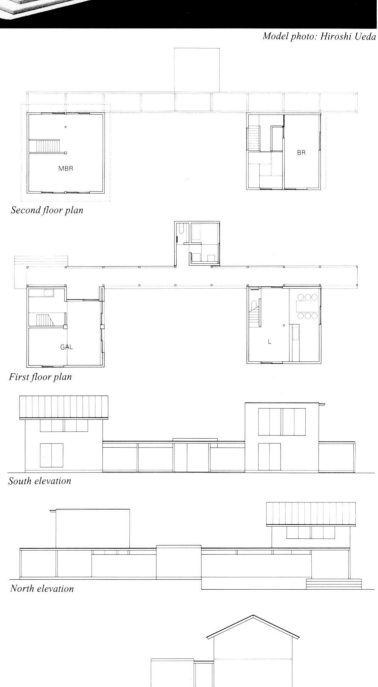

Second floor plan

First floor plan

South elevation

North elevation

West elevation

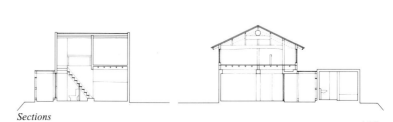

Sections

HIRO SHUDO

MIURA HOUSE
Saiki, Oita, Japan
Design: 1996
Construction: 1996

This town of about 70,000 people forms a small cluster on the northern bank of Bansho River with the densely wooded Shiroyama as the backdrop. The site is located in the town center with its long axis running north to south and paralleling, to the designer's delight, a canal that adjoins it. The situation called for the enclosing of all four sides by a wall causing a subsequent investigation as to how light, ventilation, view, etc. be best brought in. After considering the family structure and future build up in the neighborhood, it was decided that the best solution was to divide the lot, 4.8 m × 18 m, in three equal parts and place living spaces at two ends leaving the middle as an open court. The lime stone quarried nearby will pave the court with a single deciduous tree in the middle. The finish and the level of the interior will match that of the court thus bringing the exterior closer to the interior. In order to maximize the sense of spaciousness, the dining room furniture will be built into the wall. The court wall facing the canal is cut out for ventilation. Off-setting stair wall screens the opening to regain privacy, and the same wall supports the over-bridge that yields a calm view of the canal.
Hiro Shudo

人口7万人程の町は，原生林で覆われた城山を背景に番匠川の北岸に小さくかたまっている。敷地はその中心部にあり，南北に細長く幸運にも一辺が水路に面している。

建物は敷地の形状から，まず四方を壁でふさぎ，その中にいかに自然を取り込めるか検討された。最終的には寸法が4.8M×18Mと与えられ，家族構成や周囲が密集することが予測されるなどの点から，建物を3分割しその南と北の部分に個室を，はさまれた中央部分にコートを配置することで解決した。

そのコートは近くで取れる灰石で敷きつめられ中央には落葉樹が植えられる。ダイニングルームの建具は広がりを持たせるために壁の中に引き込まれ，床の仕上と高さはコートに合わされている。これによって内と外の空間はさらに関わりを増すことになる。コートに面した西側の壁はベンチレーションも兼ねて水路に向いて大きく開けられている。階段の壁はコートのプライバシーを守り2階のブリッジからは静かな水面が見える。　　　　（首藤廣剛）

計画：三浦邸／大分県佐伯市
用途：専用住宅／夫婦＋子供2人
建築主：三浦肇
建築設計：首藤廣剛／アルカイック
　　　　担当／首藤廣剛，岩切訓子
構造設計：常廣構造設計事務所　担当／常廣俊治
敷地面積：131.9m²／住居地域
建築面積：67.5m²／建蔽率51.1%
延床面積：123.83m²／容積率93.8%
建築規模：地上2階，最高高さ4.9m
主体構造：鉄筋コンクリート造
外部仕上：床／吉野石敷込み　壁／コンクリート打放し
内部仕上：壁・天井／コンクリート打放し

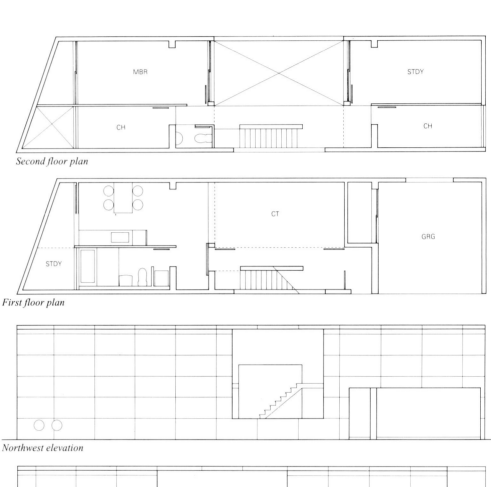

Second floor plan

First floor plan

Northwest elevation

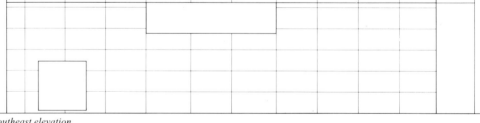

Southeast elevation

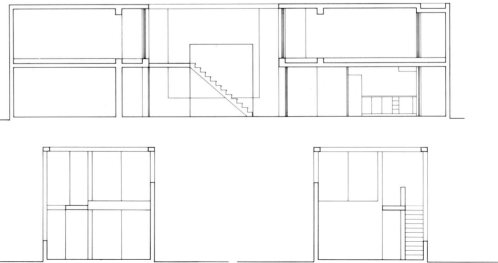

Sections

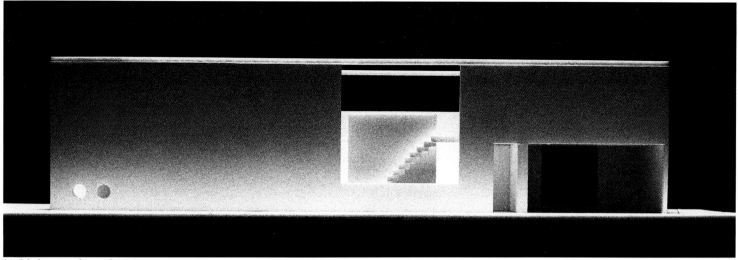
Model photo: northwest elevation

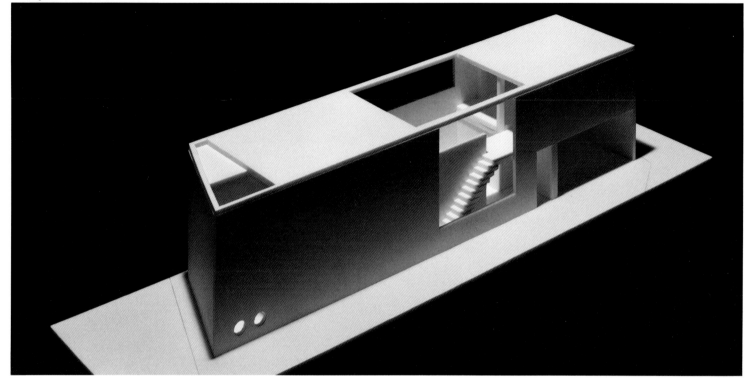
Overall view

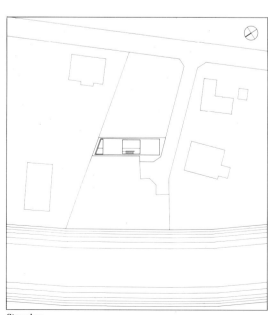
Site plan

Open court

Model photos: H. Ueda

SZYSZKOWITZ + KOWALSKI

HOUSE RIZZI
Carinthia, Austria
Design: 1996
Construction: 1996–97

この住宅の真の中心はヴォイドである。それはリヴィング・スペースと壁のあいだにつくられたコートなのだが，その機能において，何よりもまず内部的な存在である。外部構成での参照点となっているのは，遠くに見える，オーストリア・アルプス山麓の丘の上に建つ二つの城である。一戸建ての住宅地によくあることだが，さまざまな性格をもつ建物との境界は，特に意識せずに知的な処理がなされている。リヴィング・スペースは横手をコートに向け，縦方向には谷を向いている。これらの部屋には，遠くの丘がよく見晴らせるように，鋭角に延びるベイが付いている。住宅の谷側は2階建てで，ゲスト・ルームと小さなユニットが置かれている。

独立柱に支持された大きなアーチ型の屋根が斜面から延び，その下の部屋部屋の上に架け渡されている。荷重を受けるアーチが建物を分節し，その間に屋根を，そしてその上には日除けを支えている。建物全体がさまざまな階調のグレイで包まれている。壁のグレイ，ガラスのグレイ，屋根タイルのグレイ。家の内部だけに，艶のあるシエナ・レッドを使うつもりである。

Architects: Szyszkowitz + Kowalski—Paul Pilz, principal-in-charge; Bernd Kuschetz, Elisabeth Eder, project team
Client: Dr. Rizzi

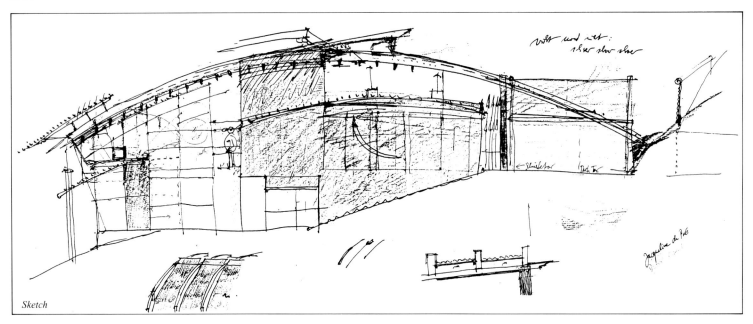
Sketch

The true center of the house is a void—a court between living spaces and walls and as such is primary an internal affair. The external reference points are two distant castles built upon the foothills of the Austrian Alps. And as is so often the case in single-family housing areas: the immediately bordering edge with all of its various yet heterogeneous buildings is intellectually handled without specific regard. The living rooms are loosely arranged alongside the court and lengthwise towards the valley. They have been given a series of sharp-edged bays as vantage points from which the far-lying hills can be seen. (The valley-side of the house is, by the way, two-stories high for guest rooms and small apartments)

A large arched roof rises out of the slope and, resting lengthwise upon independent columns, it bridges over the formation of the rooms below.

The load-bearing arches articulate the structure and carry between them the roof and above them the shade-casting elements. The entire house is gray; gray in its many variations: gray-render, glass-gray, roofing-tile gray; only the inside of the house will perhaps glow sienna-red.

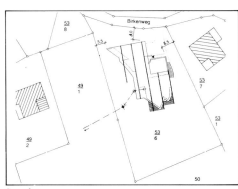
Site plan

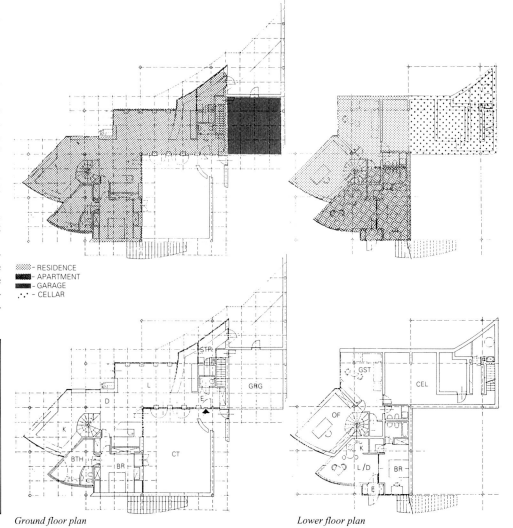
Ground floor plan   *Lower floor plan*

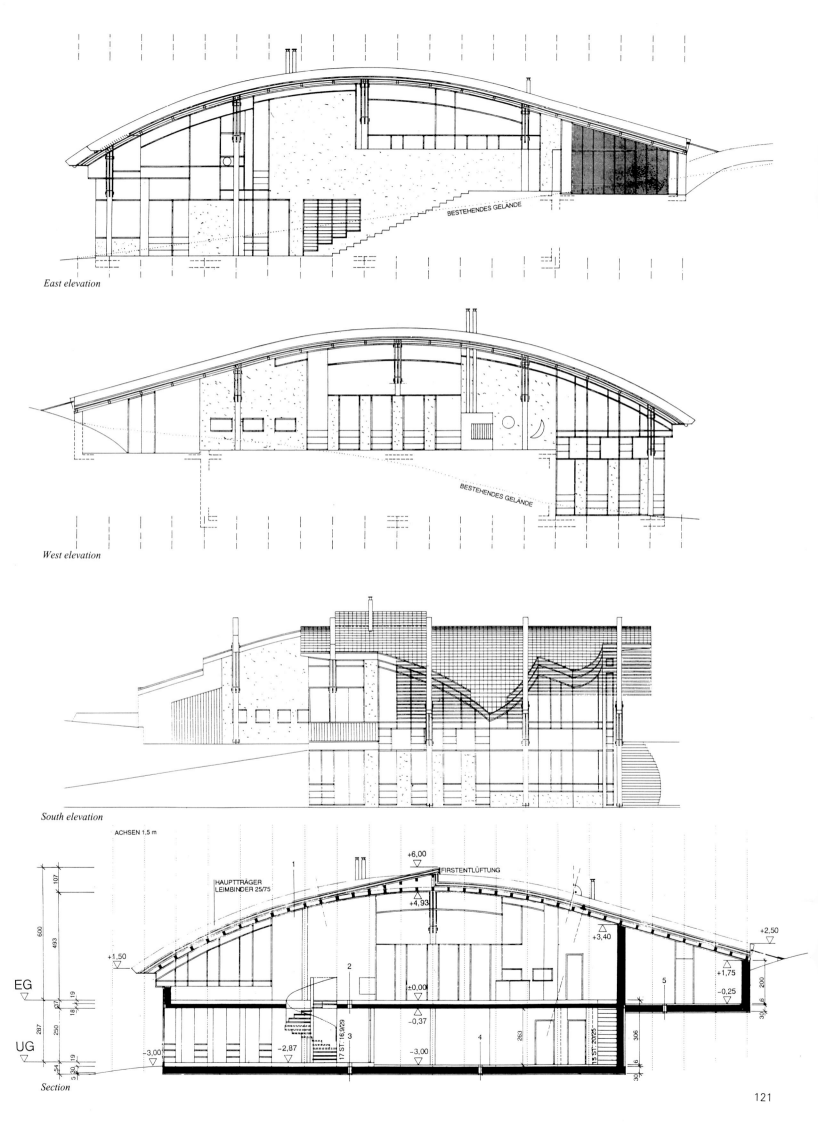

East elevation

West elevation

South elevation

Section

JOSEPH VALERIO

CINCINNATI DREAM HOUSE
Suburban, U.S.A.
Design: 1993

The rooms

The rooms are the city. They do not form houses, which do not form blocks, which do not form neighborhoods. The hierarchy of the traditional city is exchanged for a system of increasing entropy. There is space for individuals, but not communities.

Rooms crisscross the landscape extending to the horizon. They define a fabric where the sense of what is yours and what is mine becomes blurred and ambiguous. Although each room belongs to someone, it is uncertain which rooms belong to whom.

The land is spared or at least excused. It is no longer the leftover, unseen space between inward-looking houses. Instead, the earth becomes a sanctuary which always has a presence in the surrounding rooms.

The enigma

Once the land and culture conspired to make every place different, while people belonged to communities, where everyone was the same. Modernism makes everyone different, making the meaning of every place ambiguous.

People are individuals, no longer belonging to communities. Lost is the collective memory which both defined community, and gave meaning to the land. Without a shared memory, different people find it impossible to agree on the meaning of things. What is not possible for

Model photos

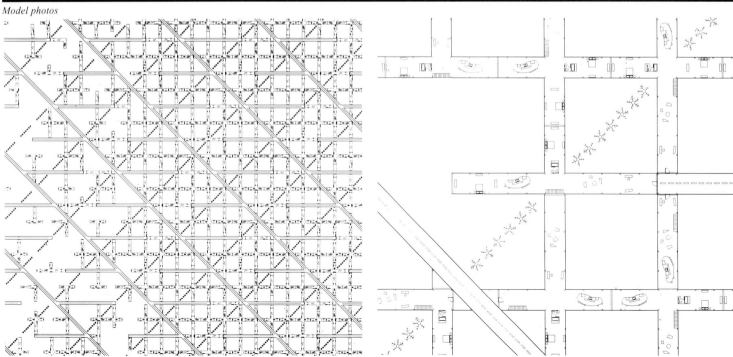

Plans

many people, is not necessary for an individual; an enigmatic design reflects the innocence of the American culture, where the total absence of history and tradition affords a person a perfect naive freedom.

Architects: Joseph Valerio, FAIA–Joseph Valerio, principal-in-charge; Randall Mattheis, David Jennerjahn, Michael Cygan, project team
Clients: The Contemporary Arts Center, Cincinnati

＜ルームズ＞部屋は都市である。部屋は家を形づくらない，ブロックを形づくらない，近隣を形づくらない。伝統的な都市の階層構成は増大するエントロピーのシステムに交換される。個人のためのスペースはあるが，コミュニティのためのスペースはない。

部屋は風景のなかを縦横に横切って地平線へと広がっていく。あなたのモノ，私のモノという感覚がぼんやりと曖昧なファブリックの境界を明示する。それぞれの部屋は誰かに所属しているのだが，どの部屋が誰にということは不確かである。

土地は予備として残され，もはや残余空間，住宅の間の見えない空間ではない。代わって，大地が周囲の部屋のなかに常に存在する聖域となる。

＜謎＞かつて土地と文化はそれぞれの場所を異なったものとしてつくろうと共謀した。そこでは，人々がコミュニティに所属し，誰もが同じであった。モダニズムは，あらゆる場所の意味を曖昧にして，誰をも異なったものとする。人々は個人となり，もはやコミュニティには所属しない。失われたものは，コミュニティを定義し，土地に意味を与えた，集合的な記憶である。共有する記憶なしに，異なった人々が，物事の意味に同意することは不可能である。多数にとって不可能なことは，個人にも必要ではない。この謎のデザインには，アメリカ文化の純潔性——歴史と伝統の全面的不在が，個人に完全な生得の自由を与える場所が反映されている。

Model photos: Cabanban

CARLOS ZAPATA

KLEIN RESIDENCE
Miravalle, Ecuador
Design: 1995–96
Completion: 1997

On the edge of a magnificent inclined site characterized by 180 degree views of the valley of Miravalle and the Andes Mountains, five minutes outside of Quito, Ecuador, CZDS is designing a private residence for a young couple and their two children. The site is part of an exclusive development of 80 parcels of land. This particular site is 50,000 square feet. The area of the house is approximately 7500 square feet with an addition of a pool contemplated as a second phase.

CZDS has separated the service quarters, consisting of two bedrooms, one bathroom, storage and a four-car garage into two additional structures which push towards the limits of the site, act as visual and sound buffer zones between the site and the neighboring parcels. Additional buffer zones are provided by careful planning of the landscape.

At the clients' request, CZDS selected not to suspend the house in the inclined terrain in order to accentuate the perceptual feeling of levitation experienced from the interior of the house. By keeping it away from the edge of the flat land, the rest of the development seems to disappear and the views consist of the Andes Mountains in the background, and an immense voiced distance in between. We have, however, pushed parts of the house beyond the edge of the inclined terrain (the dining terrace and the pool) in order to establish a dialogue between the land and the built form. The house is a receiver of the hill as much as the hill accepts the house placed on it and continue its line up and down.

The house is an assembly of fluid, energetic, puzzle-like fragments which together fuse with the terrain and accentuate its natural contours. The resulting composition is therefore brought together with a powerful gesture inherent in the terrain itself.

The house functions are distributed in two V-shaped floors, split apart by the main staircase opposite to the main entrance. The first wing of the first floor contains a semi-formal living room adjacent to a family room and separated from it only in extreme occasions by a movable translucent wall; otherwise, both rooms will act as one. The second wing of the first floor contains a formal dining room, an informal dining room adjacent to it and divided by a movable wall which allows the two dining rooms to become one for special functions; an interior garden next to the main entrance; the guest bathroom; the kitchen area; the laundry with exterior patio; a guest room with complete bathroom shared by a playroom; storage areas; and a pool (planned as a second phase expansion). The playroom and future pool are linked by a secondary stair to the children's wing located directly on top of the dining room and game room wing. The children's wing contains two bedrooms with their respective bathrooms and walk-in closets. The second wing of the second floor contains the master bedroom; a painter's studio adjacent to it; the master bathroom adjacent to an open private garden directly accessible from the master bathroom; two walk-in closets; a safe room; a hair-stylist room; and a gymnasium, strategically placed next to the children's wing.

The materials used in the house are poured-in-place concrete, stucco, glass, granite, zinc, stainless steel, and local woods.

エクアドルのキートから郊外に5分、アンデス山脈とミラヴェルの谷間を望む眺望が180度見渡せる、美しい斜面に、二人の子供をもつ若い夫妻のために住宅を設計した。敷地は80区画からなる5万sq.ft.の開発地のなかの一区画である。住宅は約7,500sq.ft.で、第二期として、プールをつくることを予定している。

2寝室、1浴室、収納、4台収容できるガレージからなるサーヴィス・クォーターを、2つの付加的な棟へと分け、敷地境界に引き寄せて配置する。ここは近隣の区画との視線や音の遮断ゾーンとしての役割を果たし、ランドスケーピングがそれをさらに補強する。

クライアントの希望により、室内での空中に浮かんでいるような知覚を強調するために、建物を斜面の敷地に浮かすようなことはしなかった。平坦な土地の端から建物を引き離しておくことによって、アンデス山脈を背景にした景色とそのあいだに広大な虚の空間をおいて、他の開発地区は消え去ったように見える。しかし、この土地と建物のあいだに対話をつくりだすように、住宅の一部を(ダイニング・テラスとプール)傾斜地の端より先に押し出した。丘が住宅をその上に置き、上へ下へと続いていくことを受け入れると同じように、住宅もこの丘を受けとめる。

この住宅は、土地と融合し、その自然の等高線を強調する、流体のような、エネルギッシュな、謎のような断片の組み合わせである。ここから、この土地そのものに備わっている、力強い形態と一つになった構成が生まれる。

各部屋は、メイン・エントランスの反対側にある階段によって切り裂かれたV型のつくる2本の翼棟に配分されている。一番目の翼棟の1階は、セミ・フォーマルなリヴィング・ルームで、ファミリー・ルームが隣にあり、特別な場合だけ、半透明の可動壁で分けられる。その他の場合は両者は一室空間として使われる。二番目の翼棟の1階はフォーマルおよびインフォーマルなダイニングが並び、可動壁によって、特別なときには一つにできる。メイン・エントランスの隣は室内庭園。ゲスト用浴室。キッチン。パティオの付いた洗濯室。遊戯室と共有の浴室の付いたゲスト・ルーム。収納。プール(第二期工事として予定)。遊戯室と将来のプールは、ダイニングとゲーム・ルーム翼の上に位置する子供の翼棟への階段でつながれる。子供の翼棟には寝室2つとそれぞれに浴室、ウォーク・イン・クローゼットが付いている。2番目の翼棟の2階には、主寝室、その隣に絵のスタジオ、直接でられるプライヴェートな庭の付いた主浴室、2つのウォーク・イン・クローゼット、金庫室、美容室、そして子供の翼棟の隣にジムがある。

現場打ちコンクリート、スタッコ、ガラス、花崗岩、亜鉛、ステンレス・スティール、地元産の木材などを材料として用いる。

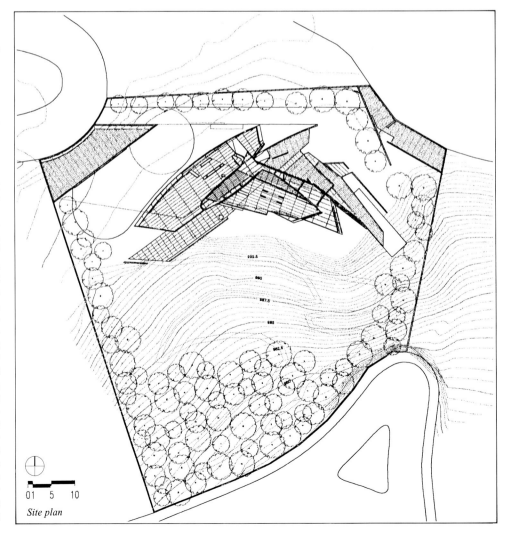

Site plan

Model photos

Architects: Carlos Zapata Design Studio—
Carlos Zapata, design direction; Pamela Torres,
Rolando Mendoza, Fred Botelho, Dania
Saragovia, design contribution
Clients: Daniel and Carmen Klein
Engineer: Luis Roggiero Gil

Model photos: Th. Delbeck Photography

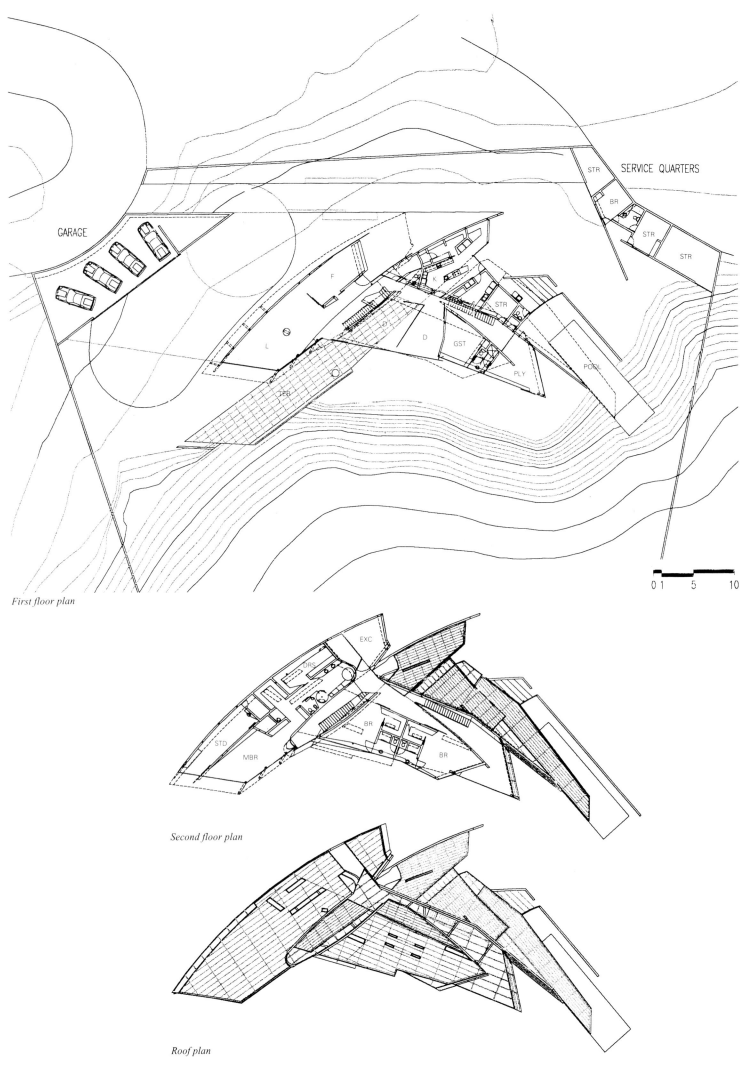

First floor plan

Second floor plan

Roof plan

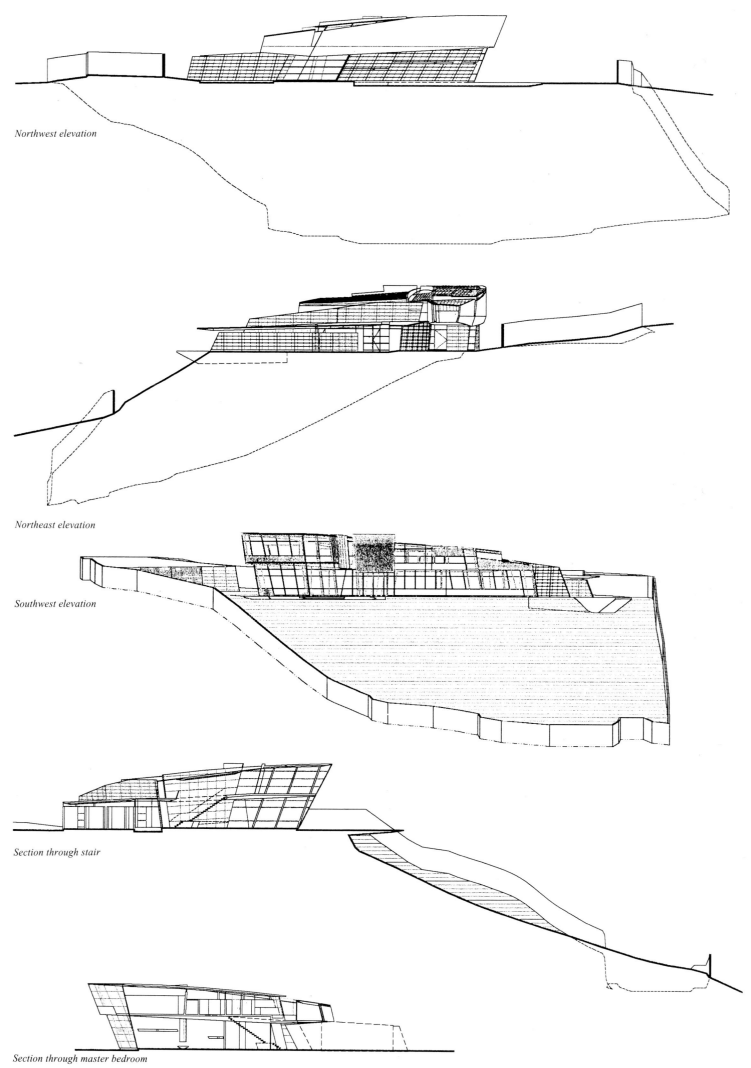

Northwest elevation

Northeast elevation

Southwest elevation

Section through stair

Section through master bedroom

PETER ZELLNER

JETTY HOUSE
Milang, South Australia
Design: 1993–95

This is a recent project, but also the second version of a house set between land and sea. The house, like its namesake, explores the moment of crossing between ground plane and liquid surface. It works like a circulation zone across it entire length.

The Jetty House is composed of three elements: 01–Concrete rectangular "pier" house circulation zones, living area etc. 02–Float metal containers: kitchen, master bedroom. 03–Plywood shields break sunlight cover portions of roof-garden.

This project is specifically about the relation between land, water, light and architecture in Australia.

陸と海を結ぶ住宅プロジェクトの改訂版である。突堤の家というプロジェクト名のように、この住宅は、地面と水面の間を渡って行くひとときを探索するものだ。その全長が一種のサーキュレーション・ゾーンである。突堤の家は3つのエレメントで構成されている。01．コンクリートの長方形の＜埠頭＞。サーキュレーション・ゾーン、リヴィング・エリアなどを収容。02．浮かんでいるメタルのコンテナー。キッチン、主寝室が入る。03．合板の楯。屋上庭園を覆い、日差しを遮る。

陸地、水、光、そしてオーストラリアの建築ということに特に思いを巡らしたものである。

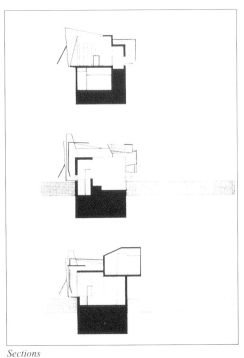

Sections

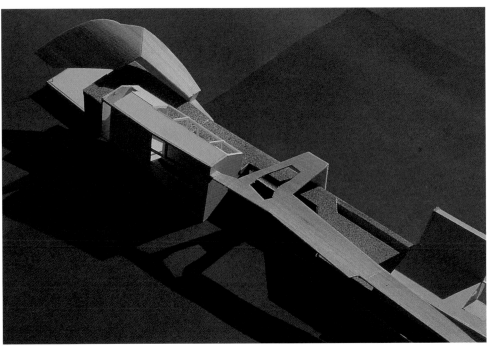

Model photo: east edge

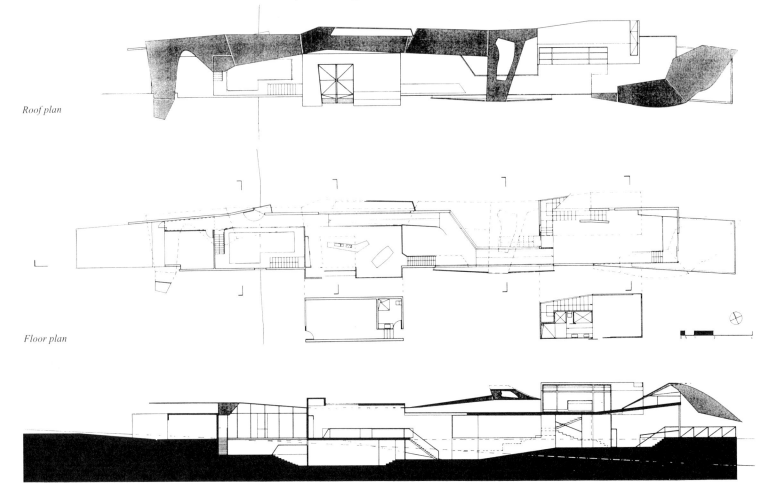

Roof plan

Floor plan

Section

Southeast view

Architect: Zellner [ark]:zellner architectural research kollaborative—Peter Zellner (design), principal-in-charge; Lei Li (design assistant), project team

Bird's eye view

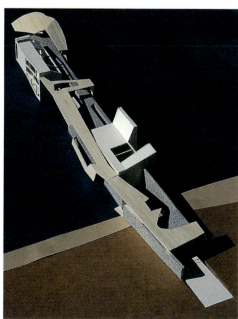
Bird's eye view

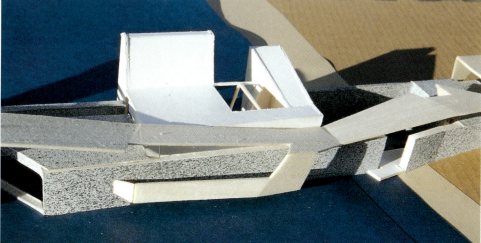
North view

PETER ZELLNER

MOTOHOUSE [HOUSE FOR A MOTORCYCLIST]
Melbourne, Australia
Design: 1995

Experimental house for an urban Dweller/Nomad
This project deals with the insertion of a three meter wide; two level dwelling into a dense inner city locale.

The house is conceived of as a series of event-spaces along a linear circuit. The dweller may enter by foot or by motorcycle; eat, sleep, work or relax according to his/her daily cycle.

The geometries of the project are derived from an interest in speed, warped space and contemporary motorcycle form.

＜都市住民／遊牧民のための実験住宅＞
高密度な都市のなかに，幅3m，2階建ての住宅を装填しようというものである。

リニアー・サーキットに沿って並ぶイヴェント空間として考えた。住人は，徒歩であるいはオートバイに乗ったまま室内に入り，彼または彼女の生活サイクルに従って，食べ，眠り，働き，休むだろう。

建物の形は，スピード，ねじれた空間，そして現代のオートバイの形に対する関心から生れている。

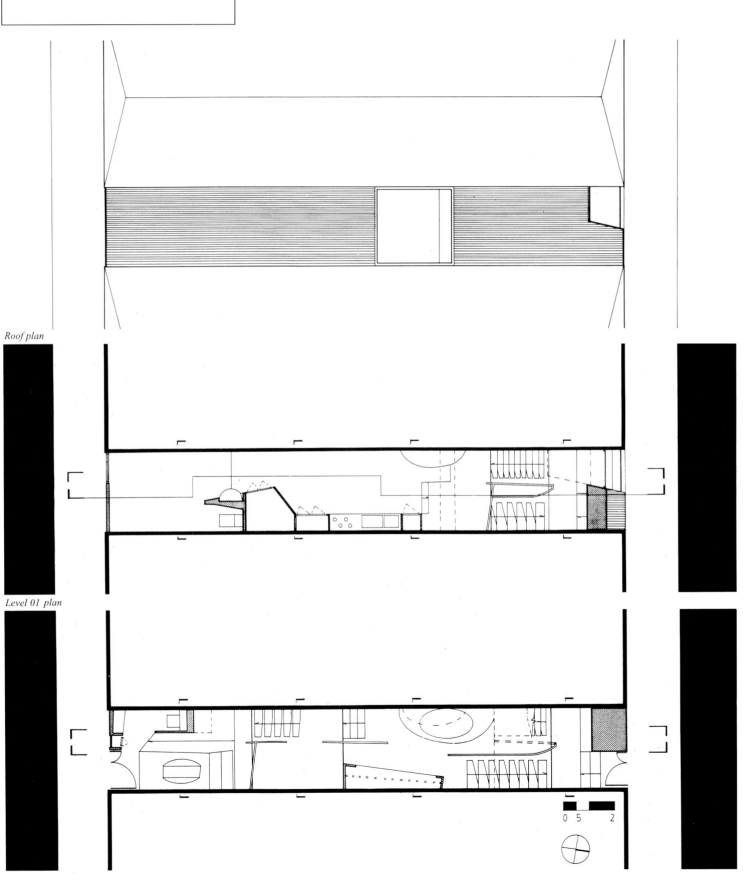

Roof plan

Level 01 plan

Ground floor plan

Architect: Zellner [ark]: zellner architectural research kollaborative—Peter Zellner (design), principal-in-charge; Gerald Yeo (computer modeling), Laurel Porcari (project assistant), project team

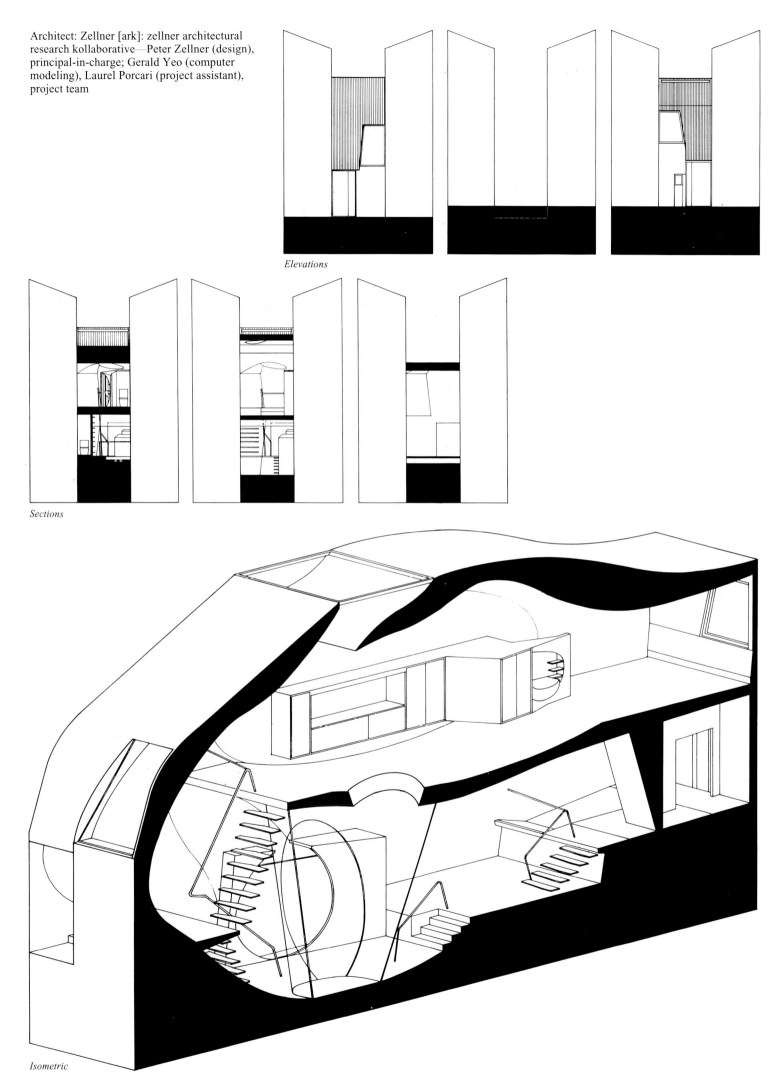

Elevations

Sections

Isometric

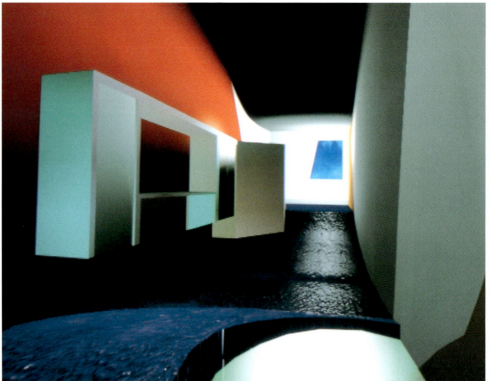
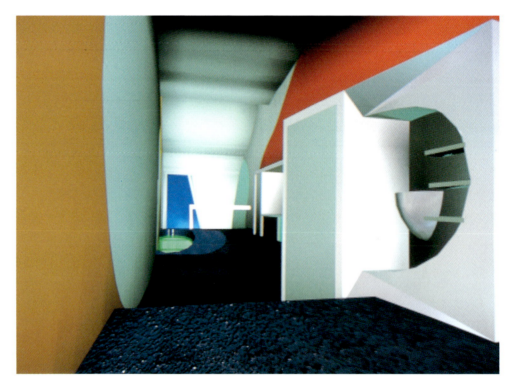

CG: interior

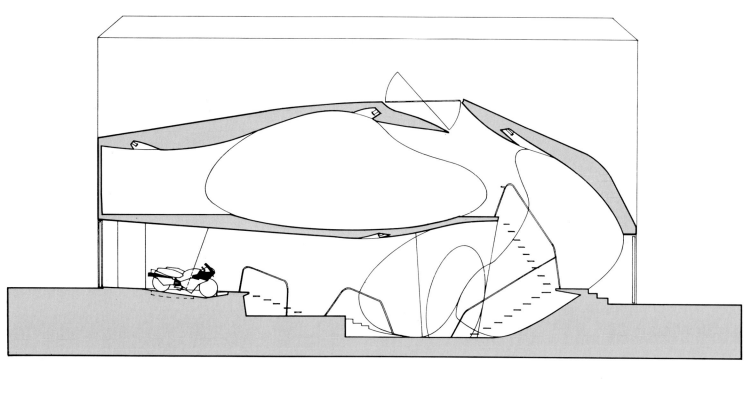
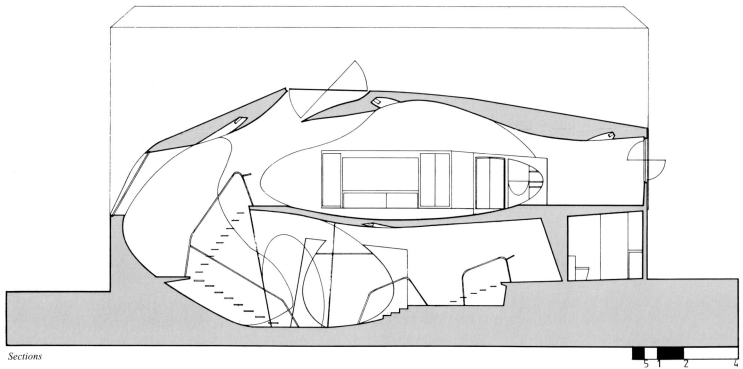

Sections

FREDERIC BOREL

HOUSING PROGRAM AND SCHOOL
Paris, France
Design: 1995
Construction: 1997

View from boulevard

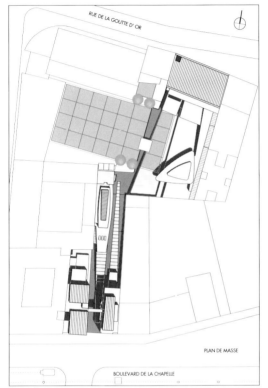

Site plan

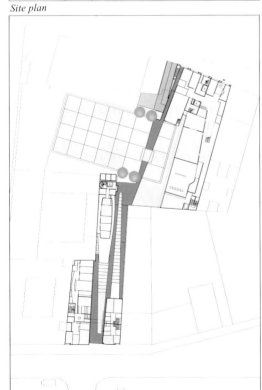

Third floor (on boulevard wing) plan

Sketch

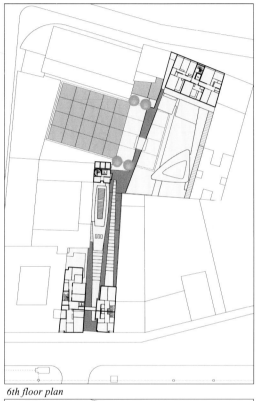
6th floor plan

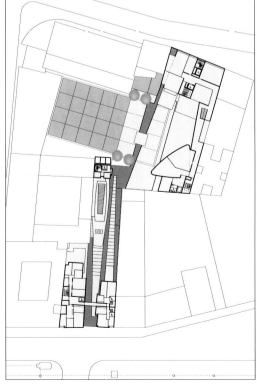
5th floor plan

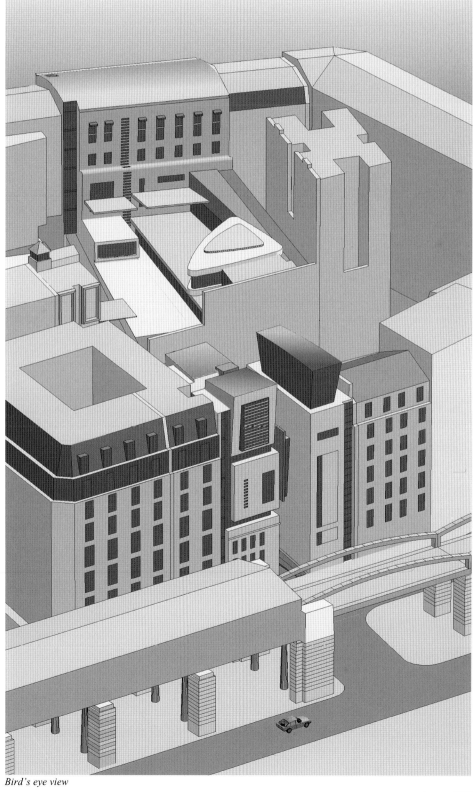
Bird's eye view

135

Symbolic, Real, Imaginary

This hybrid project, comprising a school, a housing program and car park, occupies two independent sites which nonetheless interconnect. The first overlooks one of the great boulevards created in the eighteenth century, along what had hitherto been the perimeter wall; the second fronts a quiet street leading to a neighborhood that forms an autonomous entity. With its overhead Métro and dense automobile traffic, the Boulevard de la Chapelle marks an imposing space and a visible break between the old city and its *faubourgs,* Rue de la Goutte d'Or, on the other hand, is a typical instance of the *corridor* stigmatized by Le Corbusier.

The project forges an interface between the boulevard as an "outside," and the Goutte d'Or district as an "inside." In the manner of Janus, the God of doors and thresholds, the project has two distinct faces. The first is heroic, with a ceremonial entrance open to the boulevard, forming a gateway not unlike the city gates of yore; the second is veiled, a contextual envelope that carefully respects the rhythms of existing facades and preserve the fragile equilibrium of the street fabric—testifying to the survival of a plural, "popular" city, despite simplistic visions of Paris as a world capital.

Caught between these two opposite worlds, the heart of the site creates a third. The hybrid nature of the brief (school, housing, car park) generates mixity of forms. The built volumes are deliberately dislocated; forming a syncopated continuity along the edges of the site—cadenced visual sequences. The housing block resembling vestiges of old fortifications; the library positioned on the school roof like some flying saucer waiting for the instant of improbable takeoff—these "objects of poetic reaction" (to use Le Corbusier's phrase) articulate the two autonomous plots and transform their random juxtapositions in a calculated relationship. These sculptural punctuations reveal the dreamlike character of any courtyard worthy of the name.

The project therefore dissociates the three key instances involved in the creative act (symbolic, real and imaginary), and assigns to them closely defined roles. The symbolic invests the expressive boulevard front, reflecting the intrinsic heterogeneity of this busy thoroughfare. The real is anchored in existing facts, and respects the social rites of this modest neighborhood. And the imaginary forms the in-between; its atomized forms create a framework for the school, conceived of as a "children's republic."

Richard Scoffier (English translation: Kenneth Hylton)

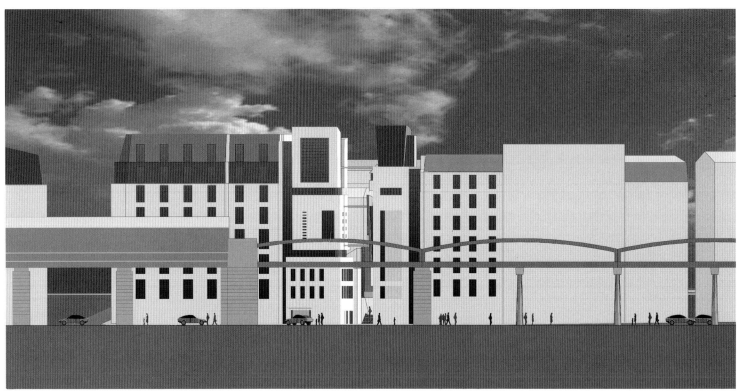

South elevation

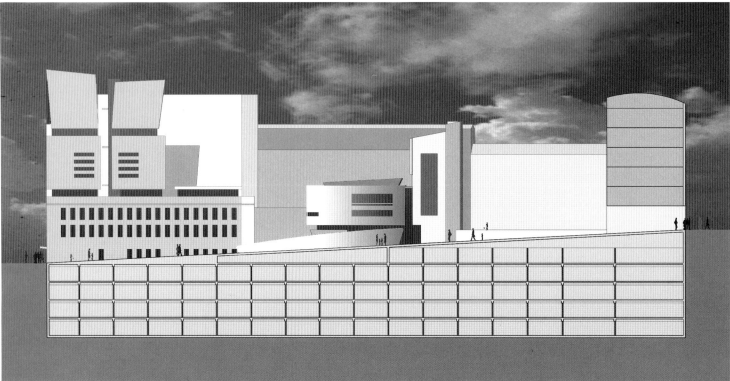

Section

<象徴性，現実性，想像性>
学校，ハウジング，駐車場からなる複合建築計画。奥で繋がっている2つの独立した敷地を占めている。敷地の一つは，今まで境界壁であった場所に沿って18世紀につくられた大通りの一つを見渡している。もう一方は，独立したブロックを形づくっている近隣へ導く，静かな道に面している。頭上をメトロが走り，交通量の多いブルヴァード・ド・ラ・シャペルは堂々たる空間，旧市街とその市壁の間の目に見える切れ目を印し，一方，リュ・ド・ラ・グゥト・ドーはル・コルビュジエが非難した狭い道路（コリドー）の典型例である。

このプロジェクトは，＜外側＞であるブルヴァードと＜内側＞であるグゥト・ドーの間に界面をつくりだす。戸口と敷居の神，ヤヌスのように，2つの異なった顔を備えている。一つは英雄的な顔――ブルヴァードに開いた儀式的なエントランスがあり，昔日の市門に似たゲートを形成する。2つ目の顔は，既存ファサードのリズムをこわさないように注意し，この街路構成のもつもろい均衡を守るように配慮した，曖昧でコンテクスチュアルな被膜である――世界の首都としてのパリという単純きわまりない構想にもかかわらず，多元的な＜ポピュラー＞都市の存続可能性を立証しようというものである。

これら2つの対照的な世界にはさまれて，敷地の中央部は第3の世界をつくりだす。設計要綱のもつハイブリッドな性格（学校，ハウジング，駐車場）が異種交配的な形態をうみだした。各ヴォリュームは故意にずらして置き，敷地周縁に沿ってシンコペートしながら続いて行き，律動的な視覚の流れをつくりだす。ハウジングは古い要塞のなごりをとどめているようにみえ，図書館は，起こりそうにもない離陸の瞬間を待つ空飛ぶ円盤のように学校の屋上に位置を占める――これらの＜詩的反応を誘うオブジェ＞（ル・コルビュジエの言葉を借りれば）は，2つの自立した区画を分節し，そのランダムな並置を計算された関係へ変貌させる。これらの彫刻的な句読点は，その名に値する中庭のいずれもが備えている夢幻的な性格を見せてくれる。

従ってこのプロジェクトは，創造的な作業（象徴，現実，想像）に関わる3つの主要な事例を分離させ，それぞれに緊密に定義された役割を配分するものである。象徴性は，この交通の激しい大通りの異種混合性を反映した，表現性をブルヴァード側ファサードに付与する。現実性は既成事実につながれ，この質素な近隣の社会習慣を尊重する。そして想像力は，中間的な存在を形成する；その原子に分かれた形態は，＜子供たちの共和国＞と見なして構成した学校のフレームワークとなる。　　　　（R．スコフィエ）

Architects: Frédéric Borel; Joakim Larson, Massimo Mattiussi, Marc Younan architects, project team
Client: OPAC
Consultant: GII.SIBAT

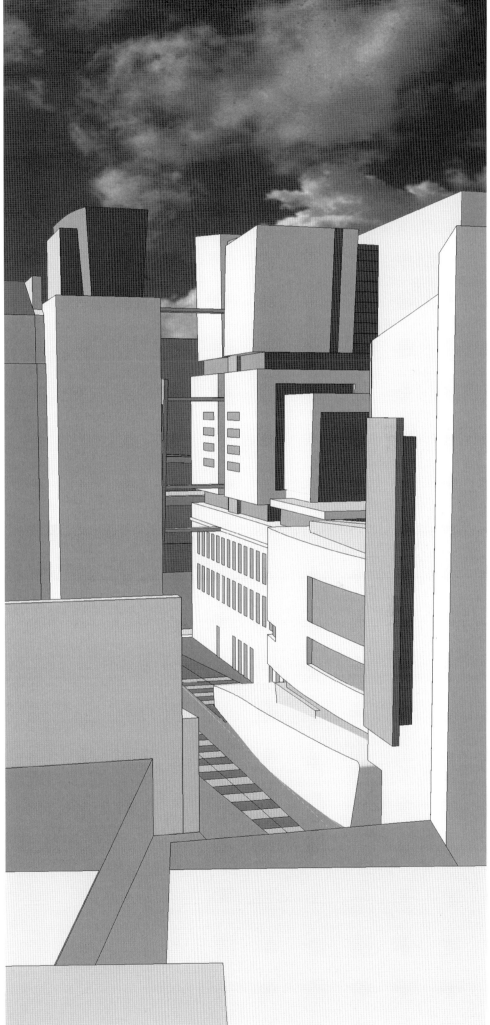

View toward boulevard

EBNER ODER ECKERSTORFER

STUDENTS' HOUSING
Salzburg, Austria
Design: 1995
Construction: 1995–97

The city center of Salzburg is shaped by the surrounding topography. The area with its rich history was settled in an arena between three characteristic ridges and a river, the Salzach, which further divided the area into two sections. Sheer cliff walls constitute the backdrop for many buildings in the old inner city. The walls of the mountains and those of the buildings interact with each other, thus creating a main theme for the typical architecture in Salzburg.

The students' hostel which is used as a hotel during the summer season, incorporates business premises and a farmers market on the ground level. The financial revenues of the hotel help to reduce the boarding cost for the students. The diverse needs of the occupants had to be respected, so that the lifestyle of the young scholars is not effected by the simplistic style of a hotel, and this is what gave this project such a wide spread definition.

The farmers market offers agricultural products directly from the producers. Each of the building's three usages is clearly defined in the project by a unique design. The translucent ground floor, above which the living quarters are located, is made up of crystalline structures containing the business premises, thus catching the visitor's eye. They appear as boulders, which have fallen off the mountain, now resting below the softly curved building unit with its cellular living quarters. The curvature of the building not only allows for two differently sized, dynamic squares, but at the same time it follows the natural curve of the Kapuzinermountain.

The facade, facing north towards the square, mirrors the parallel sequence of the hotel/student rooms in a discrete glass facade, which guarantees sufficient light in the mountain's cast shadow. The entrance divides the building into two sections of different size. The front door portrays a tunnel, which opens up to a spacious hall, offering a wide view of the mountain.

The numerous references to the mountain, in a metaphorical sense, the form of the building, as well as the visual design create a new reference point in the topography of the city of Salzburg.

Materials, construction
The students' hostel is constructed with concrete and surrounded by a glass facade, which is divided into three zones: the balustrade is paneled with translucent, the window area with transparent, and the lintel area again with translucent insulated glass.

The business premise are partially built with glass and a lightweight panel construction. The paneling consists of either Niroster-steel of Corten-steel.

Roman Höllbacher, Christine Wolff

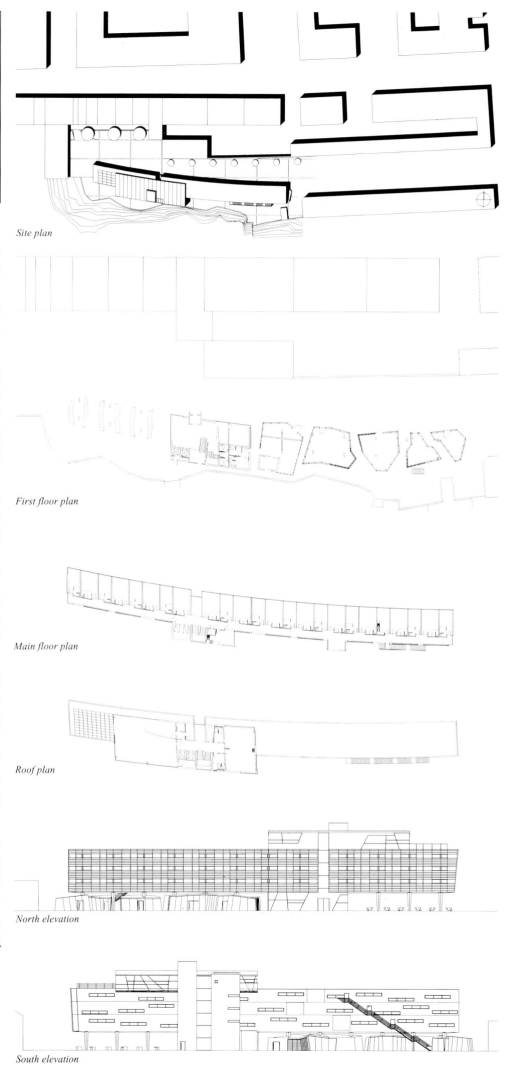

Site plan

First floor plan

Main floor plan

Roof plan

North elevation

South elevation

ザルツブルクの中心部は周辺の地形によって形づくられている。豊かな歴史をもつこの地域は，3つの特徴のある尾根に囲まれ，ザルツバッハ川がさらに2つの区域に分けている。切り立った崖が，旧市街の多くの建物の背景となっている。山とこれらの建物は相互に影響しあって，ザルツブルクの典型的な建築の主題をつくっている。

学生寮は，1階のビジネス施設や農家の市場と合体して，夏のあいだはホテルとなる。ホテルからの収入は学生の寮費を軽減する助けとなる。ここに宿泊する人の多様な必要に対応しなければならないので，若い学研の生活スタイルは，ホテルの単純なスタイルには有効ではなく，このことが，建物に広範な性格を与えることになった。

ファーマーズ・マーケットには産地直送の農作物が並ぶ。特徴のあるデザインによって建物のもつ3つの用途が明快に区別されている。上階が宿泊施設である，半透明の1階はビジネス施設が置かれ，結晶体のような構造によって訪問者の目を集める。山から落下してきて，細胞状の宿泊施設からなる緩やかにカーヴする建物の下に静止した丸石の集まりのように現れる。建物の湾曲は，違う大きさの二種類のダイナミックな四辺形を受け入れると同時に，カプツィーナ山の自然の曲線に沿ってもいる。

北側の広場に面したファサードは，ホテル／学生室の平行する連なりを，分離したガラス面に映している。このガラス面によって，山の落とす影のなかでも充分な光が内部に入る。エントランスが建物を大きさの異なる2つの部分に分けている。正面扉はトンネルのようで，山が見渡せる広いホールに開いている。

山との関わりが，メタファーとして数多く使われている。建物の形，視覚的なデザインがザルツブルク市の地形に対する新たな参照点をつくりだす。

材料・工事：コンクリート造にガラスのファサード。ファサードは3つに分割されている。手摺は半透明パネル。透明な窓。窓の上部も半透明の断熱ガラス。ビジネス施設エリアは一部がガラスと軽量パネル造。コールテン鋼パネルを併用。

Architects: E.o.E.—Peter Ebner, Günter Eckerstorfer, principals-in-charge, design; Schmid & Schmid/Bischofshofen, project architects; Edith Hitsch, Helmut Grill, Peter Schurz, Christine Wolff, Wilhelm Brugger jun., Thomas Gollackner, Helge Kirchberger, Andreas Traufellner, Roman Höllbacher, assistants
Clients: Studentenförderungsstiftung, Wenzi-Hartl
Consultants: Spirk & Partner

Model photos: bird's eye view

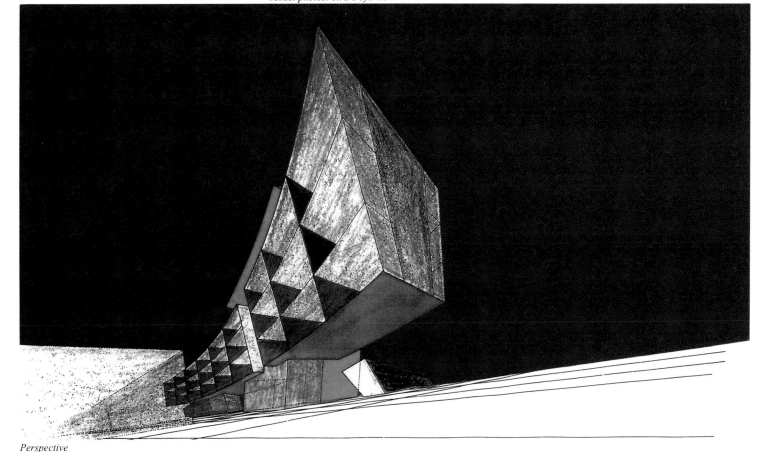

Perspective

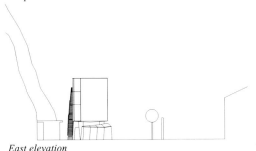
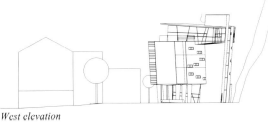
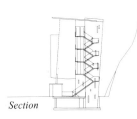

East elevation   *West elevation*   *Section*

COOP HIMMELBLAU

HIGHRISE BUILDING WITH CLIMATE FACADE
Wagramerstrasse, Vienna, Austria
Design: 1994–96
Construction: 1996–98

The planned highrise building is located adjacent to the "Alte Donau" metro station.

The project creates a new urban space in conjunction with two other highrise buildings and a school/apartment building, which captivates with height and with the quality of its space. The highrise buildings differ from one another in typological concept.

The major considerations for the outer form of our building can be seen as followed:

The highrise building is made up of two building components divided at the level between building class V and building class VI.

This enables an economic plan solution leading to a positive relation between usable surface area and gross surface area. A skylobby occurs at the intersection of the two components. This is used as common space for the accommodation of venues, billiards, table tennis, sundecks, playgrounds etc.

The linking element between the two components is the climate facade. This is a SW-S-SE oriented glass facade, which is integrated with the core to allow the circulation of air. This regulates the climate during all seasons. A further aspect of this glass climate facade, hung over the whole elevation, is the creation of an eco-social living space, by means of loggias, green spaces, and communication areas. The inner space of the building allows gardens, three levels high, which are similar to winter gardens.

The site is very wind-intensive. In order to achieve high living comfort and to be able to open windows without any pressure we chose a parallelogram as the ground plan. The parallelogram is oriented so that its long sides coincide with the direction of the wind in order to minimize pressure and suction forces. Therefore, the choice of form, orientation and the special facade offer an opportunity to achieve passive energy profits, to raise living quality and to optimize running costs.

Architects: Coop Himmelblau—Wolf D. Prix, H. Swiczinsky, principals-in-charge;
Weichenberger (project architect), Mostböck, Myndl, Pean, project team
Client: Seg Vienna
Construction planning: Argei Eiger Nord Vienna—G. Rieder, principal-in-charge; Enk, project team

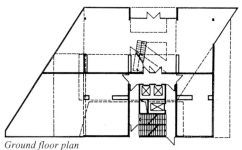

Ground floor plan

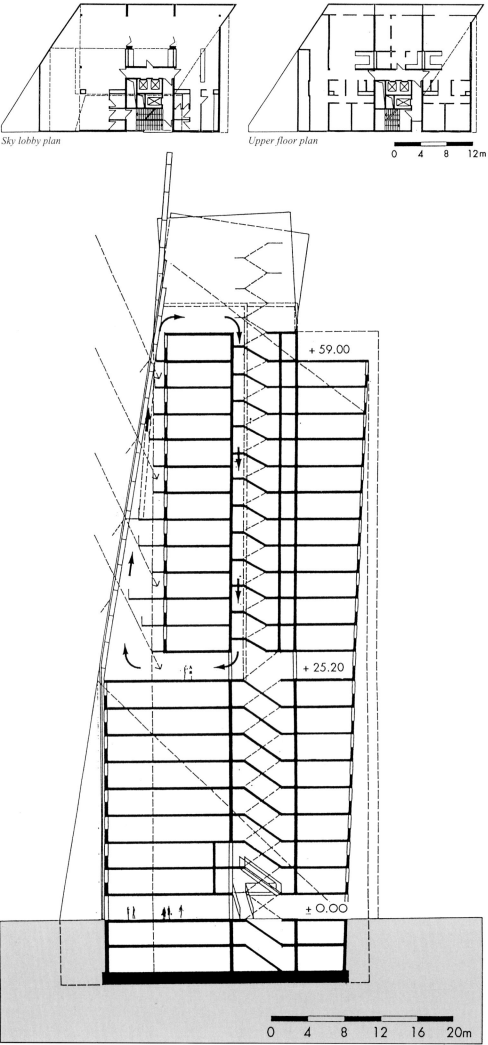

Sky lobby plan *Upper floor plan*

Section

計画された高層建築は，地下鉄の「アルテ・ドナウ」駅に隣接している。

このプロジェクトは，他の2つの高層建物と学校／アパートからなる建物と連係して，その高さと広い空間によって他を魅了する新しい都市空間をつくろうというものである。

われわれの建物の外形に対する主要な考え方は以下の通りである。

高層の建物は，ビルディング・クラスⅤとビルディング・クラスⅥの間のレヴェルで分割された2つのビルディング・コンポーネントで構築される。

これによって，建築可能エリアと芝生のエリアの間に建設的な関係へと導くことのできる経済的な平面計画が可能となる。2つのコンポーネントの交差部にスカイ・ロビーを配置する。ここはビリヤード，テーブル・テニス，サンデッキ，運動場などのための共有空間として利用する。

2つのコンポーネントをクライメット・ファサードが連結する。これは，南西，南，南東を向いたガラス面で，大気が環流するコアで統合され，四季を通じて気候を調節する。立面全体に掛けられたこのガラスのクライメット・ファサードはさらに，エコ・ソシアルな生活空間を，ロッジア，グリーン・スペース，交流の場などによってつくりだす。建物の内部空間にはウィンター・ガーデンのような3層吹き抜けの庭園をつくることができる。

敷地には非常に強い風が吹く。居住性を高め，風圧を感じずに窓を開けられるように，平行四辺形の平面とした。平行四辺形は，その長い方の辺を，風圧と吸引力を最小にするように，風向に一致させた。形態，方位，特殊なファサードの選択は，省エネルギー効果をうみ，生活の質を向上させ，ランニング・コストも効率的なものとすることができる。

Model photos: Markus Pillhofer

COOP HIMMELBLAU

GASOMETER B2
Simmering, Vienna, Austria
Design: 1995–96
Construction: 1997–2001

Architects: Coop Himmelblau—Wolf D. Prix, H. Swiczinsky, principals-in-charge; Weichenberger (project architect), Mostböck, Besendorfer, Pillhofer, Wiscombe, Zottl, project team
Consultant: Di Fritsch–Chiari, structural

General information
In an outer district of Vienna called Simmering, there are four Gasometers which originally housed the tanks for the gas supply of Vienna. After the closure of these Gasometers, the interior elements were dismantled and tanks were emptied. The unusual type of space and the industrial site led to the fact that the Gasometers were often used for diverse activities such as clubs, exhibitions, etc.

The aim of the competition was to study the feasibility of reusing these old shells as a new multifunctional complex for housing, cultural and commercial activities.

Three architects won: Jean Nouvel, Manfred Wehdorn and Coop Himmelblau.

The location of the project represents a spatial opportunity to develop the urban structure of Vienna.

Summary
The project is a new formulation of the topic "living in direct connection with culture and commercial facilities" within a historical framework. Because of the high density within the site and because of the infrastructural connections, an urban environment is generated. This environment exists close to nature. (The Prater is in 700 meter walking distance.)

The layering of periphery, urbanity, and history is a chance to reform the environment in a complex, dynamic way.

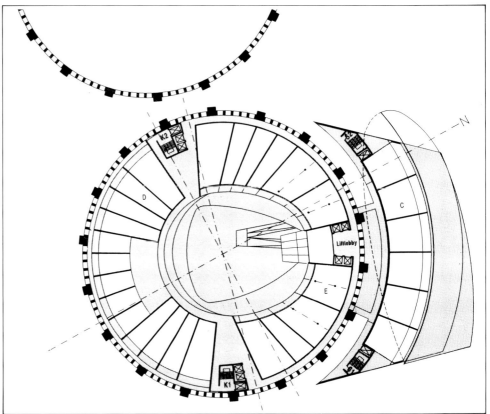

Upper floor plan

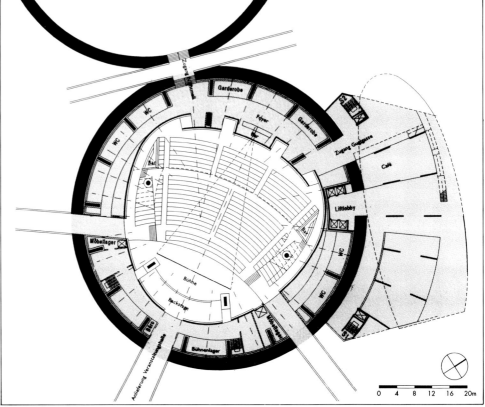

Entrance floor plan

Model photo: northeast view

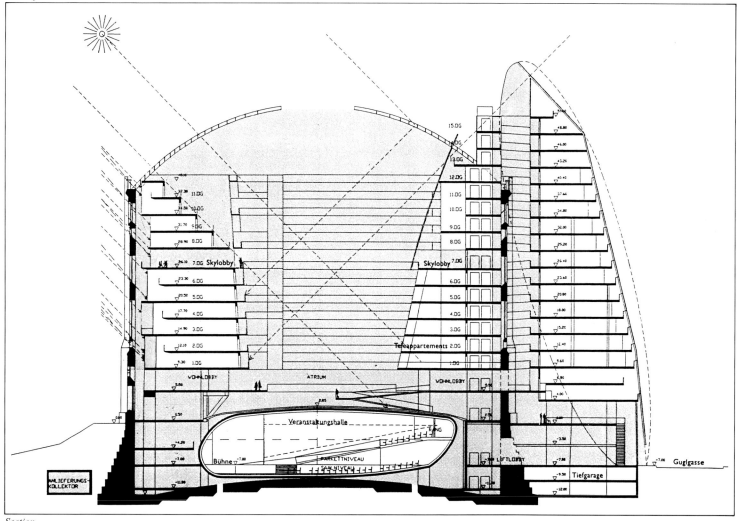
Section

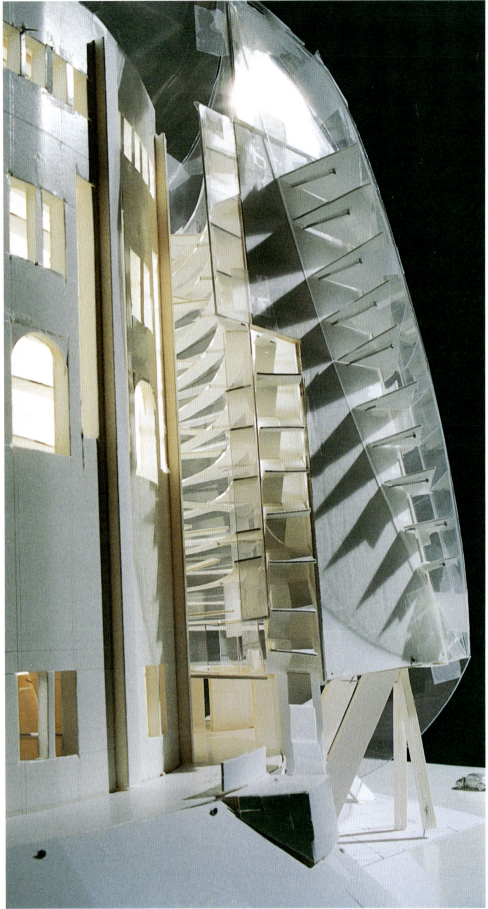

East view

Overall view

Model photos: Markus Pillhofer

COOP HIMMELBLAU

APARTMENT BUILDING REMISE VORGARTENSTRASSE
Vienna, Austria
Design: 1994–96
Construction: 1996–99

Urban housing in a dense area

The goal was to achieve an urban edge towards the Danube within this heterogeneous development. Special conditions for this apartment complex are the unique location within the urban structure and an excellent infrastructural network.

The project should be seen as a contrast to conventional housing blocks, offering an opportunity for an open, differentiated form of living.

We chose to raise our building, while keeping the same density as a low building. Reserve spaces are offered inside the apartment building at various levels.

These reserve spaces, which are situated within the building complex like airpockets, are a clear improvement in living quality for the inhabitants. The most distinctive formulation of these spaces can be seen in the "Orangerie" in the rooftop zone (building class V, +26,00 m). This zone shows how the relationship between the density of program and the provision of open space can be improved remarkably.

The chosen housing form with crosswise joint maisonettes and a central circulation passage enables an extensive glazing of the outer wall. This outer wall allows, in connection with the glass loggias, passive energy gains.

Furthermore, the differentiated formulation of the rooftop landscape and the sloping and tilted superstructures offer the possibility for a solar-collector roof. The energy collected from the roof could be redirected into conditioning the glazed loggias in areas with less sunlight.

The housing structure appears within its immediate and indirect urban environment as a "raising edge" in a newly developed district.

It is an exemplary model for the future of urban living.

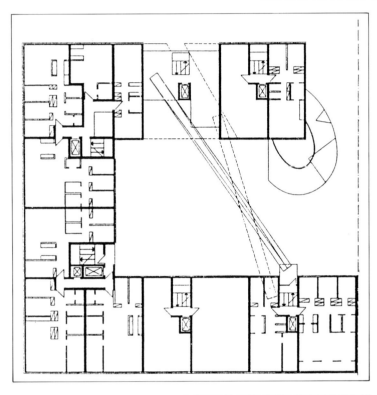
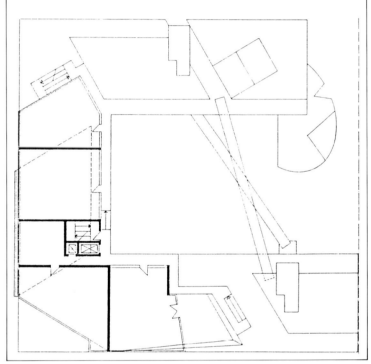
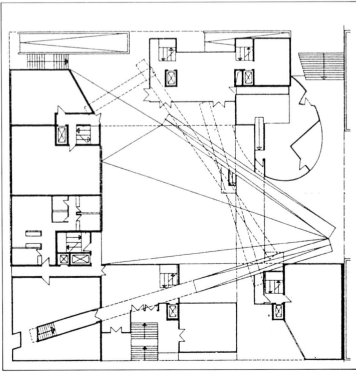
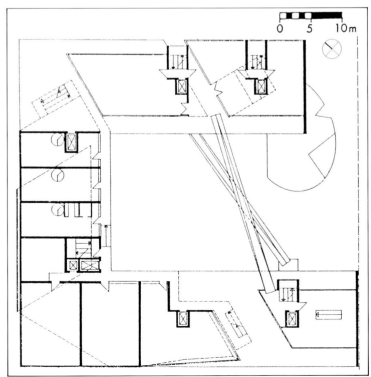

Plans

＜高密度地区の都市集合住宅＞
この異種混合的な開発によって，ダニューブ川に向かう都市のエッジをつくるのが目標である。このアパートメント・コンプレックスの敷地に備わる固有の状況は，都市内の特殊な性格をもつその位置と完備したインフラ設備網である。

従来のハウジング・ブロックとは対照的な，開放的で多彩な生活環境を提供する。

低層の建物と同じ密度を保ちながら，高層にすることを選択した。アパートメント・ビルディングのさまざまな階に，予備的なスペースを残してある。

これらの予備スペースは，エア・ポケットのように，住民の生活の質を明らかに向上させる。これらの空間が最もはっきりと表現されているのは，屋上（ビルディング・クラスⅤ，+26.00m）にある＜オランジェリー＞内である。このゾーンはプログラムの密度に対するオープン・スペースの配給の関係がいかに住環境を向上させているかを示している。

メゾネットの十字形配置と中央の動線通路というハウジング形態によって外壁に広いガラス面が可能となった。この外壁はガラスのロッジアとつながって太陽熱を利用できる。

さらに，屋上の個別的な配置構成，傾斜し傾いた建物形態は，太陽熱収集装置として屋上を使うことも可能である。屋上で集められた太陽エネルギーは，日差しの少ないエリアにあるガラス張りのロッジアへ送ることもできよう。

建物は，新しい開発地区のなかの＜高く立ち上がったエッジ＞として，すぐ隣のまた間接的な都市環境のなかに現れる。

これは未来の都市生活のためのハウジング・モデルである。

Architects: Coop Himmelblau—Wolf D. Prix, H. Swiczinsky, principals-in-charge; Weichenberger (project architect), Mostbröck, Myndl, Pean, Turner, project team
Client: SEG VIENNA
Construction planning: Arge Eiger Nord Vienna—G. Rieder, principal-in-charge; Fusseneger, project team

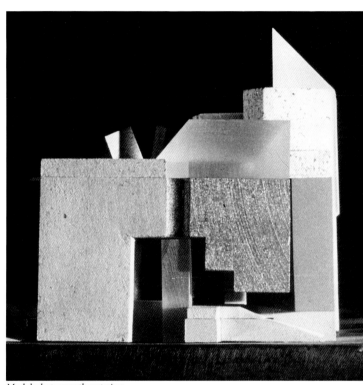
Model photo: northeast view

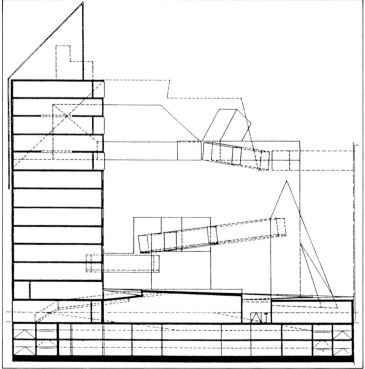
Southwest view

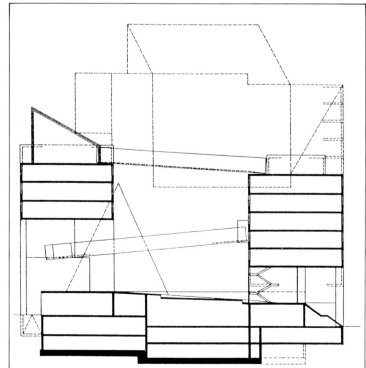
Sections

South view

East view

Model photos: Markus Pillhofer

MARK MACK

VIENNA HOUSING
Vienna, Austria
Design: 1995

Four Points of Departure

1. Exposure to outdoor space

Each unit is intentionally given a relatively large exterior component—loggia, balcony—which can easily converted into usable space through temporary enclosures per season. Roof garden and ground floor garden also extend the living spaces of the individual units. Most units also face public open spaces thus expanding views and increasing exposure to sun and light.

2. Differentiated common space

Courts, green spaces, gardens, play areas for children and adults offer a variety of semi-private and public spaces. Interior connection (Coop Himmelblau shared lobby and core) and exterior connection (Sorkin Gate, connecting walkways) through the adjacent sites provide access to recreational and social amenities (kindergarten, school, gym, work place.) This accessibility reinforces the open webbed design and creates an equally accessible environment for the district as well as the adjacent developments.

3. Urban conditioning

The Wagramerstrasse is recognized as the most visible urban gesture. Therefore, new development along the street follows transitional methods in creating high value, multifunctional, and urbanistically varied spatial development which allows openings into the interior site. This open gesture would yield a defined and faceted approach towards the issues of private and semi-private connections through the site and with other developments, effectively challenging the nineteenth century definition of a perimeter block development. Towards the interior of the site, the scale of the building decreases while the private character increases. Public spaces (plaza and playgrounds, etc.) and outdoor spaces, together create a larger public environment both soft and hard. To the north (Coop Himmelblau site) the connections become more determined—a possible shared parking structure, a shared entry and hallway system, a possible creation of a non-housing development which relieves the monotony of a large housing estate. The new commercial development may further develop new jobs in the human service industry. To the south (Sorkin site) a gate like character is developed between the curved high-rises and the articulated building edges allowing for the public to enter both the buildings and the site. In addition, the mixed use quality of the Wagramerstrasse building. (live-work, retail, offices, services) enclosure a vital and multiple use of the immediate urban space as well as to connect to previously established elements of the site (transportation, access, district center).

4. Flexible housing space

To combat increasing cost of housing and to address the ever changing needs of housing demographics, flexible housing units are set within a rigid structural building system. The units are mostly maisonette type duplexes oriented to the interior of the site (noise/privacy). This ensures light and air from only one direction (south or west) and reduce the building depth. Interior layout of the units can accommodate different household situations, i.e., loft type living, 1-2-3-bedrooms, live/work, etc. The changes in interior layout would also be reflected in the exterior perception of the units with changing balcony sizes, winter gardens, different window layouts. The flexible elements, windows, doors, and enclosures are made of wood or steel in order to allow later alterations by an owner or a renter. It is especially useful for student housing (Veterinary University) and temporary housing for athletes from a future ice rink. Some of the units might only be equipped with plumbing and electrical hookups to ensure variety of uses and improvement. Access to the units can also be varied to avoid long corridors and shared spaces. Ground floor units have direct access from the site. In addition the Wagramerstrasse building (building A) offers a variety of uses, housing, retail, live/work, offices can all be integrated yet separately accessed if required. Smaller units facing the loud street may be used for more commercial activities.

＜新しい試みについての4つの要点＞

1．戸外へ開く

各ユニットには，意図的にロッジア，バルコニーなどのかなり広い外部要素を付ける。このスペースは，季節ごとに一時的な囲いを設置することで，簡単に利用しやすい空間に転換できる。屋上庭園や1階の庭もまた，各ユニットの居住空間を拡げてくれる。ほとんどのユニットが公共空間に面しているので，広い眺望と豊かな陽光を受けられる。

2．多彩なコモン・スペース

コート，緑地，庭園，子供や大人の遊び場は，変化に富んだセミ・プライヴェート／パブリック空間を提供する。隣接する敷地同士での内部での接続部（コープ・ヒンメルブラウ設計の建物とのロビー，コアの共有），外部での接続部（ソーキン設計のゲート，連絡通路）はレクリエーション施設や公共施設（幼稚園，学校，ジム，ワーク・プレイス）へのアクセスを提供する。こうした往来のしやすさは，オープン・ウェッブのデザインを補助し，隣接する開発地区やこの地域にもまた，近づきやすい環境をつくりあげる。

3．都市的な調整

ヴァグラマー大通りは都市の構成要素として最も目立つ存在である。このため，この道路に沿った新しい開発においては，敷地の内側に空き地をとれるような，高度で，多機能的で，都市的にも変化に富んだ空間構成をつくりあげる，変転していくような方法に従う。この開かれたジェスチュアは，このプロジェクトそして他の開発地区全体を通してのプライヴェートとセミ・プライヴェート間のつながりという問題に対し，明快な輪郭をもち，小さな面に分かれた方法，つまり周縁ブロックという19世紀的な境界の付け方に対する有効な挑戦である。敷地の内側に向かうに従って，プライヴェートな性格は増していき，建物のスケールは小さくなっていく。パブリック・スペース（広場，遊び場など）とアウトドア・スペースは一体となって，ソフト，ハードの両面で大きな公共空間をつくりだす。北側（コープ・ヒンメルブラウ担当の敷地）に対しての接続部は他より徹底している。パーキング，エントリー，廊下を共有でき，大規模な団地の陥りがちな単調さを和らげ，非集合住宅的なハウジングをつくることができよう。新しい商業地区開発は人に対するサーヴィス産業に，さらに新しい仕事をもたらすかもしれない。南側（ソーキン担当の敷地）に対しては，湾曲する高層棟と分節された建物端部の間がゲートのように構成され，そこから両方の敷地や建物に入ることができる。さらに，ヴァグラマー大通りの建物には生活／仕事，小売店，オフィス，サーヴィスなどさまざまな機能が入った複合的な性格をもっているため，敷地内に既に設置されている，交通機関，アクセス，地区センターへの接続や近隣周辺の都市空間の備えている，活気があり，多彩な活動を保持することになる。

4．柔軟な住空間

増加し続けるハウジングの建設費に抗戦し，変化し続けるハウジング人口統計の必要とするものに取り組むために，固定的な構造システムのなかに，フレキシブルなハウジング・ユニットを設置する。ユニットは大半がメゾネット・タイプのデュプレックスで，敷地の内側に向いている。（騒音／プライヴァシー）。これによって，光や空気は片側（南または西）からのみ流入し，建物の奥行きも浅くなる。ユニット・プランは居住者の条件によって変えることができる――ロフト・タイプ，1-3寝室タイプ，職住併設タイプ等など。室内のレイアウトの変化は，バルコニーの大小，ウィンター・ガーデン，窓割の違いなど，外部にも反映されている。窓，ドア，被膜などフレキシブルな要素は，オーナーや借り手によって後から変更できるように，木あるいはスティール造である。これは，学生用ハウジング（獣医学校）と将来のアイスリンクとなる，運動選手のための一時的なハウジングに対しては特に有効である。ユニットのいくつかは，多様な使い方や器具の進歩に対応できるように，配管配線のみが設備されることになろう。長い廊下や共有空間を避けるために，各ユニットへのアクセスも多様なものとした。1階にあるユニットには地面から直接アクセスする。さらにヴァグラマー大通りの建物（A棟）はハウジング，店舗，住居兼仕事場，オフィスなど多様な用途に対応でき，全体がまとまっているが，必要に応じて別なアクセスを設定できる。騒音の激しい通りに沿った小さなユニットは，商業的な活動の場として使われることになろう。

Architects: Mack Architects—Mark Mack, principal; Frances Moore, Tim Sakamoto, Gloria Lee, Peter Ebner, Arden Young

Overall view

Building E

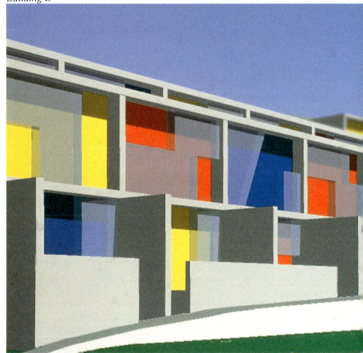

Southwest view

Site plan and section

Bird's eye view

Building A and building C

ENRIC MIRALLES

SEASIDE RESORT IN SARDINIA
Buggerru, Sardinia, Italy
Design: 1994

This beautiful part of the west coast of Sardinia was used for mining until some years ago, when the city decided to transform the land into a tourist resort. The interventions we are presenting are fragments of a bigger urbanization scheme planned by the city of Buggerru. It is a group of six small villas and a residence with thirty small living units, unified by a commercial center (which we will not present in this issue).

Group of six small villas
A group of six villas is imposed on the steep land as a stairway, where the perimetral walls divide one property from the other and retain the earth. We designed these horizontal walls to be as long as we could. The villas insert themselves in this pentagram of walls developing in the longitudinal sense and creating a series of courtyards, rooms and skylights compressed in a line. The villas move their position each one in respect to the next, allowing beautiful views of the sea from every villa. The vaults and the retaining walls are the most important constructed elements. The group of the vaulted villas creates a new topography on this virgin land. Each villa measures about 90 square meters and can hold up to seven people.

Residence
This is a center created by 30 small living units. Each unit is elevated from the land, which we can imagine as a small floating house: ...floating bed, floating sofa, floating chimney, floating bathroom and floating windows... The units are connected by an elevated corridor and are protected externally by a wooden vault. This group of living units creates a new topography, leaving the existing one as it is. This building tries to be as respectful as possible to this astonishingly beautiful virgin land.

Retaining walls
All these projects are done using a special kind of concrete retaining walls. The form of the retaining wall is with "vaults" in plan, so that the elevation looks like a fragment of a classical column. We think that these walls are good to build a new landscape in the landscape.

Architects: Enric Miralles, Benedetta Tagliabue; Josep Miàs, Victoria Garriga, Mary Rose Greene, Sybille Maurer, collaborators; Ottmar Dodel, Hans Buchlmann, Henning Jordens, models

Site plan: six villas and residence with 30 small living units

サルデーニャ島西海岸のこの景勝地は、数年前にここをツーリスト・リゾートに変身させることに市が決定するまでは鉱山町であった。われわれが提案した案は、ブッジェッル市によって計画された広大な都市化案のなかの断片を形成するものである。6つの小さなヴィラ、30の小さなリヴィング・ユニットからなる住宅グループを商業センター（ここでは紹介していない）でまとめようというものである。

＜6つの小さなヴィラからなるグループ＞
6つの小さなヴィラは急斜面に段をつくりながら並び、それぞれの周回壁がお互いの敷地を分け、擁壁ともなる。これらの水平の壁はできる限り長くなるようにデザインした。ヴィラはこの壁のつくる、長軸に沿って展開し、1本の線のなかに圧縮されたコートヤード、部屋、スカイライトの連なりをつくりだす星形五角形のなかにはめこまれている。各ヴィラは隣にくるヴィラに配慮して位置をずらしているので、どのヴィラからも美しい海が見える。ヴォールトと擁壁は最も重要な要素である。ヴォールト屋根のヴィラはこのまだ手の付けられていない土地に、新たな地形をつくりあげる。各ヴィラは約90平米で、7人を収容できる。

＜レジデンス＞
30の小さなリヴィング・ユニットで構成される。各ユニットは地上から持ち上げられている。小さな浮かんでいる家を想像してほしい……浮かんでいるベッド、浮かんでいるソファ、浮かんでいる煙突、浮かんでいる風呂、浮かんでいる窓……。各ユニットは持ち上げられている廊下で結ばれ、木のヴォールトに包まれている。これらのリヴィング・ユニットの集合は、既存の土地をそのまま残したまま、新たな地形をつくりあげる。これらの建物は、この美しい未開の土地を可能な限り尊重しようとしている。

＜擁壁＞
これらのプロジェクトでは、特殊なコンクリート造の擁壁を使っている。擁壁の形は、平面が＜ヴォールト＞状であるため、立面は古典的なコラムのように見える。こうした壁は、風景のなかに新しい風景を構築するのに適切なものだと思う。

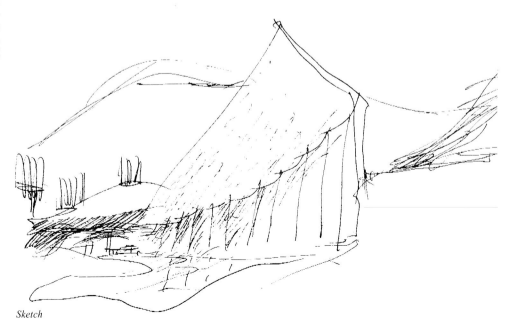

Sketch

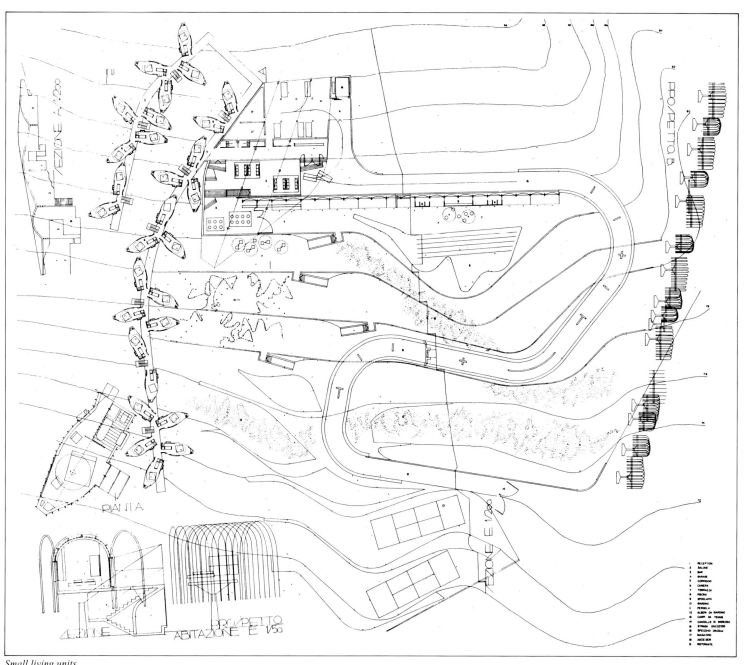

Small living units

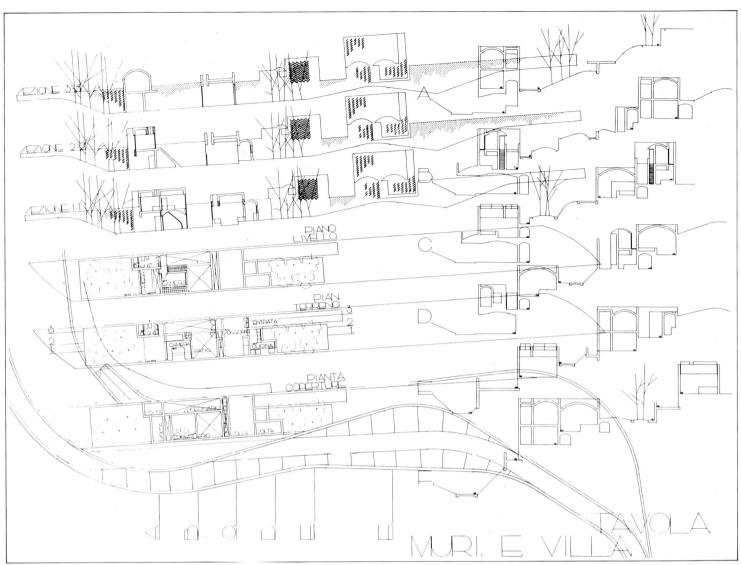

Villas

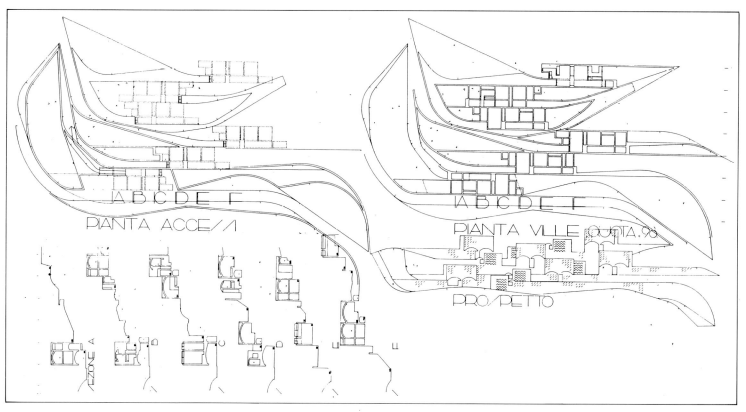

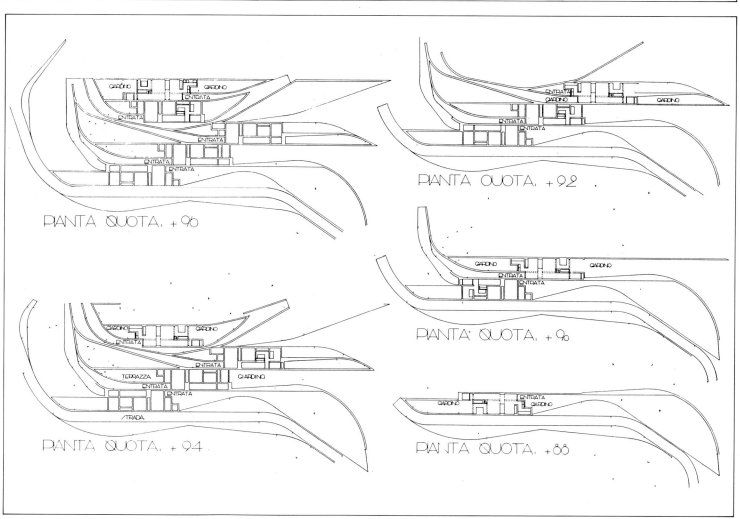

ERIC OWEN MOSS

VIENNA HOUSING
Vienna, Austria
Design: 1995

The project proposes a total of 70 housing units in two buildings on two sites. Building 1 on the corner of Wagramerstrasse and Doningasse has the greatest public visibility. Building 2, just off the corner of Anton-Sattler Gasse and Doningasse is also a prominent site because of its corner adjacency.

The project begins with a strategy that associates the architect's concept of Chinese calligraphy with the design of the two Vienna housing blocks. The architectural calligraphy correlates a conceptual-pictorial language with an invented form-language for the design of the buildings. Just as the combining of calligraphy symbols results in pictographic written concepts, the combining of the building "calligs" coalesce in a sequence of concept/forms that organize the design of the project.

The architectural calligraphy choreographs the buildings, the individual units, and the inter-relationship of one site with another. The first "callig" is the SANDPIPER, a bird that inhabits the transitory seashore zone between water and land. The Sandpiper callig is an analogue for the shifting design concepts that govern the project. The Sandpiper image crosses both sites in a pattern called the RICOCHET, the second callig, a strategy of lines that influences the organization and design of both vertical volumes and horizontal surfaces.

Additional calligs are as follows:

MOVE a curving, horizontal line that rises and falls in section connecting critical destination points on all sites.

HORTICULTURE, a theoretical enclosure that protects the existing trees on the first site, and contributes to the organization of the interior courtyard/gardens on both sites.

HOW HIGH a concept for a theoretical roof that would cover the entire site; the roof form is premised on, but not identical to, the height limits for the property as given by Vienna zoning regulations.

IDIO-DESCARTES, an order of points following the Move curve and the two site center lines, that assists in the determination of the position of columns, beams, and walls in both buildings.

ANOTHER BRICK IN THE WALL is the mechanism for positioning units in section and elevation in each building block. The units are conceived as adjoining, irregular bricks in a wall, the building as the wall itself.

BUBBLEGUM is an analogue image representing the joining of disparate pieces of building by "sticking" them together.

BUILDING 1 on the Wagramerstrasse has two apartment blocks or wings, one on Wagramerstrasse containing 14 units, one on Doningasse containing 23 units. A subway stop is anticipated below this site, so direct pedestrian access to the subway is provided. The Doningasse wing at both ground floor and subway levels offers 840 square meters to be leased as retail, office, or restaurant space.

The central portion of the Building 1 site area is a partially covered, private garden/courtyard. An open stair and elevator enclose the west edge of the court, and connect the courtyard with housing units above, or retail and subway below. The stair itself has large landings that double as observation platforms. So it is possible to climb to the top of the stair or to stop on intermediate levels to view the city beyond or the courtyard garden below.

Access to individual housing units is up from the courtyard by stair or elevator and across bridges. All units have both city and courtyard views. Units in Building 1 vary in size and accommodate a variety of living arrangements. Corner units are stacked at regular floor levels. However, there are no continuous floor planes in the central portion of the elevation of each of the two building blocks. These units (the majority of the project) are to be built with each unit at a different floor elevation. Stairs and bridges accommodate the changes in floor levels. So the conventional order of housing units on regular floor planes is supplemented with a free sectional organization.

A triangular portion of the site bordering Wagramerstrasse and Doningasse remains unexcavated in anticipation of the future subway stop. West of this triangle is a spherically excavated garden and children's play area surrounded by the rising, curving walk. The garden connects by stair to the courtyard above. The sphere garden also has direct entry to the subway and to retail space at the subway level.

The first floor of the Wagramerstrasse block contains a theater space with seating for 220 people. The space can be used as a conventional cinema or could accommodate meetings and discussions. The cinema space has its own stair and elevator with public access from the Wagramerstrasse.

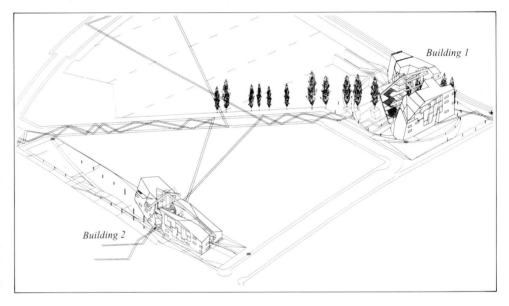

プロジェクトは，2つの敷地に2棟の建物，総計70戸のハウジング・ユニットを提案している。ヴァグラマー大通りとドニン小路の交差する角地にあるビルディング1は町中から非常によく見える。アントン=ザットラー小路とドニン小路の角から少し離れたビルディング2もまた，角地に近いことからよく目立つ敷地である。

書についてのコンセプトを，ウィーンに計画されたこの2つのハウジング・ブロックのデザインに結びつけるというストラテジーから設計を始めた。建築の〈書法〉は，概念的な象形文字と，この建物のデザインのために創造された形態言語とを相関させる。漢字を組み合わせるように，絵文字で書かれたコンセプトに帰結し，建物の〈書法〉の結合は，このプロジェクトのデザインを組み立てるコンセプト／フォームの連なりのなかに合体する。

建築書法は，建物，個別のユニット，一つの敷地ともう一つの敷地との相互関係を振り付ける。一番目の〈書法〉は，水辺と陸の間，浜辺という転換的なゾーンに住む鳥，サンドパイパーである。

サンドパイパー書法はこのプロジェクトを支配するシフトするデザイン・コンセプトの類似物である。サンドパイパーのイメージは〈跳飛〉と呼ばれる模様を描いて両方の敷地を横断している。〈跳飛〉は2番目の書法で，垂直方向のヴォリューム，水平に延びる面の双方のデザインと構成に影響する線のストラテジーである。

この他の書法は以下の通り。

〈動き〉すべての敷地の最も重要な目標地点を結んで，上昇し降りて行く，弧を描き，水平を描く線。

〈園芸〉一番目の敷地の既存樹木を保護する理論上の囲みで，両方の敷地において内部にある中庭や庭園を組み立てるのに貢献する。

〈ハウ・ハイ〉敷地全体を覆うことになる理論上の屋根のためのコンセプト。屋根の形は，ウィーンのゾーニング法がこの敷地に規定している高さ制限を前提としているが，全面的にではない。

〈イディオ=デカルト〉動きの曲線と敷地の2本のセンター・ラインに従ったポイントの配置規則。これは，両方の建物の柱，梁，壁の位置を決定する助けとなる。

〈壁のなかの別の煉瓦〉両ブロックにおいて，断面立面上におけるユニット配置のためのメカニズム。ユニットは壁のなかの隣合う，不規則な煉瓦と見なす。壁そのものである建物。

<ビルディング1>ヴァグラマー大通りに面しては2つのアパート・ブロックあるいはウィングがある。一つはヴァグラマー大通りに面し，14戸から成り，一つはドニン小路に面し，23戸から成る。地下鉄駅がこの敷地の下に予定されているので，地下鉄への直接のアクセスを設置する。ドニン小路に面するウィングは1階と地下鉄レヴェルで，計840sq.m.が店舗，オフィス，レストランなどに賃貸される。

ビルディング1の敷地の中央部分は部分的に屋根の付いたプライヴェートな庭／コートヤードとなる。オープンな階段とエレヴェータがコートヤードの西端を囲み，上のハウジングや下の店舗や地下鉄と連絡する。階段には広々とした踊り場があり，展望台の役割も果たす。つまり，階段の上まで昇っても，途中で止まっても，市街や下のコートヤードを見晴らすことができる。

個々のハウジング・ユニットへはコートヤードから階段，エレヴェータ，ブリッジから行ける。各戸からは市街と中庭が見える。ビルディング1のユニットはさまざまな大きさがあり，室内の配置も変えられる。角に位置するユニットは規則的な階高のところで積み重ねられている。とはいえ，2つの棟とも，その立面の中央部分では連続する床面は存在しない。これらのユニット（このプロジェクトの大半であるわけだが）はそれぞれ異なった床高をもつように建設されるだろう。階段とブリッジが床高の変化に対応する。つまり，規則的な床高をもつハウジング・ユニットの慣習的な秩序は，自由な断面構成によって捕足される。

ヴァグラマー大通りとドニン小路を縁取る敷地の三角形の部分は将来の地下鉄駅を想定して根切りせずに残しておく。この三角形の西側は，球形に掘り込まれた庭園と子供の遊び場で，高くなった，カーヴする散歩道に囲まれている。この庭と上のコートヤードを階段が結んでいる。球形の庭には地下鉄と地下鉄階にある店舗への直接の入り口が付く。

ヴァグラマー大通り側の棟の2階には220席の劇場がある。ここは映画の上映にも，集会にも使える。映写場にはヴァグラマー大通りから専用の階段またはエレヴェータで入れる。

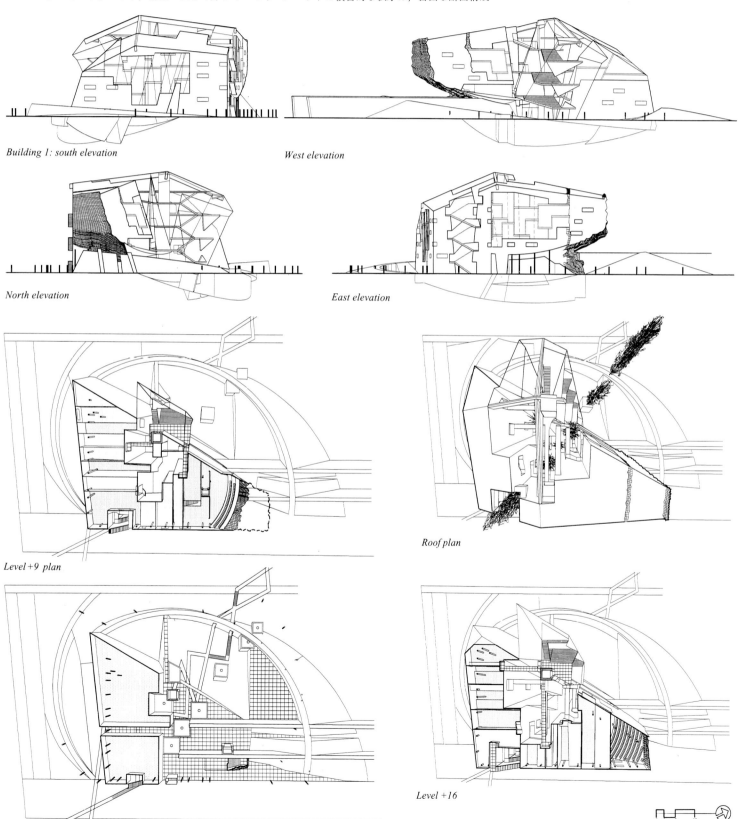

Building 1: south elevation

West elevation

North elevation

East elevation

Level +9 plan

Roof plan

Level +0

Level +16

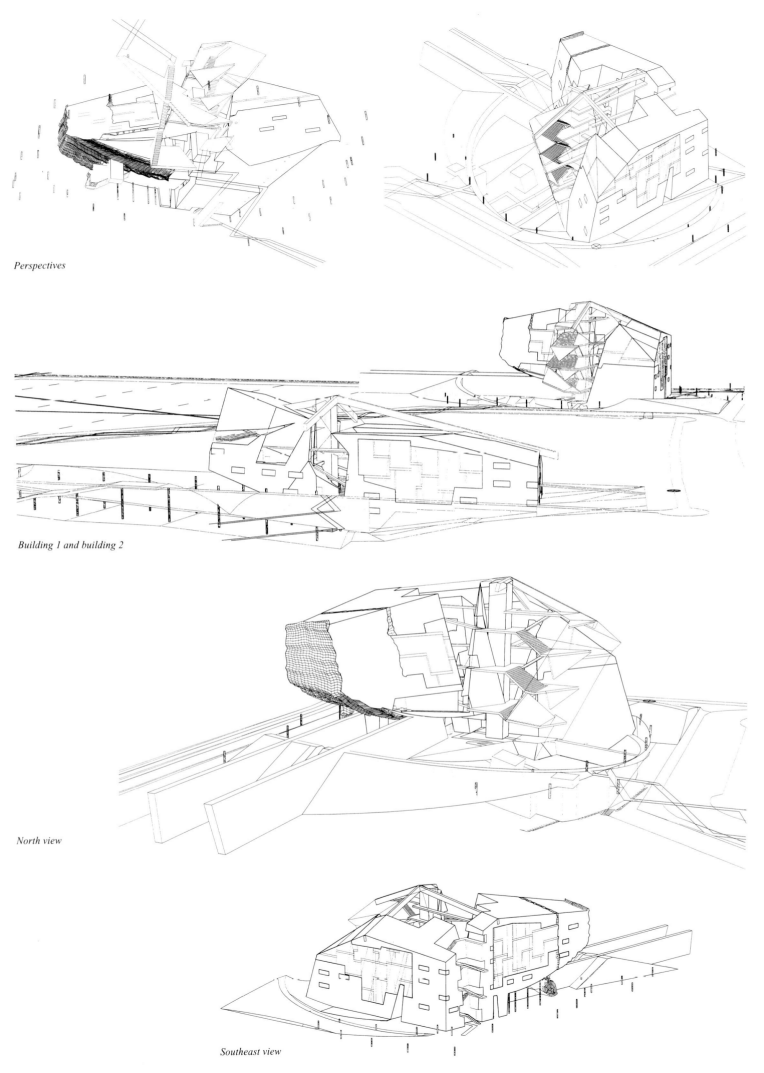

Perspectives

Building 1 and building 2

North view

Southeast view

BUILDING 2, just off the corner of Anton-Sattler Gasse and Doningasse, is to be constructed over a basement level garage. The building holds 33 units with a range of sizes and types.

Access to the units is through a central stairwell and elevator core which leads directly to walks, bridges and units. As in Building 1, corner units are stacked at regular floor heights. Other units are organized freely, each individual unit on its own floor level.

The central vertical circulation connects to the garage, and adjacent streets. An interior landscape courtyard, the roof of the garage, steps down gradually toward the north, dividing the units into three groups: the block which terminates the courtyard at the north end and contains 8 units; the block on the west side of the court with 11 units; third, the block with 14 units which forms the east perimeter of the courtyard. From the south end of the courtyard a pedestrian walk extends, facilitating pedestrian circulation to the park on the south side of the Doningasse. The parking garage is accessible from Doningasse.

On the top floor of the north block a multipurpose public gathering space seating 80 people is proposed. This space can be used for public meetings or classes or children's day care. An exterior space, partially covered, protected children's play, is to be built outside under the raised north block.

The proposed apartment blocks will provide all of the essential housing amenities in investigatory design framework. So the housing will offer both typical and atypical living conditions. Like the multiple environments of the Sandpiper, those who live here will inhabit convention and unconvention simultaneously.

＜ビルディング２＞はアントン-ザットラー小路とドニン小路の交差する角から少し離れ，地下駐車場の上に建設される。一連の大きさとタイプから成る33戸で構成されている。

ユニットへのアクセスは，歩行者路，ブリッジ，ユニットへ直接通じている中央階段室とエレヴェータ・コアからである。ビルディング１と同じように，角にくるユニットは規則的なレヴェルのところで積層されている。他のユニットは自由に構成され，各ユニットは独自の床高をもっている。

中央の上下動線はガレージと隣接する通りへつながれている。内部にある修景された中庭つまりガレージの屋根は北にゆるやかに段になって降りて行き，このユニットを３つのグループに分割する。中庭の終点にある北端の８戸；中庭の西側の11戸；そして中庭の東側を囲む14戸。中庭の南端から歩行者路が延び，ドニン小路の南側にある公園へ簡単に出られる。駐車場へはドニン小路から入れる。

北側のブロックの最上階には80席の多目的な集会室を提案した。ここは公共的な集会や，教室，保育所などに使える。子供たちの遊べる，部分的に屋根の付いた戸外スペースが，北側の高く持ち上げられたブロックの下につくられる。

ここに提案したアパートメント・ブロックは，学校のようなデザインの枠組みのなかに，ハウジングの必要とする基本的なアメニティをすべて提供するだろう。このハウジングは，典型的な，そして非典型的な居住条件をどちらも提供するだろう。サンドパイパーの住む多面的な環境のように，ここに住む人は，古い習慣のなかに，新しい住み方のなかに，同時に生活することになるだろう。

Model photo: H. Ueda

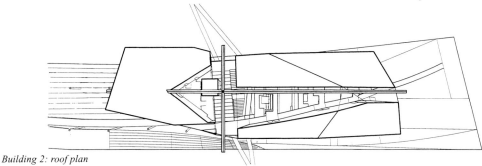

Building 2: roof plan

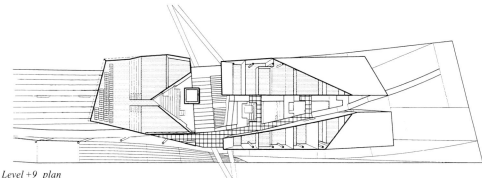

Level +9 plan

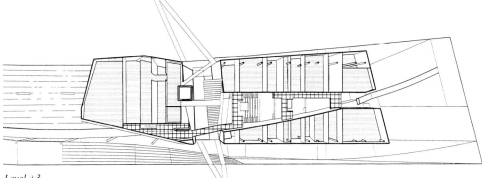

Level +3

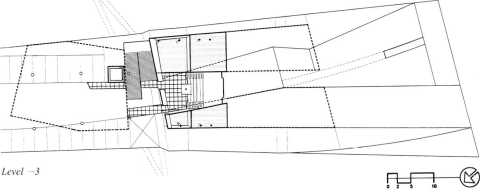

Level −3

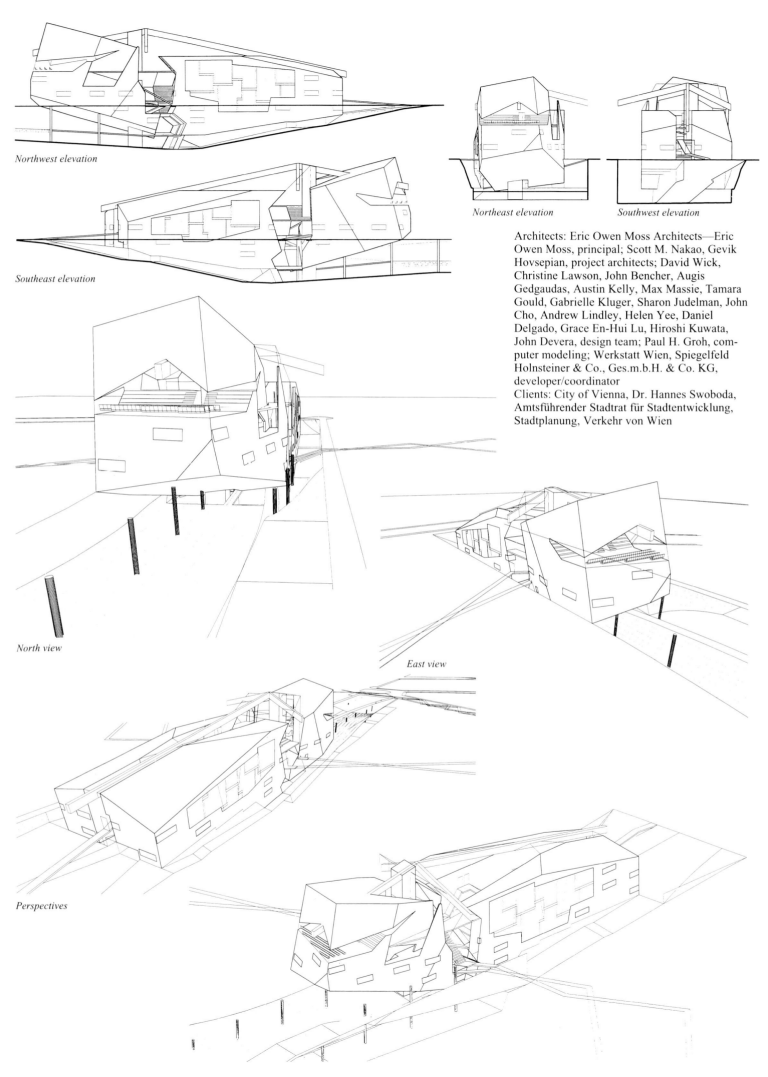

Northwest elevation

Southeast elevation

Northeast elevation

Southwest elevation

North view

East view

Perspectives

Architects: Eric Owen Moss Architects—Eric Owen Moss, principal; Scott M. Nakao, Gevik Hovsepian, project architects; David Wick, Christine Lawson, John Bencher, Augis Gedgaudas, Austin Kelly, Max Massie, Tamara Gould, Gabrielle Kluger, Sharon Judelman, John Cho, Andrew Lindley, Helen Yee, Daniel Delgado, Grace En-Hui Lu, Hiroshi Kuwata, John Devera, design team; Paul H. Groh, computer modeling; Werkstatt Wien, Spiegelfeld Holnsteiner & Co., Ges.m.b.H. & Co. KG, developer/coordinator
Clients: City of Vienna, Dr. Hannes Swoboda, Amtsführender Stadtrat für Stadtentwicklung, Stadtplanung, Verkehr von Wien

ERIC OWEN MOSS

GASOMETER D-1
Vienna, Austria
Design: 1995

In district 11, five minutes on the autobahn from the airport in Vienna are four cylindrical Gasometers, each 60 meters in diameter and 65 meters high. The Gasometers, constructed in 1896, are neoclassical masonry facades designed to surround cylindrical steel containers of natural gas which was piped into the city. The gas has long been abandoned, the steel liners are gone, and the tanks are used sporadically for exhibits and rock concerts. No permanent solution for their re-use has been offered untill now.

Because of their longevity and neoclassic design, the Gasometers are protected monuments in Vienna. Any design proposal for re-use must retain the exterior structure intact and untouched. It will be possible, however, to remove portions of the roof—a wood and steel dome—so long as the original dome profile remains unaltered.

The masonry walls have a regular rythm of windows and doors and these apertures must be retained and used as sources for natural light, air, and view. No other openings may be cut in the masonry, though added natural light may be introduced through new openings in the roof dome.

Four architects were selected, one for each of the Gasometers, to develop designs for re-use. The primary program element is social housing. Building ownership and design and construction

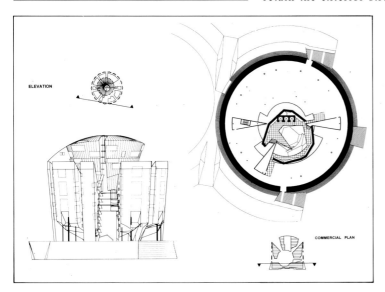

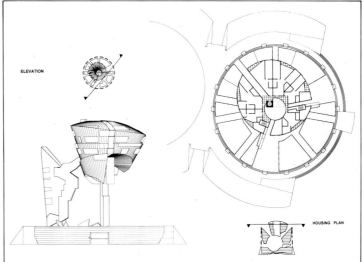

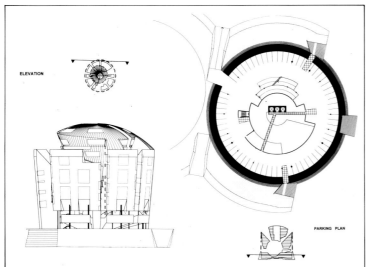

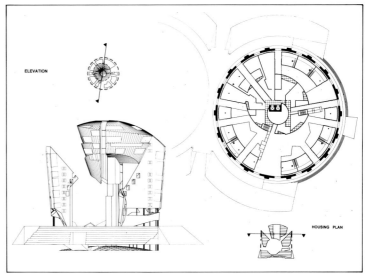

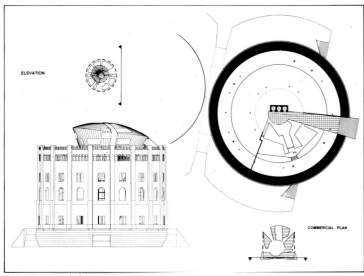

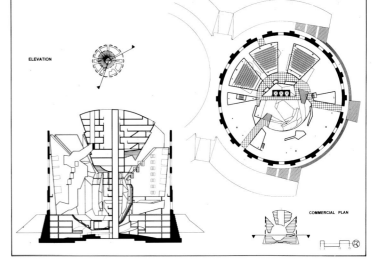

Floor plans and elevations

costs are shared between private developers and the City of Vienna.

The program for this Gasometer—D-1— is 15,000 square meters of social housing, with units averaging 100 square meters. In addition there will be 5000 square meters of retail shops and small offices, along with public gathering space, a circulation lobby, and three cinemas. Parking for 200 cars is required.

The design problem is to position multiple social housing structures within the Gasometer, without altering the exterior of the original cylinder and without relying on the existing masonry wall for support. In addition, the Vienna lighting code for housing mandates the angle and duration for the penetration of natural light into every useable living space, bathrooms and stairs excluded.

The project is a complicated puzzle: how to

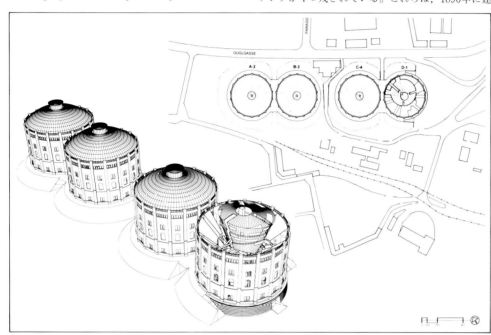

fill the cylindrical void with housing without touching the original shell, while conforming to the requirements of the lighting code?

Conceptually the design solution fills the Gasometer D-1 with three space-making components. The first is a Pentasphere, an analogue-sphere made of five-sided pieces of varying sizes, which creates an enormous interior volume for public circulation and gathering. The interior space is essential so that natural light can pass through the old perimeter windows and new roof holes to light the second component—the Wedges. The Wedges'shape —almost triangular in plan—is a consequence of light entry through the perimeter wall. Wedges are formed by the plan interval between the exterior windows. Where the light is, the Wedge isn't. The Wedge walls are located by drawing radial lines from the window edges through the plan center of the circle (cylinder).

The final component is the Gyro, an inverted cone with the (original) domed roof profile (on top), deformed to allow light to enter through the roof, between Gyro and Wedges, lighting the perimeter walls of the Gyro and the radial sides and tops of the wedges below.

The Pentasphere form hollows out a portion of the Gasometer's base, the walls of the Wedges, and the underside of the Gyro to form the interior volume which opens the interior uses to natural light.

The gasometers were originally placed on an earth berm, raised nine meters above the existing grade. Retail and cinemas are located on the main entry level, accessible from an exterior pedestrian walk at nine meters, that will serve all four tanks. Below that, from 0-6 meters, are two levels of parking enclosed within the original foundation walls of the cylinder. Wedges, and Giro above hold the social housing.

The project for Gasometer D-1 represents an absolutely unique opportunity to combine a dated but pedigreed piece of Vienna's built history with a revised and progressive new use— social housing. The Gasometer is intriguing both because of the intricate design criteria to which it must conform, and the intricate politics it will have to circumnavigate in order to succeed.

ウィーンの空港からアウトバーンで5分の所に位置する11区に、直径60m、高さ65mの円筒形をしたガスタンクが4つ残されている。これらは、1896年に建設され、市内に供給する天然ガスを貯蔵していたスティール製の容器を新古典様式の煉瓦造のファサードが取り巻いている。天然ガスの利用は長いあいだ放棄されたままで、容器も取り外され、タンクは散発的に展覧会やロックコンサートに使われてきた。現在まで、恒久的な再利用のための提案はされてこなかった。

長い歴史をもち、新古典様式のデザインであるため、ウィーンのモニュメントとして保護されている。再利用のためのいかなる提案も、外側の構造体はそのまま保全しなければならない。しかし、元の輪郭が変わることなく残っている、木とスティールでつくられた屋根のドームの一部は、取り除くことが許されている。

煉瓦壁には規則的なリズムを刻んで窓やドアがあいており、これらの開口は保存し、自然光や空気、眺望の取り入れ口として使わねばならない。煉瓦壁には新たに開口をとれないが、ドーム屋根に新しく開口をつけて、そこから自然光を導くことができるだろう。

4人の建築家が選ばれ、各自一つのタンクを担当して再利用のデザインを提示することになった。最優先のプログラムは公共集合住宅である。建物の所有権と設計及び工事費は民間業者とウィーン市間で折半される。

ガスタンクD-1に対しては、平均100sq.mのユニットで構成される、全体で15,000sq.mの公共集合住宅。加えて、公共の集会スペース、動線ロビー、シネマ（3）、店舗、小オフィスなどに5,000sq.m、200台分の駐車場が要求されている。

設計上の問題点は、元の円筒形の外被を変更せず、かつ煉瓦壁を耐力壁として頼らずに、多層のハウジングを設置すること。さらにウィーン市のハウジングに対する採光規定では、浴室、階段を除いたすべての居室に、自然光が浸透する角度と時間の長さを制定している。

このプロジェクトは複雑なパズルのようなものである。どのようにオリジナルの殻に触れずに、その円筒形のヴォイドのなかに、採光規定を満たしたハウジングを設置したらよいか。

コンセプトとしては、このデザイン解は、ガスタンクD１を３つのスペース・メイキングのための構成要素で充填するものだ。一つ目は、＜五角球＞—それぞれ大きさの違う５つの断片からなる球の類似物で、公共動線と集いのための巨大な空間をつくりだす。内部空間は本質的な性格をもち、自然光は周囲を囲むオリジナルの煉瓦壁の窓から差し込み、屋根に新たに開けられた穴から二番目の構成要素である＜楔＞に浸透する。ほぼ三角形平面をもつ＜楔＞の形は、周縁の壁を通ってくる光の参入の結果である。＜楔＞は外側の窓と窓の間に生まれる平面形から形成されている。つまり光が入るところには、＜楔＞は存在しない。＜楔＞の壁は窓の縁から円（円筒）の平面上の中心に引かれた放射状の線によって位置づけられる。

３つ目の構成要素は＜ジャイロ＞である。これは（もとの）ドーム屋根の輪郭が（上に）付いた逆円錐で、屋根から、ジャイロと＜楔＞の間に光が入るように変形され、ジャイロの周回壁、放射状の側、下の＜楔＞の上に光があたる。

＜五角球＞の形は、ガスタンクの底、＜楔＞の壁、＜ジャイロ＞の下側の一部を掘り抜き、内部で自然光が利用できるように開かれるインテリア・ヴォリュームを形成する。

ガスタンクはもともとは、地盤面より９m高くなった盛り土の上に設置されていた。店舗とシネマは、4つのタンクを結ぶ、9mの高さの屋外歩行通路から入れるメイン・エントリー・レベルに配置する。その下、0から6mまでは、元の円筒形の基礎を構成している壁に包まれた2層の駐車場である。その上に位置する＜楔＞と＜ジャイロ＞はハウジングとなる。

これは、時代遅れではあるが、ウィーンの建築史上、由緒正しい構築物を、公共集合住宅という進歩的な用途へと改訂しようという、非常に希な機会を提供してくれるプロジェクトである。それが従わねばならない複雑な設計基準、そしてそれを成就させるために周航しなければならないであろう複雑な政治的条件ゆえに、非常に興味を引かれる計画である。

Architects: Eric Owen Moss Architects—Eric Owen Moss, principal; Scott Nakao, Gevik Hovsepian, project associates; Paul Groh, Christine Lawson, Augis Gedgaudas, Austin Kelly, John Bencher, Scott Hunter, Joseph H. Tiu, Sharon Judelman, Sally Riggs, Hao Ko, Tae Kim, Phillipe Marmillod, Juan Garcia, Curt Simmons, David Wick, project team

Model photos

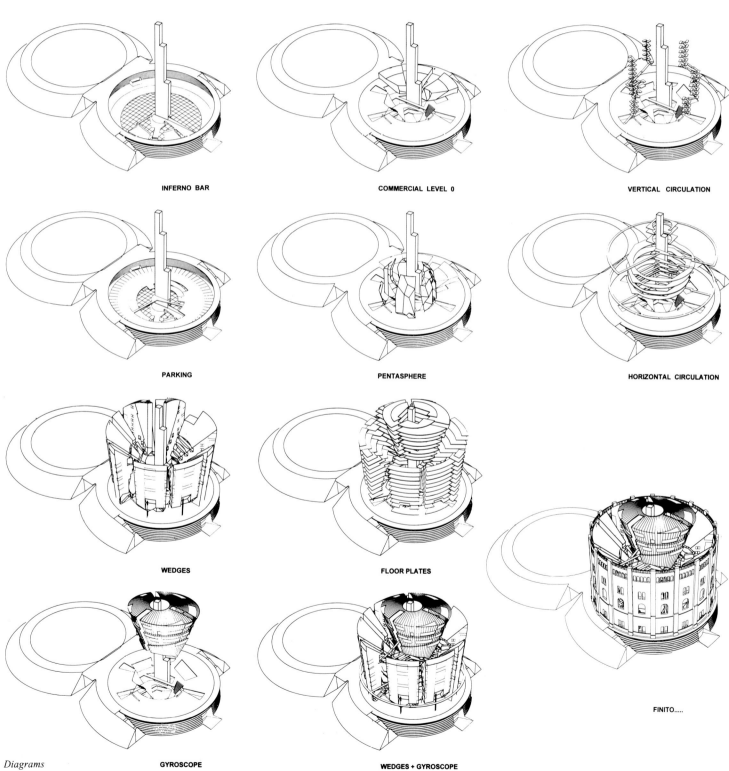

Diagrams

PAUHOF

NEW URBAN COMPLEX
Linz, Austria
Design: 1991–92
Construction: 1996–

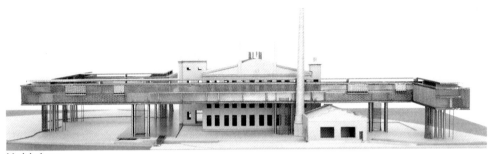

Model photos

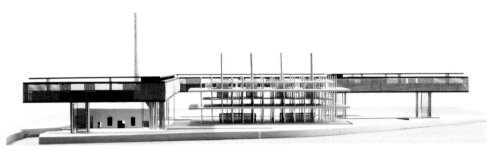

After the construction of the new residential district, the site of the textile factory will be the last green "island" occupied by a historical building; the only place remaining in the area with its own historical identity. This import consideration, affecting the whole of the Auwiesen residential district, was the departure point for our reflections concerning the design and location of the new housing block which, resting on a series of double pilotis, leaves the existing green zone practically intact. At the same time, it deliberately avoids the traditional urban subdivision into street, square and block. The decisive characteristic of the project is the design of a new structure that forms a synthesis with the historical context and becomes incorporated into a unitary group, while at the same time standing apart in order to create potential visual relationships with the site itself.

1. In the project both the present exterior image (the skin) and the structural system (the skeleton) of the old factory are maintained without modifications. The hollows cut into the floor-ceiling structures serve to light the offices crosswise, as ducts for the installations and as supports for the platforms necessary for the new closing wall. Thus great flexibility is obtained for the distribution of office space. On the first and second floors, next to the new lighting hollows, perimetric galleries are constructed suspended from the existing floorceiling structures.

2. The ground floor of the former textile factory should be set aside for communal amenities, thus providing justification for the central position of the building within the complex. The office area is extended along the northern facade on the same level as the sanitary blocks, occupying part of the new residential building. This is where the smaller offices will be, the existing

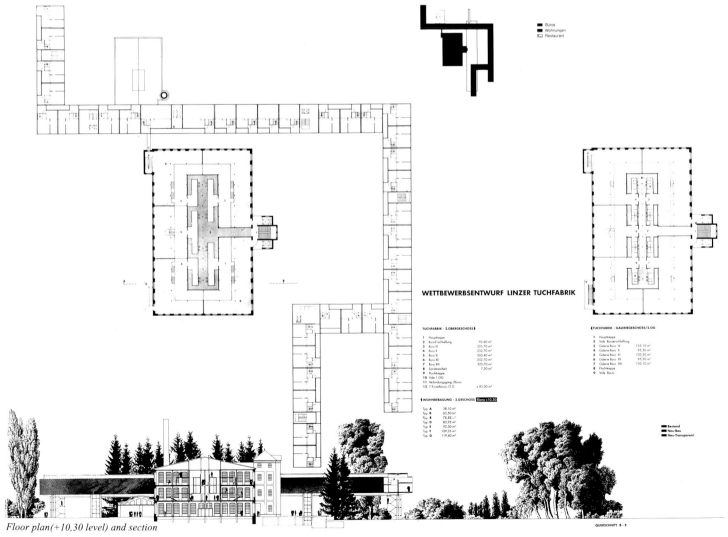

Floor plan (+10,30 level) and section

tower providing a link with the former factory.

3. The new two-story building on pilotis will contain forty-eight flats of seven different kinds which, by maintaining a fixed bay of 3.5 meters, can be combined in any way, whatever the needs of the occupants. The complex formed by a main beam, whose side is the same height as a floor, and a series of aluminum joists suspended perpendicularly from the lengthwise axis of the pillars, constitutes the structural support system for the first floorceiling structure and for the transversal subdivision plates. The transmission of loads to the foundations is carried out by double pillars held in place by steel guys (the pillars are steel tubes filled with concrete).

この新しい住宅地区の建設後は，繊維工場の敷地は歴史をもつ建物の占める，最後の緑の＜島＞――独自の歴史的アイデンティティをもつこの地区に残された唯一の場所――になるだろう。アウヴィーゼン住宅地区全体に影響を及ぼしている，こうした意味を移入しようというわれわれの配慮は，この新しいハウジング・ブロックのデザインと配置――2層の高さをもつピロティの上に乗り，既存の緑地をそのままに残した――を考える上での出発点となった。同時に，道路，広場，ブロックに細分するという伝統的な都市構成も慎重に避けている。このプロジェクトの決め手となる特徴は，歴史的なコンテクストとの総合体をかたちづくり，一つの集合体となるように一体化すると同時に，敷地そのものとの視覚的な関係を保ちつづけるために自立した，新しい構造をもつデザインであることだ。

1. 旧工場の外観（被膜）も構造システム（骨組み）も修正せずに保持する。床と天井には新たに穴を開け，オフィスを十字形に照らす照明装置，設備用ダクト，新しい仕切り壁に必要なプラットフォームの支持体の設置のために活用する。これによってオフィス・スペースはフレキシブルに配置可能となる。2階と3階には，新しく開けた照明用の穴の隣に，既存の床と天井から吊るされた周縁ギャラリーを増設する。

2. もとの繊維工場の1階は地区のアメニティのためにとっておき，この建物のコンプレックス内での中心的位置を正当化する。オフィス・エリアは，新しいハウジングの一部を占める，衛生施設と同じレヴェルに面した北側ファサードに沿って拡張される。ここには小さなオフィスが置かれ，既存のタワーは元の工場との連結部を提供する。

3. ピロティに乗った新しい2層の建物には，7タイプからなる48戸のフラットが入る。3.5mに固定されたベイは，居住者の必要に応じて結合できる。コンプレックスは，メイン・ビームによって構成され，その側面は床と同じ高さをもち，柱の長手軸から直角に吊るされた一連のアルミ製ジョイストが，最初の床天井の構造支持システムと，横方向の分割プレートを組み立てる。基礎へかかる荷重は，張り鋼で地盤に留められた二重柱で受ける（柱はコンクリートを充填した鋼管である）。

Architects: PAUHOF—Michael Hofstätter/Wolfgang Pauzenberger
Client: Maculan Holding AG

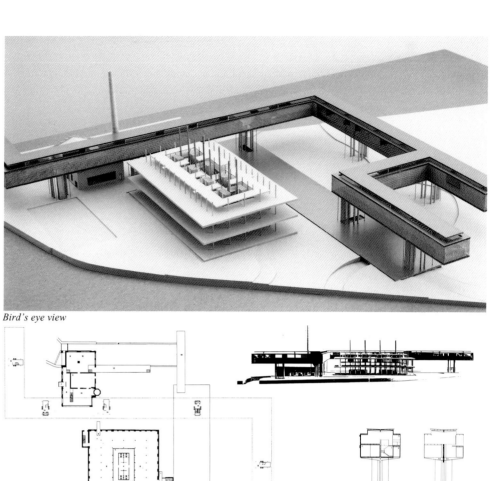
Bird's eye view

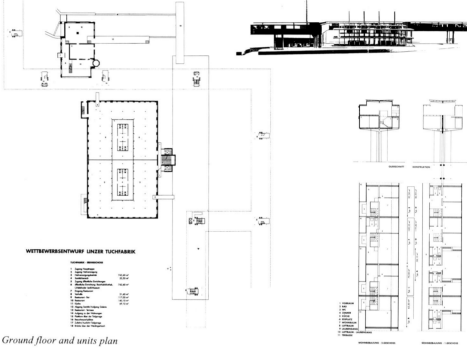
Ground floor and units plan

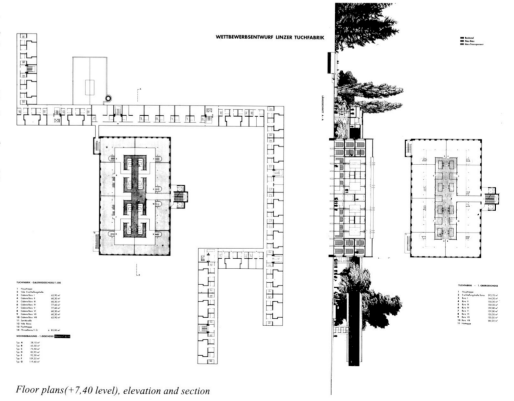
Floor plans (+7,40 level), elevation and section

MICHAEL SORKIN

VIENNA HOUSING
Vienna, Austria
Design: 1995

Our project for the Wagramerstrasse is evolving, in development. The larger site condition, of course, is predicated on a series of revisings meant to address the artificial autonomies of the initial division into property-like strips and to capitalize on the opportunities opened by the work of our collaborators. Our first scheme was built continuous from front to back of the site and struck us as too much of a barrier to the lateral movement both of bodies and space. The second scheme fragmented the project into a space-managing colony of seven buildings of uniform plate and varying heights. Their small-scale plan form was generated from a sense of motility and orientation and by a desire to have pairs of floor-through apartments, each exposed to an open southerly view and to a series of intimate internal visual connections with nearby buildings.

The current version seeks to preserve many aspects of its predecessor while consolidating the apartments into a smaller number of buildings and making the slightly stiff, repetitive feeling of the regular shapes more sinuous. The elaborated forms of the revised project accommodate a larger number of apartments and step down toward the best light in order to provide a greater area of terrace space. Collective use—a cafe, a shop, and a children's center are located in the ground floors of the buildings. As the project progresses and as the surrounding conditions unfold and reconfigure themselves, the three creature can be expected to flex and wiggle into positions which optimize views, solar exposure, neighborliness, circulation, and a more general sense of urban ensemble. We are working at the moment on the possibility of placing greenhouses on the roofs of the buildings to provide both year round gardening and solar collection for heating.

ヴァグラマー通りに対するわれわれのプロジェクトは，計画が進展するなかで徐々に発展していっている。敷地全体の状況は，最初の分割のもつ人工的な自律性を個人の所有地に似た細長い土地の断片とすることに取り組んだ，われわれの協力者の仕事によって切り開かれた好機を利用することを意図した一連の修正に基づいている。最初の計画案は，敷地の前面から背面へと連続しており，躯体と空間の両面において，側面の動きをあまりに妨げているように感じていた。2番目の計画案は，全体を一様なプレートに，高さを変えた7つの棟からなる空間を上手に操作したコロニーへと断片化したものである。これら小スケールの形態は，運動や方向感覚を考え，南面に開き，近くの建物と内部から親密な視覚的つながりをもつ対になった階をアパート全体に設置したいという願望から生まれている。

現在進めている改訂案は，前案の多くを引継ぎながら，ハウジングをいくつもの小さな建物にまとめ，いくぶん硬直し，反復する規則的な形態を，曲がりくねったものにするというものである。多数の住戸を集め，広いテラスをつくりだすために，最適の光を受けられる方向へステップ・ダウンさせていく。カフェ，店舗，子供センターなど，皆の集まる場所は1階にある。この計画が進行して行き，周囲の状況が展開し，再構成されるにつれ，この3つの棟は，眺め，日差し，親しみのある近隣，動線，さらに広い意味での都市的調和をつくっていくだろう。目下，一年中，庭いじりが楽しめ，太陽熱収集装置としても使える温室を，屋上に設置できないかと考えているところである。

Architects: Michael Sorkin Studio—Michael Sorkin, principal; Andrei Vovk, partner; Peter Kormer, Yukiko Yokoo, Rebecca Parker, Celine Condorelli

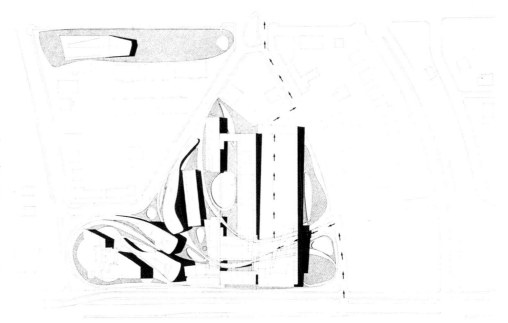

Site plan

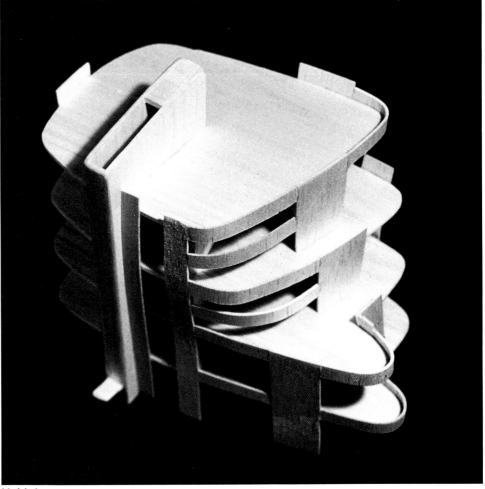

Model photo

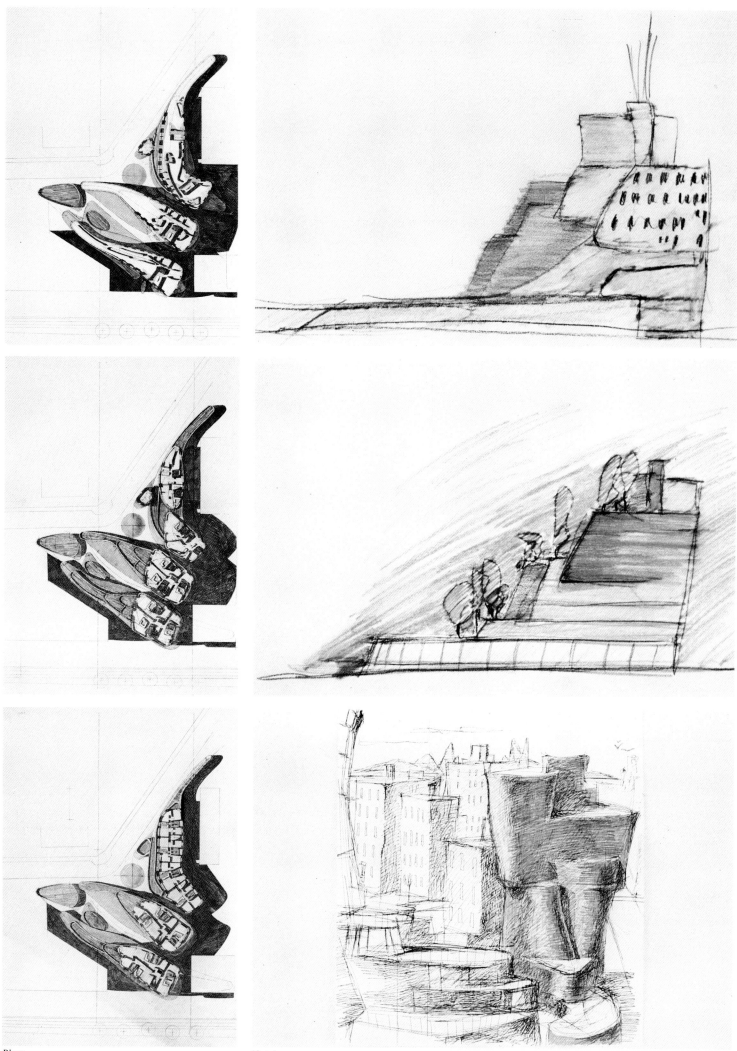

Plans　　　　　　　　　　　Sketches

DAVID ROCK-WOOD

RESIDENTIAL TOWER PROTOTYPE
Multiple locations proposed
Design: 1993–95
Completion: 1998

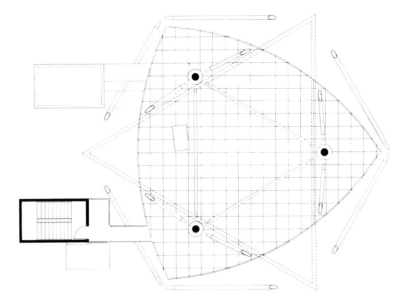
Roof plan

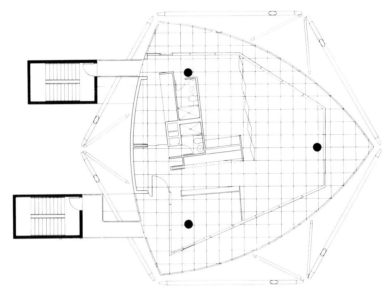
Typical apartment plan

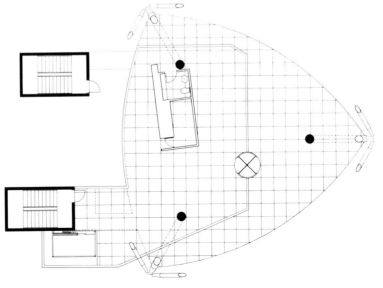
Lobby floor plan

The new city produces subjects which in turn produce the contemporary city. The new subject encounters objects which appear as psychical or physiological affects. The perspectival bias is overlaid by a spatial collapse into 2-D (e.g., the video screen), and spatial expansion into 4-D (e.g., the multiplicity of space/time events). Boundaries are transgressed in simulation, and in speed. Technology has problemitized distinctions of cultural difference, animate/inanimate, and nature/culture. Responding to sensory overload in negotiating a dispersed and complex spatial field, the subject produces active mental space; an irrational-yet-functional cognitive map is drawn, an attempt is made to determine location.

The prototype may be built repeatably on varying sites; it thus criticizes the determining authority of specific sites. Specificity is acknowledged not by *parti* order, but via selections of "optional features." Each prototype retains individuality while respecting its context.

The prototype is affirmative in its creation and proposal of form. Efficiency and rationality are celebrated: the prototype is repeatable, perfectible, economic (design and construction labor), and optimal (structural/material technology, standardization of components). Technique becomes a productive means and an outlet for the creative will. The inhabitant is empowered to literally control the "machine" to effect environmental modes interwoven with fuller life experience. The "sublime uselessness of art" remains to compensate for alienating consumerist agencies enmeshed in productive modes.

The project's affirmative quality critiques the reactive nature of practice; simultaneously, its desassociation from a singular site evokes the idea that "the work of art reproduced becomes the work of art designed for reproducibility." Presently, dialectically-framed distinctions are supplanted by relative and contingent dimensions of authority, intention, ritual, local, and originality. These relative dimensions pose both opportunities and threats to the architect's role, and the conception and perception of the architectural object.

Materiality is not sublimated such to elicit preferred conceptual readings. *Techné* does not fully succeed in wresting natural force from material. Brought to the limits of expensive force, material relinquishes its corporeality—the Gothic stones become ineffable.

Four spatial conceptions are overlaid: a centralized space (a triangle, inscribed in a hexagon, is inscribed in a three-columned *aedicule*); an interference space (massive service elements effect a "gravitational" shift overlaying a virtual, unmarked center upon the Cartesian/Euclidean center); a topological space (an approximate Klein bottle—a space simultaneously inside and outside); a kinetic space (a double-helix spiral traces a spatial unfolding during construction).

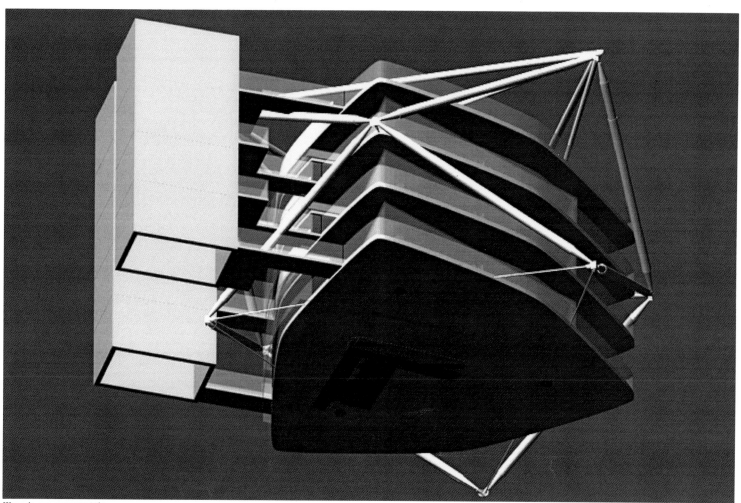
Worm's eye axonometric

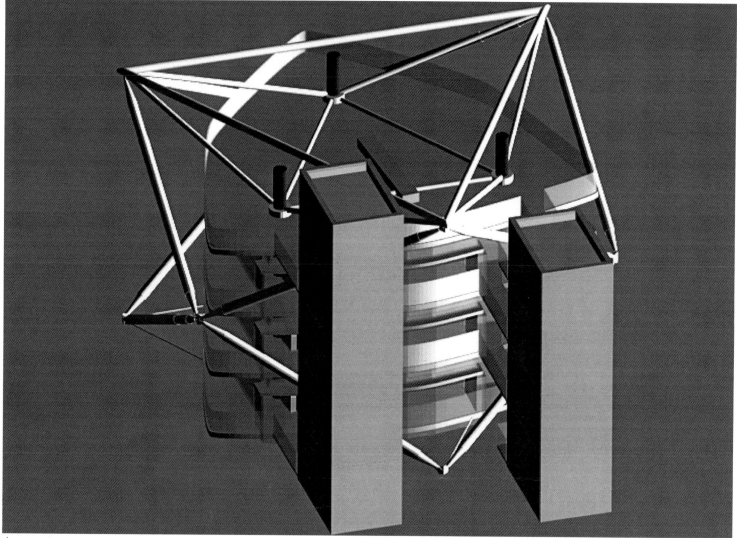
Axonometric

171

工産的な方式にからめとられている情質に走る代理店を遠ざけるための代償として残す。

プロジェクトの肯定的な質は，慣習の復古的な性格を批判する。同時に，特定の敷地とは無関係であることは，「複製された芸術作品は複製可能性のためにデザインされた芸術作品」という考えを引き起

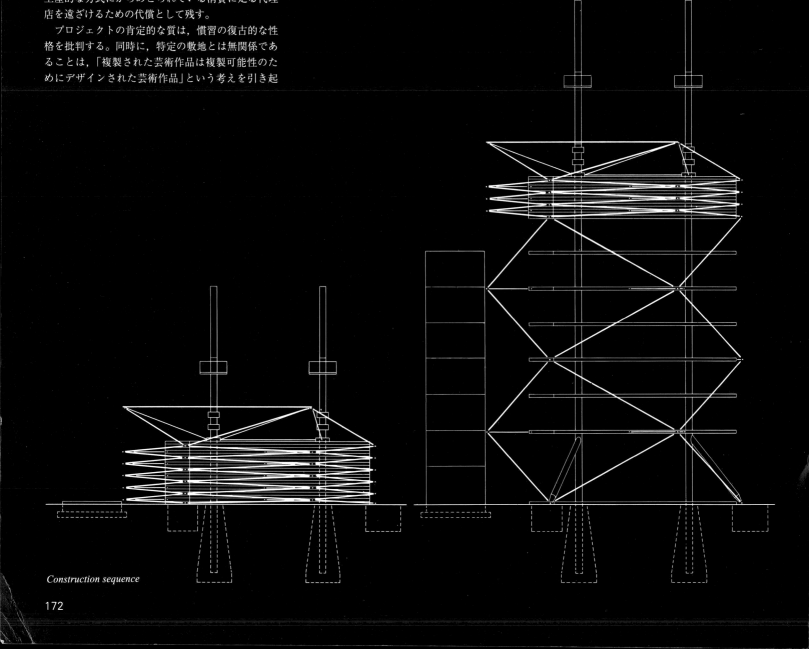

Construction sequence

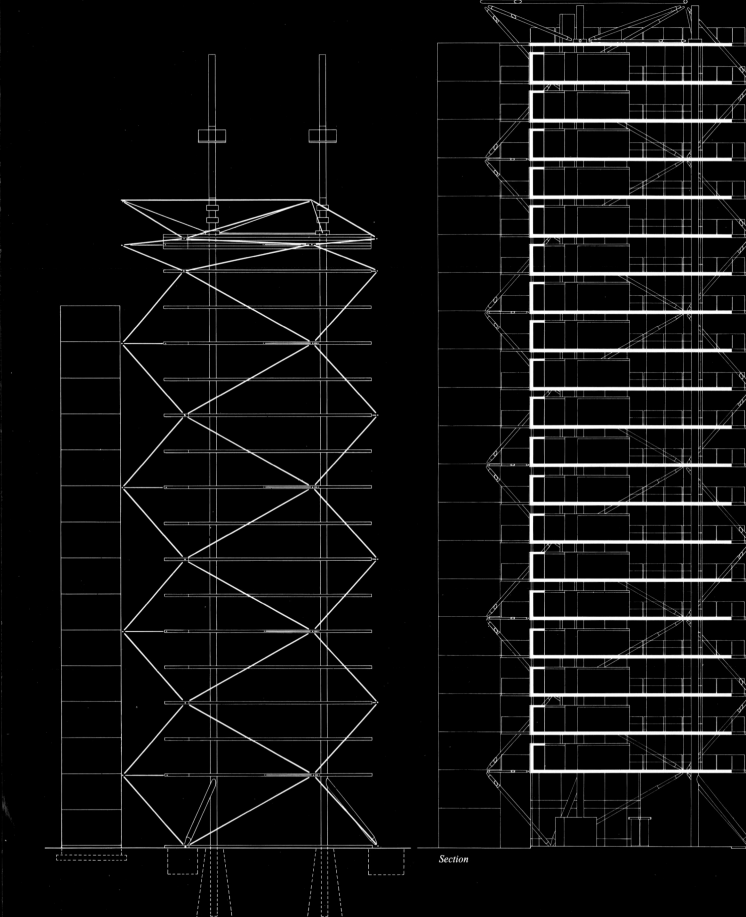
Section

FRANK LLOYD WRIGHT
12 vols.
フランク・ロイド・ライト全集
全12巻

Edited and Photographed by Yukio Futagawa
Text by Bruce Brooks Pfeiffer
企画・編集・撮影：二川幸夫
文：ブルース・ブルックス・ファイファー
翻訳：安藤正雄，小林克弘，榎本弘之，玉井一匡

In the course of his 70-year career, F. L. Wright continued to influence modern and contemporary architectural design. This 12-volume series of monographs presents all of his realized buildings as well as unrealized projects—a collection of over 1,000 works—in what is surely the most definitive series of books on Wright the world wide. This was made possible through the cooperation of the Frank Lloyd Wright Foundation and our over twenty years of experience photographing Wright's architecture. Volumes 1–8 combines photographs and original drawings in a visually dynamic format, defining the most complete monograph of his work to date. Volumes 9–11 are a selection of preliminary studies, examining the design process of his most famous works. Volume 12 presents 200 examples of Mr. Wright's highly expressive architectural renderings.

この全集は，現代建築に多大な影響を与え続けた巨匠フランク・ロイド・ライトの70年にも及ぶ設計活動から，プロジェクトを含め1,000を超える作品全体を通史というかたちで編集した世界で唯一のものであり，ライト・ファンデーションの全面的な協力と20数余年にわたる実施作品の取材，撮影によって初めて可能となった決定版である。第1巻から第8巻を構成するモノグラフは，多数の写真と図面により，ヴィジュアルなかたちで実施作品と計画案の大部分を網羅した作品集。第9巻から第11巻を構成するプレリミナリー・スタディは，特に重要な位置を占める作品を取り上げ，その設計過程を深く掘り下げた図面集。第12巻のレンダリングは，芸術作品と呼ぶに相応しい雰囲気を備えた透視図を中心に，膨大な図面の中から200点を厳選したドローイング集。これまで捉えきれなかった全貌を明らかにしたこの全集はライト研究に必要不可欠な定本であり，新たな発見と貴重な示唆とが得られる豊かな資料庫となろう。

- vol. 1 MONOGRAPH 1887-1901
- vol. 2 MONOGRAPH 1902-1906
- vol. 3 MONOGRAPH 1907-1913
- vol. 4 MONOGRAPH 1914-1923
- vol. 5 MONOGRAPH 1924-1936
- vol. 6 MONOGRAPH 1937-1941
- vol. 7 MONOGRAPH 1942-1950
- vol. 8 MONOGRAPH 1951-1959
- vol. 9 PRELIMINARY STUDIES 1889-1916
- vol.10 PRELIMINARY STUDIES 1917-1932
- vol.11 PRELIMINARY STUDIES 1933-1959
- vol.12 IN HIS RENDERINGS 1887-1959

Hard cover: vols. 1, 2, 5–8, 12 are out of print 絶版
Paper back: vols. 1–3 are out of print 絶版

Size: 227×307mm／220-408 total pages (24–156 in color)
¥8,505 (vols.1–5, 9–11), ¥9,797 (vols.6–8), ¥12,000 (vols.12)

表記価格には消費税は含まれておりません。

GA ARCHITECT

This is a new series of monographs in which each issue is dedicated to an architect and is a complete chronological account of the architect's work to date. GA ARCHITECT is presented in a large format full of arresting photographs most of which are taken soley for the purpose of illustrating the articles and are heretofore unpublished. Each volume features texts by foremost architectural critics, historians or fellow designers, and the architect's own account of the works.

現代建築界で活躍している建築家の全貌を，気鋭の批評家書きドろしの作家論，現地取材の写真，建築事務所の全面的な協力を得た詳細な図面，簡明な作品解説により立体的に編集した大型サイズの作品集。巻末には作品リスト，文献リストを収録。変貌を続ける現代建築家の肖像を現時点で正確に把握，記録することを試み，現代建築家全集の最新決定版を意図した。各巻は建築家それぞれの個性を最大限に表現できるよう多彩な構成をとっている。

Size: 300×307mm

1 ケヴィン・ローチ／ジョン・ディンケルー
KEVIN ROCHE JOHN DINKELOO AND ASSOCIATES

Planned issue 企画中

2 グナー・バーカーツ
GUNNAR BIRKERTS AND ASSOCIATES

論文：ウィリアム・マーリン／グナー・バーカーツ　翻訳：山下泉／難波和彦　作品：ミネアポリス連邦準備銀行／ダルース公立図書館／ヒューストン現代美術館／IBM社コンピューター・センター／IBM社屋／コーニング・ガラス博物館／ミシガン大学法学部棟増築／他
Text: William Marlin, Gunnar Birkerts　Works: Federal Reserve Bank of Minneapolis; Duluth Public Library; Contemporary Arts Museum, Houston; IBM Computer Center; Museum of Glass, Corning; and others;
228 total pages, 36 in color

Out of print 絶版

3 マリオ・ボッタ
MARIO BOTTA

論文：クリスチャン・ノルベルク＝シュルツ　翻訳：井出章　作品：リヴァ・サン・ヴィターレの住宅／モルビオ・インフェリオーレの高等学校／カプッチーニ修道院図書館／クラフト・センター／フリブール州立銀行／スタービオの住宅／他
Text: Christian Norberg-Schulz　Works: One Family House at Riva San Vitale; Secondary School at Morbio Inferiore; Craft Center; State Bank at Fribourg; Office Building at Lugano; One Family House at Stabio; and others
236 total pages, 42 in color

Out of print 絶版

4 リカルド・ボフィル
RICARDO BOFILL

論文：クリスチャン・ノルベルク＝シュルツ　翻訳：三宅理一　作品：ラ・マンサネラ／ウォールデン7／タリエールのスタジオ／メリシェルの聖所／レ・アール計画／湖畔のアーケード・橋／アブラクサスの宮殿・劇場・凱旋門／アンチゴネー／他
Text: Christian Norberg-Schulz
Works: La Manzanera; Walden 7; La Fabrica; The Sanctuary of Meritxell; Le Jardin des Halles; Les Arcades du Lac; Les Espaces d'Abraxas; Antigone; and others
200 total pages, 54 in color

Out of print 絶版

5 ザハ・ハディド
ZAHA M. HADID

序文：磯崎新　インタヴュー：アルヴァン・ボイヤースキー　翻訳：彦坂裕(他)
計画案：マーレヴィッチのテクトニク／19世紀博物館／アイルランド首相官邸／イートン・プレイス59番地／ラ・ヴィレット公園／ザ・ピーク／トラファルガー広場計画／他
Introduction: Arata Isozaki　Interview: Alvin Boyarsky
Projects: Malevich's Tektonik; Residence for the Irish Premier; 59 Eaton Place; Parc de la Villette; The Peak; Trafalgar Square Grand Buildings; and others
120 total pages, 48 in color

Out of print 絶版

6 磯崎新
ARATA ISOZAKI 1 1959-78

論文: ケネス・フランプトン　翻訳: 三宅理一／渡辺洋
作品: 大分県医師会館／大分県立中央図書館／岩田学園／福岡相互銀行本・支店／群馬県立近代美術館／北九州市立美術館／北九州市立中央図書館／神岡町役場／NEG／他
Text: Kenneth Frampton
Works: Oita Medical Hall; Oita Prefectural Library; Fukuoka Mutual Bank; Gumma Prefectural Museum; Kitakyushu Central Library; Kamioka Town Hall; and others
264 total pages, 42 in color　　　　　　　　　¥9,660（上製）¥6,767（並製）

7 磯崎新
ARATA ISOZAKI 2 1979-86

論文: ケネス・フランプトン　翻訳: 三宅理一／渡辺洋
作品: つくばセンター・ビル／ロサンジェルス現代美術館／西脇市岡之山美術館／武蔵丘陵カントリー倶楽部／パラディアム／サンジョルディ・パレス／他
Text: Kenneth Frampton
Works: Tsukuba Center Building; The Museum of Contemporary Art, Los Angeles; Okanoyama Graphic Art Museum; The Palladium; Sant Jordi Sports Hall; and others
Forthcoming issue 近刊

8 安藤忠雄
TADAO ANDO 1 1972-87

論文: ケネス・フランプトン　翻訳: 隈研吾
作品: 双生観／住吉の長屋／領壁の家／六甲の集合住宅／フェスティバル／小篠邸／城戸崎邸／タイムズ／OLD NEW 六甲／六甲の教会／水の教会／渋谷プロジェクト／他
Text: Kenneth Frampton
Works: Soseikan; Row House in Sumiyoshi; Wall House; Rokko Housing; Festival; Koshino House; TIME'S; Old New Rokko; Chapel on Mt. Rokko; and others
248 total pages, 24 in color　　　　　　　　　*Out of print* 絶版

9 高松伸
SHIN TAKAMATSU

論文: 三宅理一　英訳: 渡辺洋／ウィリアム・ティンギー
作品: 織陣／修学院の家／西福寺／ARK／PHARAOH／WEEK／DANCE HALL／KIRIN PLAZA OSAKA／ICHIGOYA／SYNTAX／OKTAGON／他
Text: Riichi Miyake
Works: Origin; House in Shugakuin; Arc; Pharaoh; Week; Dance Hall; Kirin Plaza Osaka; Ichigoya; Syntax; Oktagon; and others
196 total pages, 36 in color　　　　　　　　　*Out of print* 絶版

10 フランク・O・ゲーリー
FRANK O. GEHRY

序文: ロバート・A・M・スターン　翻訳: 青木淳, 他
作品: ゲーリー自邸／ノートン邸／ウィントン・ゲストハウス／カブリロ水族館／チャットデイ, メインストリート／ヴィトラ美術館・家具工場／アメリカン・センター／他
Text: Robert A.M. Stern　Works: Gehry Residence; Norton House; Winton Guest House; Cabrillo Marine Museum; Chiat/Day Main Street; Vitra Museum Factory; American Center; and others
204 total pages, 66 in color　　　　　　　　　¥5,806

11 スティーヴン・ホール
STEVEN HOLL

文: 伊東豊雄, スティーヴン・ホール　翻訳: 渡辺洋（英訳）, 玉井一匡（和訳）
作品: コーン・アパートメント／ストレット・ハウス／ハイブリッド・ビルディング／ネクサスワールド集合住宅／ベルリン図書館コンペ案／ポルタ・ヴィットリア計画／他
Text: Toyo Ito, Steven Holl
Works: Cohen Apartment; Stretto House; Hybrid Building; Void Space/Hinged Space Housing; Berlin AGB Library; Porta Vittoria Competition; and others
168 total pages, 36 in color　　　　　　　　　*Out of print* 絶版

12 安藤忠雄
TADAO ANDO 2 1988-93

論文: トム・ヘネガン／作品解説: 安藤忠雄　翻訳: 速水葉子／ブライアン・アムスタッツ
作品: 水の教会／光の教会／ライカ本社ビル／兵庫県立子供の館／直島コンテンポラリーアートミュージアム／六甲の集合住宅II／真言宗本福寺水御堂／熊本県立装飾古墳館／他
Text: Tom Heneghan
Works: Rokko Housing II; Church on the Water; Water Temple; RAIKA Headquarters; Naoshima Contemporary Art Museum; Japan Pavilion Expo '92/ Sevilla; and others
228 total pages, 30 in color　　　　　　　　　¥5,806

13 原広司
HIROSHI HARA

論文: デイヴィッド・B・ステュワート／作品解説: 原広司　翻訳: 高島平吾
作品: 慶松幼稚園／粟津邸／原邸／城西小学校／田崎美術館／游喜庵／ヤマトインターナショナル／飯田市美術博物館／梅田スカイビル／内子町立大瀬中学校／地球外建築／他
Text: David B. Stewart
Works: Hara House; Josei Primary School; Tasaki Museum of Art; Yamato International; Iida City Museum; Umeda Sky Building; Ose Middle School; and others
252 total pages, 36 in color　　　　　　　　　¥5,806

14

Key to Abbreviations

ALC	alcove
ARCD	arcade/covered passageway
ART	art room
ATL	atelier
ATR	atrium
ATT	attic
AV	audio-visual room
BAL	balcony
BAR	bar
BK	breakfast room
BR	bedroom
BRG	bridge/catwalk
BTH	bathroom
BVD	belvedere/lookout
CAR	carport/car shelter
CH	children's room
CEL	cellar
CL	closet/walk-in closet
CLK	cloak
CT	court
D	dining room
DEN	den
DK	deck
DN	stairs-down
DRK	darkroom
DRS	dressing room/wardrobe
DRW	drawing room
E	entry
ECT	entrance court
EH	entrance hall
EV	elevator
EXC	excercise room
F	family room
FPL	fireplace
FYR	foyer
GAL	gallery
GDN	garden
GRG	garage
GRN	greenhouse
GST	guest room/guest bedroom
GZBO	gazebo
H	hall
ING	inglenook
K	kitchen
L	living room
LBR	library
LBY	lobby
LDRY	laundry
LFT	loft
LGA	loggia
LGE	lounge
LWL	light well
MAID	maid room
MBR	master bedroom
MECH	mechanical
MLTP	multipurpose room
MSIC	music room
MUD	mud room
OF	office
P	porch/portico
PAN	pantry/larder
PLY	playroom
POOL	swimming pool/pool/pond
PT	patio
RE	rear entry
RT	roof terrace
SHW	shower
SIT	sitting room
SHOP	shop
SKY	skylight
SL	slope/ramp
SLP	sleeping loft
SNA	sauna
STD	studio
STDY	study
ST	staircase/stair hall
STR	storage/storeroom
SUN	sunroom/sun parlor/solarium
SVE	service entry
SVYD	service yard
TAT	tatami room/tea ceremony room
TER	terrace
UP	stairs-up
UTL	utility room
VD	void/open
VRA	veranda
VSTB	vestibule
WC	water closet
WRK	workshop/work room

TADAO ANDO
DETAILS
安藤忠雄ディテール集
EDITED BY YUKIO FUTAGAWA／CRITICISM BY PETER EISENMAN

企画・編集：二川幸夫／論文：ピーター・アイゼンマン

翻訳：渡辺洋（英訳），丸山洋志（和訳）

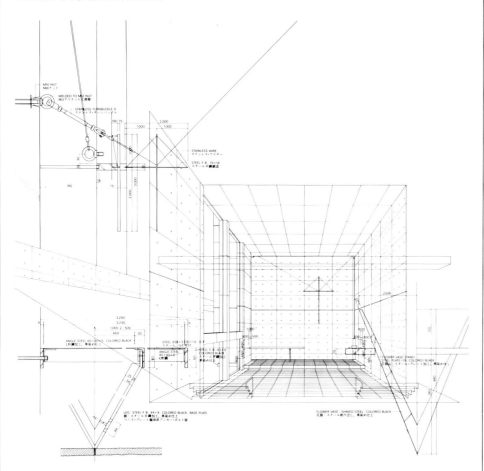

From "Row House in Sumiyoshi" to "Church with the Light," this book contains Ando's architectural details in his unique expressions of drawings.

住吉の長屋から光の教会まで，安藤忠雄が編み出した独自の表現方法によるディテール集。

LIST OF WORKS
Row House in Sumiyoshi (Azuma House), Osaka, 1975-76
Wall House (Matsumoto House), Hyogo, 1976-77
Glass Block House (Ishihara House), Osaka, 1977-78
Rokko Housing I, Hyogo, 1978-83
Koshino House, Hyogo, 1979-81/1983-84 (addition)
Festival, Okinawa, 1980-84
BIGI Atelier, Tokyo, 1980-83
Townhouse in Kujo (Izutsu House), Osaka, 1981-82
Iwasa House, Hyogo, 1982-84/1989-90 (addition)
Kidosaki House, Tokyo, 1982-86
TIME'S I/II, Kyoto, 1983-84/1986-91
JUN Port Island Building, Hyogo, 1983-85
Old/New Rokko, Hyogo, 1985-86
Chapel on Mt. Rokko, Hyogo, 1985-86
Church on the Water, Hokkaido, 1985-88
Church with the Light, Osaka, 1987-89

Size: 300×307mm／168 total pages
¥4,806

表記価格には消費税は含まれておりません。

La Maison de Verre
Pierre Chareau EDITED & PHOTOGRAPHED by **Yukio Futagawa** TEXT & DRAWINGS by **Bernard Bauchet** TEXT by **Marc Vellay**

ガラスの家：ダルザス邸
企画・撮影＝二川幸夫
文・図面＝ベルナール・ボシェ／翻訳＝三宅理一

Built in the center of Paris, La Maison de Verre is neither a work which can be overlooked for its avant-garde qualities, nor as a landmark in the history of Modern Architecture. This volume attempts to give an overall picture of this major work with photographs and survey drawings.

1932年，パリの中心部に建てられた＜ガラスの家＞は，スチールとガラスブロックの大胆な構成で，近代建築史上，その前衛性からも注目すべき建築である。光の浸透というテーマがどのような構成の原理と空間構成のテクニックのうえに成立しているのか。特別撮影の写真と実測図面により解明する。

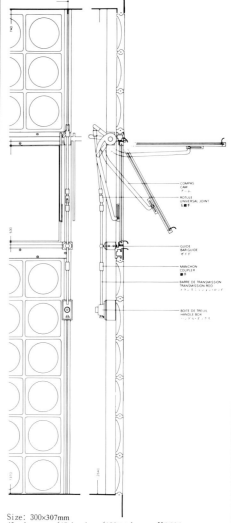

Size: 300×307mm
42 color pages／47 drawings／180 total pages　¥5,806